THE WINNING MOMENT

PART 1

Becoming a Wild and Wooly Warrior

By Steve Adkins, Paul Adkins & Danial Adkins

The Winning Moment - Part 1

Becoming a Wild and Wooly Warrior

Steve Adkins, Paul Adkins & Danial Adkins

ISBN (Print Edition): 978-1-54396-672-5

ISBN (eBook Edition): 978-1-54396-673-2

In the middle of the night

In the middle of nowhere

If you play your cards right

You just might spot the Dancing Bear

"Let's go do something we will never forget," said my room-mate, Mike.

"I'm game," I said.

"Let's go running," he suggested.

"I don't know if you've checked, but it's midnight, and it's freezing out there," I replied.

Mike was hell-bent on going, so I relented and bundled up. When I got out there, it was snowing. I mean, it was coming down in flakes the size of half-dollars.

We ran our mile in a winter wonderland.

I'll never forget it.

From what I understand, later in life Mike became a warrior for Christ and instrumental in leading people to God. He was well suited for that.

He was the funniest guy I ever met and incredibly dynamic.

This one's for you.

Good night, sweet prince…

Love,

Steve

PREFACE

My wonderful mother is eighty-five years old and has Alzheimer's. Over time, it has taken a toll on her. Before she really started to lose her senses, I tried to get my younger sister to videotape my mom telling her life story, packed with as many memories as she was able to remember. A videotape that contained her acknowledgment of all the helpful tidbits and phrases she learned along the way. The ones that really helped her become the incredible matriarch that she is. Life got in the way, the video was never made, and now Mom is unable to reminisce on the events that unfolded throughout her life. I really would have liked to have that video. I was thinking about what it would contain, had it been made, when out of nowhere a thought hit me like a ton of bricks. I realized that I hadn't taken the time to create something similar about my own life.

I thought about it for a while. I thought about how nice it would be to leave my kids a tangible rundown of my life. I thought about highlighting all the most influential phrases and quotes that had helped to mold me. Some of them at the most demanding times. All of my most vivid memories. Not just the good ones but the bad ones too.

I decided to do it. Although I knew it would take a lot of time, I began by thinking back to my earliest memories as a child. I'd think all day and all night about any memory I could harness. Some memories led to others. As time went on, I realized that I had a great start in my mind and that I really needed to write them down for the sake of remembering them as well as I did.

The only problem was…well, my body. Due to an unforeseen disaster that occurred when I was fifty-four years old, I am, in large part, handicapped. The memories in and of themselves are a miracle. They are memories I was told that I would never have. My body is another story. I'd lived my whole life right-handed, but the right half of my body is partially paralyzed. Still, if I could have the memories I was told I wouldn't, then I felt like I could find a way to write them down with a body that shouldn't be able to do anything at all.

Finally, I decided that the only thing to do was try. I asked my wife to purchase an iPad for me, and I began writing. It'd take me six or seven hours to write a paragraph. One memory would take me a day or two. I'd write an entire story and then accidentally erase it and, of course, have to start all over again. It was a painstaking process, but eventually I got a little faster. No matter what, I kept my eye on the prize and pushed forward. There were times when I would get a bit discouraged with how hard it was, but I was determined, and in time, I got it all down.

The Winning Moment: Becoming a Wild and Woolly Warrior chronicles my life and the most meaningful people in it. It details the hardships I have faced, the challenges I've overcome, and the fun I had in the process. Most of all, it is a work that describes, through my own stories, the mind-set that is needed to overcome obstacles throughout life no matter the shortcomings you have or the hard times you find yourself in.

Truthfully, life is not for the faint of heart. You are dealt a hand, and you'd better play it. Sure, things can happen that don't go your way. Other times, things will go your way. They are all a part of life, and that's what makes each and every experience beautiful in its own right. That's what makes each and every experience an opportunity. An opportunity to learn, grow, and overcome. I hope you enjoy the read. My biggest prayer is that, in some way, it inspires you to live a life even larger than the one you are living now.

You are braver than you believe and stronger than you think.

INTRODUCTION

The Winning Moment: Becoming a Wild and Woolly Warrior introduces you to the tragedy that occurred in the life of my family and me when I was fifty-four years old. It also details the process through which I then learned to live and describes the things in life that molded me into the persevering man that I like to think of myself as. Each and every lesson and experience has proved to be invaluable over time. I hope that you too are able to walk away from reading this with a slightly different perspective and conceptualization of what it takes to overcome adversity. Not just the smallest of hurdles but the largest ones too.

If you can find it in you to embody the things you will read about in this book, nothing in this world can stand in the way of you accomplishing something that you have decided you want to achieve. But never forget, everything we ever set as a goal must be in alignment with the true purpose that we have in this world.

With that said, anytime we feel we are defeated, as long as we are still breathing we ultimately have the opportunity to overcome. I have always tried to live my life with this line of thinking, and it has taken me further than I could ever have thought possible. If just one person is able to read this book and walk away with a similar mentality, my efforts in writing this have surely been worthwhile.

It All Begins Somewhere

May 13, 2008

Resaca, Georgia

Fifty-four Years Old

I used to consider a day successful if I hadn't gone past the mailbox. Saturdays were the day I usually succeeded. There was nothing like waking up, walking out of my bedroom, and humbly admiring what I had provided for my family in the silence of everyone being gone or asleep. The large plantation-style home with its acutely angled roof reaching for the sky, stationed on two acres of perfect land in the middle of Nowhere, USA. It was white on the outside, with beautiful columns on the front porch. On the porch sat four green rocking chairs that were perfectly matched to the shutters. Rocking chairs that you could relax in and stare out over the green pastures and the pond across the street. The dark-stained hardwoods throughout the spacious living room, kitchen, and so on. Upstairs there was an office, an extra bedroom, and bedrooms for the boys that were just a few feet smaller than our generous master bedroom downstairs, although we did have the master bath with the tiled floors, stand-up shower, and the huge Jacuzzi tub. Walk out back, and you had an awning extending from the poolside of the main house and covering the grilling and lounge area. To the right, just past the arbor and wrapped in jasmine leading to the driveway, you also had an awning covering an outdoor dining table coming off of the pool house that I had designed and had had built to match the main house.

The pool deck was something spectacular. You could look out on the rolling green hills for miles. Follow the hills with your eyes, and you'd eventually be peering out on a beautiful scape of mountains that appeared to be shaded gray in the background. Without a tree any closer than seventy-five feet from the deck, midsummer you could get sun from seven in the morning until nine at night. Around the entire house, we had beautiful landscaping, but the pool area was on another level. To the left and right, you'd see the largest lilies you've ever seen. There were angel trumpets, tulips, and butterfly bushes. Annual and perennial galore, year after year. Hedges as a backdrop to every flower bed.

The pool house had an entertainment room with a billiards table that was more than a century old, a wet bar, and a big-screen TV with a receiver that powered the surround sound throughout the house and out onto the pool deck. Through the hall was the workout room equipped with full-body mirrors, all the weights and machines you would ever need, and a redwood sauna that was my best friend when I hit the gym too hard. Upstairs, we had a guest master bedroom that accompanied a bunkroom with three full-size beds. Lastly, we had the seldom-used half-court to play basketball on until the hoop was taken down on a dunk by one of the boys' friends while they were hanging out one night. It was nestled on the other side of the pool house, at the top of the driveway, just outside the carport that housed three spaces for parking and a sizable storage room.

I woke up one sunny Saturday morning with my usual goal in mind.

Whatever you do, Steve, don't go past the mailbox.

This morning was like no other except for one key detail—I had this unexplainable double vision. Like a *ten too many by the pool while listening to Creedence Clearwater Revival with my best friends* kind of double vision. I figured I'd shake it off, so I drank my cup of Café Bustelo and went about my day.

Although the double vision was nauseating, I had yard work to do. I went outside and began skimming the leaves off the top of the pool. Next, I straightened up the pool area and walked through the pool house to open the windows and turn off the air conditioning since it was such a nice day. Then it was on to the carport to break out the riding lawn mower.

I thought to myself, *This must be what it is like to drive while impaired.*

While rolling the lawn mower out of the storage room, my vision started closing in. Everything got darker and darker. Time felt like it was slowing down for a moment. I remember wondering what in the world was happening. The sunny day melted away into a narrow hallway of pitch black.

The next thing I remember was waking up, lying on the ground with my son Paul standing over me.

He was frantically yelling, "Dad! Dad!"

I was confused and wondered what exactly had happened. The feeling wasn't unfamiliar: I had been knocked unconscious numerous times throughout my football career.

I realized that I had passed out.

Paul had just woken up about nine o'clock, and my wife Bella had called him in an attempt to get in touch with me because I had not answered my phone. When he came downstairs, he called out for me in the house. After receiving no response, he looked out and saw my car in the carport, so he came out calling for me. Still no response. He yelled through the open windows of the pool house to see if I was working out. Yet again, no confirmation. Finally, he walked around to the carport, past my car, past his truck, and discovered me lying there on the ground next to the lawn mower.

I was unconscious.

He was terrified.

He helped me up, and I walked around to the pool and sat in a lounge chair. I took it easy well into the afternoon until the double vision finally went on its merry way. Bella must have called me a hundred times that day after finding out. She, Paul, and my other son Danny were very concerned about me—and understandably so. To be honest, I was too. Although it was against my creed, being the macho man I was, I agreed to make an appointment with a doctor. I was raised during a time when going to the doctor was the equivalent to turning in your Man Card. Nevertheless, it seemed serious, and everyone wanted to know what was going on. Me included.

I will never forget that afternoon. Paul was refereeing a high-school soccer game south of Atlanta.

He called me on the way. "Dad, you've got to get this figured out. Please make a doctor's appointment. Nothing can happen to you. I don't know what I'd do without you."

I could hear the pain in his voice.

I would have done anything to make him feel better.

"Dad, promise me nothing is going to happen to you.

"Nothing is going to happen, Paul. I promise."

CHAPTER 2

1954–1959

Knoxville, Tennessee

Early Childhood

I was born the morning of Friday, March 5, 1954, in Knoxville, Tennessee, at St. Mary's Hospital. At the time, it was so small that it was basically three wings. I weighed seven pounds eleven ounces and was twenty-one inches long.

A lot was going on in the world in 1954. The US Supreme Court ruled against the Board of Education in the Brown v. Board case, ultimately ending segregation or any tolerance thereof. Ellis Island officially closed. Eisenhower was president and signed the Social Security Amendments of 1954 into law, expanding coverage to ten million more Americans. Eisenhower also signed the Communist Control Act outlawing the Communist Party in the United States. The words *under God* were added to the Pledge of Allegiance. Hurricane Hazel hit, which is considered one of the worst hurricanes of the twentieth century. *The Tonight Show* aired for the first time. *Lord of the Flies* was released and so were the first two books in the popular series *The Lord of the Rings*. Last but certainly not least, Elvis Presley began his public music career.

When I was born, we lived on Atlantic Avenue. As you headed east on Atlantic, our house was a small gray one on the left. I remember the Clancys' huge house on the corner, all redbrick. It was a Victorian-style home, if I'm not mistaken—no telling how many rooms. You could see three floors from the street. Suffice it to say, there were at least four including the basement. It was monstrous and was built on what, at the time of its construction, were the outskirts of town. Across from the Clancy mansion was an old Esso station with tall, brick columns running up to the frame roof and a screen door advertising Kern's. Inside was candy to your heart's delight, and the price was right. In 1954, the average cost of a new house was around ten thousand dollars. A new car was just under two thousand. Gas was around twenty cents a gallon. A movie ticket cost you a whopping seventy cents. And a cold Coca-Cola or a candy bar was five cents.

My dad's name was Charles Spencer Adkins, and he was born on Monday, September 30, 1929. He was an only child and grew up on Western Avenue in Knoxville. That part of town was commonly referred to as McAnally Flats. He grew up in a family dominated by men as his mom, my Grandmother Bee, was the only daughter of five children. Bee was more like an aunt than a grandparent. Aside from the fact that she was referred to as Ruby, the only things I ever really knew about my grandmother's childhood were that she had been the Knoxville marbles champion and that she was full of piss and vinegar. Stories about my dad's uncles came in fleets. While Dad was growing up, Grandmother Bee worked in the cafeteria of a plastic manufacturer. His dad, my Papaw, was the captain of Fire Hall No. 7 in Knoxville. It was located in Lonsdale, which was a more financially depressed part of town. The firehouse was a large brick building with screen doors and a basement. It had a large bunkhouse, and as a special attraction, there was the old fire-engine cab that we got to climb into and ring the bell. That was my favorite part.

Dad grew up to be the kicker for Knoxville High School, which was big deal back then. He was a southpaw because he had broken his right leg. I always loved the stories about him punting for old Knoxville High back when they played Central High on Thanksgiving Day at the University of Tennessee's Shields-Watkins Field, in what was billed as the City versus County Game. It was always a sellout crowd, according to the stories. There was only one other high school in Knoxville at the time, which was Knoxville Catholic High School. It was on Magnolia Avenue in a big Victorian house. My mother went to school there.

My mom and dad met when they were neighbors on Chickamauga Avenue. He courted her at my Grandmother Bee's urging, and inevitably ended up asking for her hand in marriage. My grandfather told him if he could wait one year, he would agree. The wait was a must because my dad was a Methodist, my mom was Catholic, and that was considered a mixed marriage. My dad had to take courses and also had to agree to raise his children Catholic before he could get the Church's blessing. Patience is a virtue, and my dad had a surplus of it regarding my mother. They got married on Friday, May 13, 1950, at Holy Ghost Catholic Church on North Central Street.

Speaking of my dad being Methodist, he was really a Methodist in theory. He mostly belonged to the Church of the No. 2 pencil. He lied about his age so he could go to work for Southern Bell before the legal age of eighteen. He climbed poles for starters as an installer. I remember him driving his Bell South truck home for lunch one day. It was a child's dream, full of all the telephone-company accoutrements and such. Basically, he was a workaholic, which is what led him to the Scarbrough family and Powell Telephone Company in Powell, Tennessee. It was started on the Scarbrough mother's porch in the mid-1950s. For most of my childhood, he worked for Bell South during the day and moonlighted for Powell at night. In between jobs, he would come home, have dinner, take a nap, and beat us with his belt for the day's transgressions. He was always ready to be in a bad mood. If you saw him going for the belt, you knew you had screwed up royally. Sometimes I felt fortunate that he loved working in the telecommunications industry. It was his career, his hobby, and his social life all rolled up into one. In other ways, it was quite unfortunate. He didn't spend much time with me doing the things a dad does with his son.

He wasn't home very often.

In his free time on Friday nights, he would hang out with his uncles at the Fraternal Order of Eagles. He was a member of the local chapter.

CHAPTER 3

As for my mom, her name is Ann Elizabeth Adkins, formerly Ann Elizabeth DeClue. She was born on Sunday, November 2, 1930. Her mom, Grandmother DeClue, or just *Grandmother*, was a caregiver to the elderly and sick. She was all a child could ever hope for in a grandmother. Her dad, my grandfather, was a manager at the Farragut Hotel. At the time, there only were two hotels downtown: the Farragut and the Andrew Jackson Hotel. The Farragut was opulent back then, with lots of granite. Even the floor was fancy by today's standards.

Every year, he would reserve a room for us on the second floor to watch the Christmas parade on Gay Street. First, the Shriners with their miniature vehicles, then the onslaught of never-ending clowns, who marched as escorts for everybody else. My family watched with glee as a myriad of floats and bands passed below our view. At some point, the University of Tennessee's Pride of the Southland Band would march by playing "Jingle Bells."

Last but not least: Santa Claus himself.

Not an impostor either.

And just like that, it was over.

Life was grand.

Mom had one brother, my Uncle David. Mom grew into a beautiful cheerleader at Knoxville Catholic High. David spent the majority of his high-school days learning firsthand about the birds and the bees. The only girl he ever loved was his high-school sweetheart. The family wasn't a very big fan of her, and eventually it led to their relationship's unraveling. A few years after high school, he went into the army. Mom spent one year at the University of Tennessee, became a beauty queen, and retired from her school days. She and my dad had married at that point and didn't waste any time having kids. Since Dad was already a working man, he took care of the finances, and she stayed home to do the child-rearing.

My brother, David Michael Adkins, aka Mike, was born on April 4, 1951. In our youth, Mike was a typical older brother—hell-bent on making my life miserable. Until me, Mike had been an only child. He liked being an only child. Somehow, somewhere along the way, he concluded that killing me, his little brother, wasn't the answer.

He sure tried, though.

My vivid memories are a testament to it.

For example, there was the time when I was barely old enough to talk that I heard Mike say, "Hey, Steve, could you come here a minute?"

I looked everywhere, but he was nowhere to be found. The basement door was open, so I thought maybe he was down there. In my tyke language I asked, "Hey, Mike, what do you want?"

At the exact same moment I peered down the stairs, he jumped out from behind the door and knocked me down the thirteen wooden steps to the basement's concrete floor. My mom came and scraped me up, dusted me off, and dragged me upstairs. She came to my aid often. I was okay: he had really just hurt my feelings. I calmed down after a while.

Later on I heard, "Hey, Steve, could you come here a minute?"

It was Mike again. When you are just a toddler, you don't put two and two together. I went looking high and low. He was nowhere to be found. The basement door was open, so I took a look and—you guessed it—I fell for it again. This time he knocked me straight to the basement floor. However, it beat the heck out of falling down each step one by one. That day, even as young as I was, I learned a valuable life lesson.

Fool me once, shame on you. Fool me twice, shame on me.

That was the obvious moral to that story.

"If he gives you any more grief, just pick up the biggest thing you can find, and hit him with it."

That was the advice my dad gave me after an evening briefing with my mom on the children's behavior of the day. The briefing was a daily activity. The next day, Mike was giving me some grief, so I picked up a big brown glass ashtray and smashed him in the head with it. It dazed him, and he fell backward without bracing himself, flat on his back, knocking the wind out of him. He thought he was dying. It was really just the equalizer for the two-day battle. My dad's advice had worked. It was all an educational experience, to say the least. The main lesson was Don't Trust Mike. These types of things were just a natural occurrence in my childhood.

I'd think to myself, "I am a toddler. What's your excuse, Mike?" On that fateful day, I was just doing as instructed. He was just being himself. But stick around; it gets worse.

As you have probably put together, I was born three years after Mike. Just after I turned one, Southern Bell, now known as Bell South, experienced a major event. The Communication Workers of America went on a seventy-two-day strike involving fifty thousand workers. The dispute was over Southern Bell trying to break the union. My dad didn't get very passionate about the issues at hand, and he loved his job way too much to spend a single second standing around with a sign in his hand. So he, being the good provider he was, crossed the picket line.

It turns out that was quite the unpopular move. That week, some strangers drove by our house with a gun and shot into our living room. Fortunately, no one was hurt. They probably only meant to scare us, to which end they succeeded. The event sparked the most influential period in my early childhood.

Shortly thereafter, we moved into a bigger place located at 708 Shamrock Avenue. It just so happened to be one of the best neighborhoods in all of America for a young buck like me, and it was the perfect place to grow up.

CHAPTER 4

Shamrock Avenue was located in the northern part of Knoxville, just south of Sharp's Ridge. We lived in the second house on the left. Our house was white except for the bottom third of the front, which was green tile and still is to this day. Our property backed up to the alley that led to Glenwood Avenue.

All of our relatives, except for Aunt Lib and Uncle Joe, lived in Lincoln Park, which was within walking distance. The Lincoln Park area started about five blocks down from our house and covered a pretty large area. First, you had my mom's side of the family. My grandparents lived twelve blocks away—the house on Chickamauga. It had cost sixty-five hundred dollars brand-new, and my grandfather made the sixty-five-dollar monthly mortgage payments for thirty years before it was paid off. They took great care of it. Their landscaping was beautiful. They had plants there that I have never seen elsewhere…most notoriously was the thornbush with two-inch thorns in the backyard. Neither of them ever owned a car. So, my grandmother made it to the patients she had and my grandfather to the Farragut Hotel by bus. In fact, they went anywhere and everywhere they had to go by walking or by taking the bus.

Incredible!

My grandfather had two reel mowers in his shed, which he called his garage. It had a giant window that connected two large, empty rooms with a dirt floor. If you owned a car, this would've been a good place to park it, assuming you could negotiate the two strands of washed concrete leading into it, which we commonly referred to as the driveway. We went there every Sunday for dinner. My grandmother would make everybody's favorite dish. She absolutely adored us. For me, the preferred menu always consisted of Mexican corn bread and roast beef. If I was around for lunch, it was the world's best pimento-cheese sandwiches with barbeque chips and a 7UP. While I ate, she would massage my feet with alcohol.

Grandmother came from a long line of dominant women who knew how to take care of their families. They had the art of being incredible women down to a science, and it showed through the generations, including in my mom. Grandmother's mom, Momma Mayes, was the matriarch. I guess Momma Mayes had no choice in being the head of the family because Daddy Mayes was a consummate alcoholic, who happened to be a painter by profession. Maybe it's due to the flexibility of the schedule, but even at an early age, it seemed to me that a lot of painters do a lot of drinking. Daddy Mayes could put'em back.

Before the Civil Rights Act, my grandmother had always had what was then called *help*. Lucas was the handyman, and he was a quiet, elderly gentleman. He could fix anything, but he was seldom there. The thing I remember most about him was that he was always smiling. There was also Clara, who did all the ironing. We loved Clara, and although she was only there long enough each day to heat up the iron and make my grandparents' clothes wrinkle-free, she was like part of the family. She grew up under and complied with the Jim Crow laws. She always entered the house by coming down the alley and through the back door. She never left the kitchen, where she ironed, and she never used the bathroom, although my grandparents hadn't forbidden it. Occasionally, she would share stories about her grandson Lawrence Clemmons, who was a popular basketball player at local Fulton High School.

Eventually, Uncle David came home from the army. During his time in the service, he did two things. He was a private, so primarily he did a ton of grunt work. And second, he went out with all of his buddies a lot and developed the ability to drink alcohol really well. After he came home, his drinking slowly got worse and worse. I remember one time he walked into my grandmother's bedroom in a drunken state while brandishing a .38 revolver.

While holding up the gun, he looked at my grandmother and said, "I bet if somebody broke in here, you wouldn't even know what to do with this thing."

At which point she snatched the .38 and *bang!*

She had perfectly plugged the center of the bedpost. She laughed hysterically, raised her eyebrows, and handed the revolver back to him. Uncle Dave, as I referred to him, looked on in dismay. Anyway, when I was a small boy, one of my sure stops on Sundays at my grandparents' house was upstairs where my uncle lived. We would reenact the Civil War on his coffee table with my box of toy soldiers. I would always be the gray guys, which was factually a bad proposition for a youngster like me. So Uncle Dave would always allow me to change the outcome and win the war.

CHAPTER 5

The other sure stop every Sunday was at Uncle Gene and Aunt Doris Woods's house. My dad was never too fond of our Sunday-dinner trips. He did, however, thoroughly enjoy his time with Uncle Gene, who always referred to him as *Snooks* (which I never did understand). They lived half a block away from my grandparents at the end of their alley. Their house was always a wreck, and when we stopped by, they were usually eating their favorite dish, which was buttermilk, in a reused jelly jar, poured over corn bread. Their children, my cousins Kathy, Kenny, and Becky, would be there. This was the main reason I liked to go. Kathy and Becky didn't really catch my attention much as a child, but Kenny was a blast.

My grandmother's sister, Aunt Becky, lived in Lincoln Park also. Her full name was Rebecca Mayes, before she married my Uncle Rector. She and Uncle Rector lived on Radford Avenue, which was located five blocks east and two blocks north of my grandmother's. Momma Mayes lived at the end of Radford. I always thought it was neat that you could see the trolley tracks in the asphalt on Radford Avenue while you were at Aunt Becky's. She used me as her handyman. The first time I went, I asked Mike if he would accompany me. The assigned task was her attic, which was like a treasure chest. We were digging around and found a pair of boxing gloves. We thought it might be fun to put them on and fight a few rounds.

I was mistaken.

It was no fun whatsoever.

Unless you classify getting the crap beaten out of you by your older brother while your whole family watches as fun. That was the last time I asked Mike to assist me.

Probably my most exciting find happened when the basement and garage were the draw for the day. I started on the basement. In it was a box of my uncle's stuff, and it was a virtual time machine. The first thing out of the box was his old baseball mitt, which was flat as a flitter and didn't have strings holding the fingers together. Next was his old bat, which was held together by a nail and electrical tape. Then came the snow globe from the Chicago World's Fair, a windup train, and a piggy bank. It was a real treasure trove, and it just kept on giving, but I realized I was wasting time, and it must be business before pleasure. I needed to put down my uncle's old toys and finish the task at hand. Unfortunately, that entailed stacking the boxes and sweeping.

Boy, did I hate sweeping.

Next, I needed to tackle the garage. It was a collection of all things yard and included a reel mower and manual hedge clippers. Remember, this was the '50s. There was a broken shovel and other implements of destruction that I had left to clean up. Well, that and, of course, whatever was in that big box in the corner. Whatever it was, it sure was heavy. The only way to move it was to take some of the contents out. Without any other option, I opened it.

Flares!

Seriously, it was full of flares. I knew that Uncle Rector worked at the Coster Shop Rail Yard fixing train cars for Southern Company. The bridge out near Lincoln Park was like the Ninth Wonder of the World. It was three miles long. A ton of leftover supplies from the build were left at his work, and I'm guessing this was how the flares ended up in his possession.

Now all I had to do was figure out how to get a couple of them out of there. I knew that the toting of the trash was always the last thing on the list. So, after I finished cleaning up, I slipped a couple in the trash. Sure enough, Aunt Becky settled up with me and paid me an extra fifty cents to boot. I walked off with the trash in hand and—*voilà!*—there were the two flares.

I would have hauled the trash for two flares alone.

Grandmother Bee and Papaw lived at 423 East Columbia Avenue, which was seven blocks from us and right off Harvey Street. As a child, I thought Harvey Street was the steepest hill in the known world. Before I was competent with the numerical system and able to read road signs, their house was still easy to find due to the trees and the whitewashed driveway. Also, they had a miniature statue of two frogs on a love seat with a red umbrella in their birdbath. Their house was quaint and roughly nine hundred square feet.

I remember most holidays being spent at Grandmother DeClue's. She was the best cook, as far as we were concerned, and she really took care of us.

The gathering place for Thanksgiving was the exception.

I remember spending Thanksgiving at Grandmother Bee and Papaw's house. We always got there early on all holidays just to visit, but on that day we would stay and feast. After all, we did have to throw my dad a bone for the amount of time spent with Mom's family. It was a Garner event, and my dad loved his Garner uncles. They were like the big brothers he never had growing up. As an adult, they were his peers, and he really enjoyed telling them about his exploits at the phone company.

The holidays were the only time I got to see my cousins Bobby and Freddy Garner. Bobby lived in Kingston, and Freddy lived in East Knoxville on McCalla Avenue. We spent a few hours with them on other holidays, but on Thanksgiving we really got to hang out. Usually, we would play outside because there were only two toys at Bee's. There was a red plastic car known as Fire Chief and a blue plastic car known as The Police. The two cars were identical except for their colors. I'll never forget one Thanksgiving when I was only a few years old. Boy, were my cousins really in for a treat. Mike, being a few years older, had really grown tired of Fire Chief and The Police, so he brought some matches for our entertainment. We all climbed into the outside crawl space, and Mike proceeded to fire a few up. We thought it was hilarious. There is a certain excitement that accompanies doing something you're not supposed to. About ten matches in, we all were dying laughing.

I guess it drew some attention because the next thing we heard was my Papaw shouting, "Hey! What are you guys doing under there?"

Need I remind you he was the captain of a fire hall? We were busted! All of the parents asked us a gazillion times why we were trying to burn the house down. Geez! We weren't trying to burn the house down. We were just lighting a few matches underneath it.

After the interrogation, we were urged to go inside, so we all marched single file and took our spots in the den. As we sat on the couch, my uncles broke out the Jack. This was when Jack was ninety-six proof, so it didn't take much. My uncles and my Papaw, who hardly ever drank, started taking shots. My Uncle Junior laughed like a maniac, my Uncle Fate sweated like a maniac, and after only a few, my Papaw needed a nap. In fact, he needed to lie down so badly that he had to take a thirty-minute power nap in the living room, which was the farthest place from quiet. Did I ever have my own questions for them! But dinner was almost ready, and I never questioned an adult's decisions when I was a kid.

I knew better.

Finally, it was time for Thanksgiving dinner. Bee was a pretty good cook, and her Thanksgiving specialty was always oyster dressing. Yum! Everyone managed to sit at the table. My immediate family was four at the time and eventually grew to six. Then you had Bee and Papaw, plus Uncle Junior and Freddy. Don't forget Uncle Fate, his wife Evelyn, and Bobby. To say space was at a premium would be a gross understatement.

As previously mentioned, Aunt Lib and Uncle Joe were the only two in the family who didn't live near Shamrock Avenue. They lived on a huge farm in South Knoxville off Sevierville Highway in Knox County. The area was commonly referred to as Seymour. Aunt Lib, formally known as Elizabeth Mayes, was another great woman raised by Momma Mayes, as she was also my grandmother's sister. Uncle Joe was a fight promoter and owned McDonald's Pool Hall, uptown on Gay Street. McDonald's Pool Hall was always a landmark, and I remember when Big Jack Haun, one of my childhood heroes, fought there one time when I was younger, and I took the purse.

When I was a kid, we only saw Aunt Lib and Uncle Joe at Christmas, Easter, New Year's, and our yearly trips to their house to watch *The Wizard of Oz*. I remember how we always watched the flying monkeys and Dorothy seeking Kansas in glorious black and white on ABC. ABC was one of three networks at the time. After all, the airwaves were free. Back then, the channel lineup consisted of 6, 10, and 26, and you had rabbit ears for fine-tuning. The first household televisions in the United States came out in 1955. Black and white was the only option, and we all thought TVs were the bee's knees. Aunt Lib lived in a big, redbrick house with a barbecue grill outside that matched. A hop, skip, and a jump away from the house was an apple orchard. Their house was on about twenty-five acres that happened to contain tracks for the Great Smoky Mountains Railroad. Way out on the southeast of the property, there was a bald spot on a ridge. It was rumored to be a Cherokee burial ground. Whatever it was, it was circular and grass didn't grow there. As a child, I thought this place had it all. At one time, Aunt Lib even had peacocks. I remember their quills all over the yard.

Uncle Joe had his own private Jamaica. He turned a big, white outbuilding into a pool room. It was equipped with his favorite pictures of the Tennessee Volunteers football players he was most fond of. It also had a nice little bar area set up with chairs for gathering around. From his pool room, you could easily get to the pasture where my Uncle JD accidentally shot my Uncle David with a Bolt-Action .22, but that's a story for another time. It was an adventure just being there. Other than watching TV, we spent most of our time just exploring. My favorite spot to explore was her basement that housed an assortment of elegant junk. One of the coolest things I ever found down there was a floor fan that doubled as an ottoman.

CHAPTER 6

As far as life on Shamrock Avenue went, I was growing like a weed. I have been blessed with a great memory, but the first few years of life are a blur even for the best of us. I remember little bits and pieces from here and there. The seasons came and went. Mainly, I remember me just becoming me, and Mike just being…well, Mike. In the beginning of winter, when I was two years old, something happened that I will definitely never forget.

I was chasing Mike while doing laps around the basement. I was on my tricycle, and he was on our fire truck. A lap started at the wooden steps and went down by the workbench that was never used. You'd hang a right and go until you got to the crawl space. Take another right, go by the washer and dryer, the water heater, and then take another right. Go through the one-car bay and take another right. Finally, you'd pass the back door, and it was back to the start at the steps.

On about the seventy-first lap, when I had finally almost caught Mike, he inexplicably came to a screeching halt. At which point I went flying over the trike's handlebars and was left hanging there, on the fire truck's ladder hooks, like a fish.

"Ann! You better get down here," advised my grandmother, who happened to be there.

Apparently, Mike had stopped for a red light. Frankly, I didn't even see the red light (because there wasn't one). Nor would the outcome have been any different if there had been. Grandmother stayed at home with Mike. Mom and I loaded into the lemon du jour and took off.

Our first stop was to pick up my Papaw on Columbia Avenue. My dad was unavailable due to being at work, of course. After Papaw climbed aboard, we took off for Dr. Stiles in West Knoxville. Dr. Stiles was able to repair the crater in my face to the tune of eight sutures. That was the last time I was guilty of Following Too Closely.It was the last thing my poor mom needed at the time. Her body was undergoing a very evident change. Through the autumn, her belly got bigger and bigger by the week. By the time the holidays rolled around, she looked like she had stuffed the pumpkin from Halloween under her shirt. Trust me when I say it was a large pumpkin.

Although my parents tried to explain to me what was happening, I didn't understand the magnitude of what was going on. My grandmother showed up on Christmas Eve to spend the night. Furthermore, Mom and Dad were both absent. On Christmas Day of 1956, our big gift was my sister Susan Elizabeth Adkins. Susan was the first girl born into the Adkins family in fifty-three years, so she was welcomed with open arms and became a favorite of my dad's side of the family. I remember being frustrated when they got home from St. Mary's after having her because my mom wouldn't let me tote Susan inside. It was completely understandable with her being a newborn baby who didn't even weigh ten pounds. Also factored into it was the fact that I was only a two-year-old.

From my point of view, I was thinking something along the lines of *She doesn't even weigh ten pounds. What's the big freaking deal?*

New Year's came and went. In 1957 I was just a little boy, and I don't remember much. Mainly just a moment here and there. Life at home was getting back to normal. Susan was just a baby and cried a lot. There was nothing that I could really do with her. At this point, she wasn't even taking bottles yet so that I could have assisted in feeding her. Truthfully, I was probably too impatient to make it through a feeding anyway. Due to the circumstances, and although I loved her, I lost interest in the new-baby thing. I was busy getting into things I shouldn't and learning the ins and outs of being a child.

Mom had adjusted to having three children. She was a jack-of-all-trades. She kept us safe to the best of her ability, tended to our bumps and scrapes when we got hurt, and kept us entertained when we weren't doing that ourselves. She got us to sleep every night, woke with us in the mornings, bathed us, and of course was our dietitian. After Susan was born, she made set meals for each night to make things easier on herself. Wednesdays were spaghetti nights, and of course, Fridays were fish nights, so we would have fish sticks with oodles of ketchup. One of my fondest memories was soup days on Saturdays and Mom ringing a bell in the open kitchen window while we were playing in the yard signaling *Soup's on!*

I guess the one big thing I remember from those days was that Dad always seemed extra ornery. I guess the combination of working night and day mixed with a newborn in the house was the perfect concoction for even worse moods than on a typical day. At the time, we had a cocker spaniel named Cocoa. I remember thinking it was a Doctor Spaniel. Whenever I got hurt out playing, I would call for Doctor Spaniel. One day, my father was walking through the garage and was pissed, as usual. Probably over something petty like us using his tools, which he stole but never used—another one of my dad's many quirks: he always got sticky fingers in the tool aisle. But hey, we had a dam to build. Anyway, walking out of the garage, he slammed the door on Cocoa's leg. Cocoa did a lot of yelping, and Dad just looked at him in disgust. That night, as we went to bed, we watched Dad and Uncle Gene load up Doctor Spaniel, and...you know. We never saw him again. I guess you could say Cocoa took the long, one-way ride.

It hurt me to know what had happened, but even at the age of three I knew that boys didn't cry. In the way of a little boy, I started to realize that if you don't get the best of the world, the world will get the best of you.

This was the old days, and you had better toughen up or it was going to be rough. It was just the way things were.

CHAPTER 7

In December, we had a First Birthday party for Susan where the entire Garner family got together to celebrate.

Just like that, it was on to 1958.

In January of 1958, Explorer 1 was launched, which was the first satellite to be launched by the United States. We were in a space race with the Soviet Union. They had launched Sputnik 1 the previous October. On February 6, 1958, the Munich air disaster took place when a British European Airways flight crashed at the Munich Airport. The flight was carrying forty-four people when it crashed soon after takeoff. Many of those on board were sports journalists and members of the Manchester United football team who were on their way home after having qualified for the semifinals in the European Cup. A total of twenty-three people died as a result of the crash, and eight of them were members of Manchester United.

A few months passed, and my birthday came in March. Just after I turned four, my dad had a moment of clarity. I guess he realized that with Susan taking up most of the attention, and that with him being at work all the time, Mike and I could use a little adventure with him. So, he had a good-father-and-neighbor moment. He took my brother and me fishing with our next-door neighbor, Lee Hedgepath. We were off to Douglas Lake, which was one of the Tennessee Valley Authority's man-made lakes just outside of Knoxville. He gave us both bait-casting reels and then got pissed because we couldn't cast them without getting backlash and a tangled line. I mean, those suckers were hard to cast. Even a veteran angler would have had a hard time doing so. I'll never forget his infamous words that day.

"You've made two trips today: your first and your last," he pronounced as he stomped about the lakeshore.

I hope that made him feel better. I didn't really see what he was so mad about. I was the ripe old age of four, and Mike was seven. Lee didn't have any male children, and if he had, he wouldn't have subjected them to that kind of humiliation. It was all just mind-boggling. What did he think was going to happen? We were going to be fishing prodigies or something? I mean, I'm not much of a fisherman, but if I took a four-year-old and a seven-year-old fishing, I wouldn't expect them to catch a lot of fish.

It wasn't exactly *A River Runs through It*, where we were going to catch the big fish if we were left on our own.

I guess this was before Zebcos were invented with their covered, push-button casting apparatus. Just maybe, had they been available, I would have been a better fisherman. Actually, *fisherkid* seems more appropriate. After we left, I felt like a complete loser, but I'd been doing the best I could. It taught me to never humiliate someone as a means to motivate them. It absolutely does not work. It wasn't the last time we went fishing together, but it definitely didn't happen for a long time. The next time we went fishing again, I was seventeen years old. Of course, this was also the time he quit fishing early so he and my brother could go look at a car at Beaty Chevrolet. It was better than fishing, even though the fish were breaking water just offshore.

But hey, what did I know?

I was no fishing expert.

CHAPTER 8

My family was fairly inhibited growing up. I was just me, take it or leave it. Between Dad and Mike, I stopped caring what others thought of me because they usually had some opinion that didn't warrant paying attention to. I started wondering if there were other kids out there I would get along with better, and I could see tons of them to question from my own yard. After all, we lived on Shamrock Avenue, and in total, there were twenty-three kids in our neighborhood, and it stayed that way until 1963.

Around the beginning of summer, Mike and I had a nice hole going before it collapsed. When I say *hole*, I mean a bunker. There was only one thing left to do, which was to gather up ammo for some imaginary foe. Mike was in charge of requisitioning the ammo from the surrounding terrain, bushes, and so forth. My job was to catch such ammo and store it in our bunker by the creek bed. By *ammo*, I mean cans, bottles, and rocks. Things were going pretty well until he threw me a broken Coke bottle. Needless to say, it made a nice hole in my hand.

I remember thinking, *My blood sure is red.* I didn't even bother crying. I just sucked it up and got it taken care of. This stuff happened so often that my tear ducts weren't able to keep up anymore. The gash was nothing that a trip to the emergency room and a couple of stitches couldn't fix. I knew the people in the ER on a first-name basis, I went there so often. In actuality, I had stitches out the wazoo, and I still have the scar on my left hand to prove it. After that, I was done with Mike being the only kid I played with on a daily basis. That day, I learned another valuable lesson in life.

Pain is temporary. Glory is forever.

I was no longer going to give him the satisfaction of seeing me cry over something he had done to me. It was really the only thing he was in it for. I couldn't stand to see him smile because of the harm he had done to me. Mike and I had our moments when we were kids where we laughed and had fun together, but those were few and far between. From that point on, I had to surround myself with kids who weren't trying to slowly but surely take my life. The limited amount of time I spent with my cousins would no longer suffice.

CHAPTER 9

Although at the ripe old age of four I had never really been out of my own yard to play, I asked my mother if I could go around the neighborhood and make some friends.

Her answer: "Be home by dark."

Back then, parents didn't have the world at their fingertips via the internet and a bazillion shows on TV reminding them of the terrible crimes committed all over the world. Furthermore, violence didn't seem as common as it is today. If they were doing things around the house and needed to keep you idle, they would let you loose, give you your boundaries, and go back to whatever they were doing. Being home by dark usually meant thirty minutes after the streetlights came on, and that was pushing it. In just the first few days venturing out, I met guys who I loved to hang out with and vice versa. It didn't matter that most of them were older than I was. Namely, the usual suspects in my clique consisted of Steve and Sonny Kivett, Mike Childress, Anthony Parrot, Jimmy Loy, Greg White, Ricky, Butch, and Rusty Henry, and you can't forget Dennis Turner. Other guys who would kick around with us from time to time were Simon Coleman, Tommy Blaylock, and his brother Larry.

We were really good when it came to creating outside games and things to do together. The sky was the limit. There were all kinds of activities that we would conjure up. If having a good imagination is a true sign of intelligence, then mark us down as geniuses. We would hang out from sunup to sundown, and there was never a moment that we weren't entertained. All was right in the world, and for a bunch of little guys, we were the furthest thing from needy. We had our own mode of transportation, which was walking, ate three square meals a day, and had a roof over our heads when needed. One day, we decided the only thing we were missing was a weapon. We were determined to come up with a system of defense, so we picked something that was readily available. One of our regular hangouts was the creek bed. About three-fourths of the way down, the ground was made up of gray clay. If you got a good chunk and rolled it up in the palm of your hand, it made a great projectile. So, now that we had ammunition, the only thing we were in need of was a way to propel it.

One thing we had in our small forest around the creek bed was a lot of tree limbs. It had to be the right limb, one which was flexible but firm. Just like that, we had a delivery system for our clay projectiles. The most logical next step was coming up with a name for our weapon. Since you would put the projectile on the limb and fling it at your target, we came up with the most fitting name, which was The Flinger.

How original, right?

In a matter of a few days of experimenting, we got pretty accurate with our Flingers. It wasn't anything to take a kid's baseball cap off with one. When we had the chance, we were practicing. Anytime there was a confrontation, one was greeted by a hail of projectiles, and everybody would charge into the woods and return with Flingers. Although they were created as our mini militia's form of defense, we only ever had the opportunity to use them on each other. The Flinger got an upgrade when we found a piece of bamboo in a roll of carpet. Add to that a projectile six inches in diameter, and you had the Bunker Buster! I sure didn't want to get hit with that bad whammer jammer! It could take an appendage off. It was a spectacle to behold.

In the first summer running around with the boys, we were really trying to come up with some games we enjoyed that would last so we could play them over and over. However, most of them were short-lived. The first game I remember that would be categorized like that was Morse code.

Believe it or not, if we went to C. B. Atkin Co. Furniture Manufacturers, we could get broken mirrors for free, so that's what we did. To this day, it still amazes me the variety of things that a little boy finds interesting and can have fun with. Anyway, after making it back to the neighborhood with our new devices, it was decided that we would climb trees and send each other messages.

So, we climbed twenty feet up into separate trees with our broken shards of glass. We flashed away, sending those time-sensitive messages. The problem we faced was that the receiver had no idea what the sender meant. Regardless, it didn't deter us from flashing our glass like little maniacs that day, but we never could figure out the message. I guess it was probably a result of the oldest of us being eight at the time and never being trained in Morse code. In the end, it wasn't worth the risk of scaling twenty feet into a tree with a broken piece of glass in your hand.

The other creation I vividly remember that falls into the short-lived genre is a game that I played once with Jimmy Loy called Fire Ranger. One person was on the ground and set blaze to a bundle of sticks with a match. At the same time, the Fire Ranger climbed up into a predetermined tree house. Once the fire really got going, you would climb down and extinguish the fire.

Simple people have simple ways.

I spied smoke first.

Good thing I was up there to keep tabs because once I got down, I took off toward the smoke and, sure enough, the entire creek bed was on fire. Once I extinguished the fire, Jimmy took his turn.

After he went, it was then decided that we would both be fire rangers at the same time. We lit a bundle of sticks and climbed into the tree house. It wasn't five minutes later that we spied smoke. We climbed down from the tree house and went in search of the fire.

There is a lot of truth behind the old saying *Where there's smoke, there's fire.*

The creek bed was on fire again—only this time, there was an eight-foot welded wire-mesh fence around the backyard of the house beside it. To make matters worse, there was a three-year-old girl playing on a tricycle inside the fence.

Can you say *Oh $#*%*? After a very brief discussion, we decided to go to the front door.

Ding dong!

The lady who lived there answered the door. "Can I help you boys?"

Nervously we replied, "Yes ma'am. We were just passing by and couldn't help but notice the large amount of smoke coming from your backyard. We just wanted to let you know it looks like it's on fire."

At which point she went running for the backyard, and we hightailed it home. End of game…forever!

I came up with a lot of the games that didn't have a lasting impact on our daily entertainment. With that said, I was always willing to join in on anything we did come up with, no matter how dangerous it was. Lasting parts of my character were being established without me even realizing it. It didn't result in my becoming the next Evil Knievel or anything like that, but I never backed down from a challenge or a situation that involved a little risk or a potentially painful ending. Also, the experience of making friends and discovering the reward of healthy relationships, as opposed to the ones I experienced at home with Mike and Dad, was helping me evolve more and more into my own person.

My family was so focused on what others thought of them and spent a lot of time being unhappy with themselves and others. Being out of the house for the majority of my time and deciding not to follow suit helped me realize that there was plenty to like about me. It also led to the cognition that I tended to be pretty good at most things I decided to take part in. As a growing child, things I was or wasn't fond of started to manifest themselves to me, and due to my self-esteem, I couldn't be persuaded otherwise. It was a powerful thing to grasp, and later in life, I came up with my own message to coincide with this important lesson that everyone should strive to learn.

Finding comfort in every facet of yourself and in being who you truly are is comparable to a permanent vacation.

Constantly living to appease the thoughts of others and finding no solace in who you've been created to be is comparable to a 168-hour workweek.

CHAPTER 10

It was late summer of 1958 that I first noticed a couple of guys who really caught my attention. I saw them every Tuesday.

"Who are those guys, Mom?"

"They are called the garbage men, honey."

I was particularly impressed with the guys on the back of the truck. They could sling garbage cans like nobody's business, and before long, I aspired to be a garbage man. This whole idea just tore my brother out of the frame.

In an attempt to discourage me, he would say, "There's broken glass everywhere on the garbage truck, even in the seats up front."

"That's okay," I would reply. "I would still like to be the garbage man."

It would frustrate Mike even more, which I admittedly relished a little bit yet didn't give it away. I got excited just thinking about getting to ride on the back bumper. Be assured that, at this point, I didn't care or have any qualms about a little broken glass.

To my benefit, Mike rarely played around the neighborhood with the rest of the guys and me. This was due to a few key facts. The first was that he was lazy. The second was that he was typically a jerk to everyone. The third was that his knack for being a bully and his laziness combined led to him being a chunky kid, which made him a target.

It didn't take the others much time to determine a nickname for him, which was Meat Market.

He hated it, and it hurt his feelings, so I usually only interacted with him when I had to go in the house for something. He would be sitting there with an empty pitcher that had been full of sweet tea just a few hours earlier and a cup that had the remains of melted ice in it next to him as he watched television.

He would wait until I came in and then yell out, "Mom! Steve came in and drank all of the sweet tea!"

I would blow it off, go about getting whatever I was in need of, and hear my mom in the kitchen making a fresh pitcher of sweet tea as I headed back out to play. The exception of Mike playing with everyone was the games which he was the best at or in control of.

A good example of this would be the time that he decided we would start a club. We modeled it after the Fraternal Order of the Eagles and called ourselves the Hawks. It was determined by our president, Mike, that as a uniform we would wear matching captain's hats that were generously donated to us by Papaw. He had found them in a pile of leftover clothes at the fire hall. They had a nice round white top with a customized drawing of a hawk, done by our one and only resident artist, Mike. Dues to be a Hawk were a stifling nickel per person, per meeting. Collecting dues was always on the agenda, and our basement was chosen as the venue. One day, I was doing as I was instructed, which was putting away everything after a Friday meeting. I made a remarkable discovery.

I asked Mike (also the treasurer), "Did you know that we have collected almost five bucks in dues?"

He must have been off his game that day because he actually looked at me and asked, "What do you think we should do with it?"

To which I replied, "I think we should go to town and spend it!"

Realizing his moment of weakness, he quickly responded, "Okay, but I am deciding where we go."

It was determined that Mom would drive Mike, Tommy, Larry, and me uptown and drop us off at one of our favorite burger joints called Blue Circle. Remember, this was before people were prosecuted for child neglect for doing such a thing and also before everyone thought that there was a 100 percent chance of your young children dying if you took them to town and dropped them off. Sunday came, and as I have previously mentioned, not every moment with Mike was terrible, and this was one of them. Although, it is worth noting that he wouldn't have gone had he not been making all of the decisions.

"What'll you have?" asked the waitress.

Mike spoke up. "We'll have five Blue Circle Burgers each and four small Cokes."

That was twenty hamburgers and a Coke for everybody. The best part was that we still had enough money left over out of our five bucks for everyone to catch a movie across the street at the Bijou Theatre after we were done stuffing ourselves.

The Bijou (which at the time I pronounced *By-joe*) was one of three theaters in downtown Knoxville at the time. The others were the Tennessee Theatre and the Riviera (which I called the *Ra-veer-ah*). That day, we saw the *Lone Ranger*—first in person and then on the big screen in the hit *Gunfighter's Revenge*. When I say in person, I mean that there was a guy dressed up like the Lone Ranger who came galloping into the theater on a horse and unloaded his dual six shooters into the ceiling as Trigger reared up on his back legs. That day, I would have sworn to you the bullets were real, and if it weren't for having to hustle outside to Mom's car after the movie was over, I probably would have checked. It was a great day to be a loyal Hawks member. We felt like we got a big bang for our buck, and Mike was proud of his five dollars well spent. It made his day for us to praise him and tell him thanks. He certainly didn't share the same sentiments a few weeks later when I reciprocated the generosity.

CHAPTER 11

"Whoa!" I shouted after spying several Tom's Potato Chips bags in a dumpster.

Whoever had thrown those away sure didn't know what they were doing. Once I shimmied inside, I realized it was better than I could have imagined. I had hit the jackpot! With the exception of the person who threw them away, everyone knew that you could get into the Tennessee Theatre on Saturday morning for just thirty-five cents' worth of Tom's wrappers. This was close to four dollars in value. We were in like Flynn and could take a couple of pals.

On Saturday mornings, Mom loaded up our brand-new blue '59 Chevy Impala with a couple of my buddies, Mike, and me. The Impala was my favorite of all the lemons we had growing up.

Mom yelled out to us when we got out of the car, "I'll be back to pick you up in this same spot at eleven thirty on the dot!"

"Deal!" we all shouted back in unison.

After getting through the ticket line, we went and got our seats. The Tennessee Theatre was majestic, but the best part was the guy who came up out of the orchestra pit and played the giant Wurlitzer. It alone was worth the price of admission.

We joined all the other 350 kids and got ready for the day's agenda.

First up was the old serial *Spin and Marty*. Spin and Marty were the Hardy Boys on horses. The Hardy Boys were the male version of Nancy

Drew. If you don't know who Nancy Drew is, then you're just out of luck here.

Next up was the serial *Sky King*. All the kids knew Sky King and Penny, as we watched them fly into our living room early on Saturday mornings. When we watched them at home, we would hit the deck when they went flying toward the television screen. Luckily, they flew high enough to miss us every time.

The main feature was *Old Yeller*. Old Yeller was a good dog, but the movie had an awfully sad ending. At the end of the feature, all I could think was what a great deal it had been: a first-rate Disney production for thirty-five cents' worth of Tom's wrappers. Better yet, I had enough left over for us all to go for the next few weeks. Mom was right on time. All the guys gave their thanks for my generosity and also for my dumpster spelunking that had allowed us the opportunity.

Not a word from Mike, though. I am pretty sure he was bitter that I was thanked at all. It is simply just the way he was. I really think that, deep down, he wanted to like me but he would never allow himself to. It didn't bother me one way or the other. The more these things happened, the more I played with the other guys in the neighborhood. Susan was still just a cute little baby and less than two years old. I couldn't do much with her besides make goofy faces and make her laugh. Besides eating, bathing, and sleeping, I didn't spend much time at home except for getting some lovin' from Mom or when we were doing something as a family.

CHAPTER 12

Around the beginning of fall that year marks my first memories of the people around me talking about something called sports. Everyone would talk about the Volunteers this and the Volunteers that. We had a bird named Beattie Feathers. Dad said he was named after the greatest player in Tennessee history.

My Uncle David would try to explain football to me, but I just didn't grasp it, and most of his explanations were followed by "Why do they do that, Uncle Dave?"

The one thing he did get across to me was that, if you lived in the state of Tennessee, you were a Volunteers fan, and there were no ifs, ands, or buts about it. He promised to take me to a game someday. The guys around the neighborhood who were a little older would talk about playing football, baseball, basketball, and so on. I was so little that they would wait to play until after I had gone in or wasn't around. But I was curious, and sometimes I would watch them from a distance as they played while I was doing family stuff. It looked fun, but I didn't understand it quite yet.

All I knew was that I wanted to play too, and everyone was scared I would get hurt. To make matters worse, Mike got to play with them. He would come back in after playing, and I'd ask him questions about it.

"What were you playing?"

"How do you play?"

"Do you think I could be good at it?"

His answer was always the same: "Shut up, Steve."

Through the beginning of fall, I had the opportunity to listen to the Volunteers on the radio and watch my first game on television. It piqued my interest even more. It was exciting, and watching it made me feel something inside I had never experienced.

Just before Christmas that year, we had company on a Saturday night. My godparents, Bobbi and Frank Mary, had come over for the evening and brought their children. We saw them at least once a month. They had a son named Bill who I liked to hang out with and two girls named Susie and Sherry. Bill and Susie were actually born in the same year and were close to my age. Bill, Susie, Sherry, Mike, and I opted for the great outdoors to find our amusement for the evening. This was common practice, and we even had a regular repertoire of games we liked to play together.

Nightfall was upon us, so the first game we played was Kick the Can, which is the ultimate exercise in futility. Throughout the game, I remember Bill telling me that he and his dad had been throwing the baseball around. Boy, was I jealous. Learning a sport and spending time with his dad—how did he get so lucky?

Next, we played Fox and Hounds. Bill was a great athlete even at an early age, and I was really determined to not get turned into a hound. We chatted as we kept from being tagged. He told me about his baseball mitt and how he had decided that one day he was going to play baseball at the University of Tennessee.

As a matter of fact, he followed through on it, too.

After Fox and Hounds and our talks about baseball, Bill wanted to show me how he could throw.

We came up with a neat game called Throwing Rocks at Cars.

So, we hid behind our giant Jacob fir and accumulated some ammo— also known as *rocks*. Bill zeroed in on a car coming, and I'll be damned if he didn't hit it on his first shot.

Bang!

The guy turned around and came back. He told Bill's dad what had happened, and he didn't take it too well. Let's just say Bill won or lost, depending on how you look at it. Frank took off his belt and proceeded to spank Bill on the spot in front of all of us. That was the last time we played that game.

CHAPTER 13

Christmas came and went. Susan was two years old and growing by the day. Dad was working all the time, Mom was raising us, Mike was being Mike, and I was trying to make my way into a sports game. In March of 1959, I turned five. It was time for something to give.

I wanted to show the kids around the block that I was just as much of an athlete as they were, regardless of how small I was. Not being allowed to join in with the older kids playing more physical sports was my only issue. I guess I forgot to mention to this point that they played everything full steam ahead: football was in pads; basketball was street ball; and there was no tee in baseball.

Although I was persistent in my efforts, I didn't get anywhere. A proverb by William Edward Hickson that I heard a long time ago is a good lesson to learn and is in alignment with my efforts.

'Tis a lesson you should heed:

Try, try, try again.

If at first you don't succeed,

Try, try, try again.

I guess I put a twist on it because, at the time, my version was more like *If at first you don't succeed, try, try, try something else.*

I had heard about track and field. This occurred when I overheard my uncles talking about how the United States dominated in the 1956

Olympics. Bobby Morrow had won multiple events where all he did was run. I didn't need permission to run. I did it every day, and I surely wasn't going to get hurt. I was knee high to a grasshopper and running wasn't in style yet. Nevertheless, I decided to go for a run.

I decided to run around the block. So, off I went past the Larrews', the Whites', the Parrots', the Henrys', the Greens', the Conners', the Daniels', up the alley, and back to the beginning. The new Converse I got for my birthday were smoldering after the first lap. I caught the attention of the neighborhood kids, and they watched with delight as I kept going.

They wore away more of the footpath in the Henrys' yard as they ran back and forth keeping up with my progress. I ended up doing eight laps—a Herculean effort and a record if only for a day. At the same time, I had completed my first sporting event, even if there were no other competitors. The cheers of my friends made me feel like a superhero. I was hooked!

The next couple of weeks yielded the same outcome in my attempt to play sports with the other kids. I didn't have much time to worry about that due to the fact that Easter Sunday was on the twenty-ninth of March that year, and I had to help my family prepare for the festivities. Before Walmart, we had Zayre, among other department stores. We shopped there sometimes and decided to go there to get a few things to take to my family's house for Easter Sunday. Zayre was a discount department store, which led Grandmother Bee to shop there exclusively. She couldn't get enough of the place. Anytime there was something to buy, she went to Zayre, and sometimes I was fortunate enough to go with her. I loved to see all of the random things they had that caught my eye.

When we got to the family Easter event, we walked in and did our usual. After we ate, it was on to my favorite part.

"Happy Easter!" said Bee.

She then presented us with a forest-green canvas tent as a gift. It was a secondhand army tent that Zayre had had on special. I still remember the smell of the canvas. It was a huge tent—at least six feet high and ten feet long. It was made for four people, and the last thing to do was try it out.

That night, we invited all of our neighborhood buddies and set up shop in the backyard by the swing set, easily the best spot for a back-yard camp-out. The whole night was great, but one part in particular was my favorite.

At about eight o'clock, my mom called me up to the house. Once I was inside, she and Dad told me to sit down. I could tell it was something as Mom started talking.

She said, "Your aunt gave you something at Easter dinner, but I didn't know whether or not to give it to you yet. I asked her about a week ago if she had anything lying around that you have been in need of. I didn't think she would come up with something so quickly, but I talked it over with your dad, and it is in your room on your bed. Go check it out."

She sounded excited for me, so I ran down the hallway as fast as I could and flung the door open. To my amazement, there on my bed was a full set of football pads, accompanied by a uniform and cleats.

I was elated.

I hooted and hollered and ran back out and hugged Mom and Dad. I felt like putting them on right then and there and running out and show-ing everyone. Mom and Dad told me not to tell anyone. Mike had told them that the guys were going to play the next day around lunch when my mother had planned to take me to get a haircut so that I wouldn't get upset. Everyone knew how badly I had wanted to play, and they were my friends, so it was their way of looking out for me. She told me that we would move my haircut to the next week and then said I could play for the first time the next day and surprise everyone.

So, that's exactly what I did.

I went back outside to a campfire and everyone lying around just inside the tent. With a smile on my face, I joined the rest of the guys and found myself in deep thought about my first backyard football game. At about midnight, a grossly inebriated man got out of a car at the corner of the street. On his way home through the alley behind our house, he kind of tripped over a tent stake as he went by. In fact, he nearly knocked the whole tent down.

Everyone happened to be awake except for me.

I had fallen asleep thinking about the next day.

There was a mad scramble as everyone tried to get out of the tent. He sure did choose the wrong night to rudely interrupt a camp-out. Once I was awake, I started thinking about my new football attire again. I was ready to tackle anything and everything. So, I led the rest of the pack in a foot chase after the guy. It looked like the villagers chasing the monster of Frankenstein; only, the villagers were on average five years old and just over four feet tall. We never did catch him, but we sure did give it our best effort. To the tune of three laps around the block to be exact, which was nothing for a record setter like me.

It was time to properly enter the next phase of my athletic career. Ultimately, that meant starting it. Watching the games on television and the guys in the neighborhood just wouldn't cut it anymore. I was so intrigued by the reactions of the fans at sporting events I watched when their favorite players made incredible plays. I got a taste of it during my run, but it wasn't enough. All sports drew the same reaction, but football was my main interest.

Thoughts would go racing through my mind. Catching the ball, tackling a guy, learning how to play. Even scoring a touchdown in front of a huge crowd. I had never in my life been so excited about something. I knew I would be capable. I knew I was better than most at the other games we played. It was finally time for me to show everyone what I was all about. It was all I could think about, and the time had come to actually take part.

The Awakening

Tuesday, May 6 – Monday, May 12, 2008

Northwest Georgia – Chattanooga, Tennessee

Fifty-four Years Old

It bewilders me that on Tuesday, May 6, 2008, at fifty-four years old, standing at six feet three and weighing 268 pounds—and being a regular madman in the gym—that I could also have had some type of serious health concern. I guess I have always felt a bit invincible and had something killed me, it would have happened in my most invincible days somewhere between the ages of eighteen and twenty-eight. It had worried me, to say the least, since the previous Saturday. A lot of my conscious thoughts had been dedicated to it. The previous day at work, I could barely focus on brokering, although I pulled out a pretty strong day for a few clients as the market closed at four o'clock. Driving up to Calhoun High School's soccer practice, where I was a coach, I sat in silence, as I usually did, deep in thought about what could be going on with me.

I determined at what point to ask around. I called a few folks I knew, and that is what led me to determining which doctors to line up an appointment with. I'm an optimist, and under further recommendations, I decided my first appointment would be with my eye doctor. The issue, after all, was double vision. I know that I passed out, but realistically, that could have been due to trying to be active while experiencing such intense double vision.

I couldn't afford for this to be something more than an irregularity with my eyes or some such thing.

Control in situations has always been my strong suit. I am a conqueror. Life has rarely presented me with a situation I couldn't handle and never one that I couldn't overcome. When I had the double vision and was unable to do what I wanted to, that was the scariest part for me because I was incapable of being in control of myself and what was happening. I thought about the inability to even protect my family if a situation presented itself.

I pulled up for my appointment and went in.

While I was waiting, I started thinking about everything going on with me and could feel the hairs stand up on the back of my neck as my mind reeled with images, like my brain was navigating through a horror-story flip-book. My throat felt like it was closing up. I could feel my claustrophobia coming on. It was frustrating and making me angry. Angry and uncomfortable. I just wanted to break out of it. I started clenching my fists and flexing my muscles. I could feel my Oxford shirt getting tighter around my biceps and forearms. For a second, I felt an immense amount of anxiety, and beads of sweat started to form on my forehead. I noticed that I was talking to myself under my breath and simultaneously pulling at my mustache.

Why had I not kept better check on my health?

Surely it was just an issue with my vision.

If something serious was going on, how could I be a rock for my family if I was unable to be a rock for myself?

Calm down, Steve. Get it under control!

"Steve Adkins," the eye doctor called, as he came to get me for my checkup.

After the usual lineup of questions, I responded with the specifics. I told him I was there due to what had happened the previous Saturday and explained the circumstances in detail. I told him about the double vision. How intense it had been, and how nauseating it was to even recall it. How I had passed out and was unaware how long I had been out before Paul woke me. I told him that someone had suggested it could be due to my eyes. So, I had made the first available appointment to figure out what was going on, to ease my and my family's minds—hopefully with some answers. After my examination, he explained to me that my eyes showed no issues. I needed to continue wearing my bifocals, but they weren't going to keep me from experiencing double vision if the problem presented itself again.

His primary suggestion was to go see my physician. Fortunately, that was the second appointment I had made, but it wasn't until the next day. There was no time to worry about that then, even though I really wished I could walk across the parking lot and already be at my next appointment. I was really banking on this being the fix. Instead, I had no clue what the hell was going on. Not only did I have to explain that to Bella and the kids, but I also had to wait. Patience is the furthest thing from being a strong suit of mine, but in fact, I had a full day ahead of me. Work for a few hours and then referee a play-off game that night. That was something I could get excited about. Not work, but the play-off game. I had really grown to love the game of soccer over the past seventeen years, and being a referee fed my love for the game and my love for exercise. Plus, I knew it would be a great opportunity to take my mind off things for at least three or four hours.

I headed to work and gave Bella the feedback via a phone call along the way. It was like a punch in the gut to hear her deflate as I told her that it was something more serious than my eyes acting up. You could tell she had been banking on it only being a vision issue as much as I was. It was easy to pick up on her imagining the thousands of diagnoses straight off the pages of the most current version of the *Merck Manual*.

It was one of the things she did.

The kids could have a common cold and she would ask me if I thought they had typhoid fever. It was in her maternal nature, and the outcome was that our children had never spent a night in the hospital that I can recall. I asked her to spare me, though. If I had gotten off the phone thinking I had three days to live, at that point that would have been the last thing I needed.

Work dragged on for a few hours, and besides getting a few things done for some of my biggest clients, I spent a while explaining to my administrative assistant, Renee, what was going on. She told me she would keep a closer eye on me while I was at the office and contact Bella immediately if I had a double-vision episode at work, whether I liked it or not. I didn't really mind, although that seemed like such a serious thing to say. Realistically, it had only been a few hours since I too had started freaking out. I guess it was understandable.

At least I knew she cared.

The stock market closed, and my workday ended. Next, it was on to refereeing. I had met the other referees two hours before kickoff as scheduled. It was relaxing to be out of my own head. We walked the field as the teams started showing up. After going into our quarters to get dressed out, we continued back onto the field with forty-five minutes left until kickoff to do our usual rundown. Check ball pressure, go over rosters, check player equipment, and so on. The more time you give yourself, the less stressful the lead-up to kickoff is. Ten minutes before kickoff, the school named the starters for both teams, everyone shook hands, and the captains came forward for the coin toss. I was an assistant referee and took my duties very seriously. This was the second round of Tennessee's play-offs, and it was understood that whoever won the game would more than likely find themselves in the finals. Finally, the game started.

As the time in the game wound down, it was an intense back-and-forth battle. With about fifteen minutes left in the game, I ran down to the goal line. The ball went out for a goal kick, and as I raised my flag to signal the call, I felt a wave pass over me. Like I had been tossed in a whirlpool, everything began spinning.

Hang on, Steve. Take a deep breath.

I could feel the sweat dripping off my face, and I tried to look down at my watch and see how much time was left in the game. As I turned my head from field level down to my wrist, I also turned and started to trot back up toward half field. As my watch came into my vision it was as if my wrist and my watch had a shadow of itself. A ghost arm, so to speak.

The double vision was back.

I deeply analyzed the situation every second of the rest of the match. The last thing I could do was just pass out as the game came to an end or miss a call that would determine the result of the game. A few times, I thought of signaling to my center official and having the fourth official take over for me.

Inevitably, it was my own personal nature that led me to pushing through. I didn't want anyone to be worried about me, and if they realized what was going on, no one could blame them for calling 9-1-1.

Going to the hospital was the last thing on my agenda.

The narrow hallway of black never came back, however. After the final whistle sounded and the game had come to an end, I tried to keep my poker face on. The referee crew and I headed in to get changed. Without giving any sign of an issue, I said goodbye to the guys as I headed out to my car. Now all I had to do was navigate the nearly fifty miles from Chattanooga to Resaca, Georgia, where home was.

Instead of feeling like I had just refereed for two hours, it felt more like I had spent the second half of my day drinking a liter of Jack. Only a mile or so into my trip home, I realized that the only viable option was closing or covering one eye to gain enough clarity to justify myself continuing to drive home. I thought about calling Bella and letting her know what was going on, but honestly, I just didn't want to have to deal with everyone freaking out. I called my referee assigner though. His name was Buddy, and I told him that I needed a replacement for my game that was scheduled for Thursday.

I told him that I was having some issues with my eyes, and he said he'd take care of it.

I alternated between covering my left and right eyes for the hour-long drive home. Thoughts rushed through my head, and the questions lingering brought back my anxiety like it had been sitting first-class in a commercial airliner. The emotions that came over me were unsettling. In my adult life, from what I can recall, I had cried only one time—when my father passed away—for a total of about three minutes. Out of frustration and due to the lack of knowledge of what I was experiencing, I started to feel a bit emotional.

Worries about something really being wrong and the inability to take care of my family and provide for the ones I loved came flooding in. There I was driving down I-75, in complete and utter silence in my car with thoughts of fear, confusion, and some form of denial swirling around in my mind. I was afraid to call my wife and tell her what was going on, not knowing what *was* going on within me, scared that I may not even make it home without passing out behind the wheel. Then, I felt tears fill my eyes and stream down my cheeks.

Something I hadn't experienced in almost a decade.

At ten minutes after nine that night, I pulled into my driveway, my lights flashing across the white house as I turned left into the driveway. My plan was simple: go inside, take a shower, tell everyone how my day had gone and that I loved them but, above all else, play it cool.

Don't let them know what is going on, Steve.

Fortunately, about a half hour after I got home, Paul told Bella and me that he loved us and headed over to the pool house for the night to hang out with some friends. Danny was in Kennesaw at his house just beside his college. He stayed with us about half the time, but when he had a big assignment or studying to do, he would stay near the school. Bella had showered just before I got home, so by the time I had gotten freshened up, she was all but ready for bed.

At about half past ten, we lay down. In my head, I hoped I would make it through the night with no big issues and that I would get some answers at my doctor's visit the following morning. Bella was asleep within five minutes. When I knew she was out, I felt relief because I was finally alone with my myself, and I lay in bed awake for what seemed like two hours. Thought after thought went through my head. I was opening my eyes every few minutes to see if the double vision had subsided. A few minutes after midnight, I remember opening my eyes for the last time and realizing the double vision was gone.

It eased my mind.

I needed sleep.

Tomorrow was a big day.

Go to sleep, Steve. Stop thinking about everything else, and just go to sleep.

CHAPTER 15

1959–1963

Knoxville, Tennessee

Childhood

Our minor encounter with the drunk guy outside of our tent only made the wait worse. The never-ending thoughts of playing football the next day came and went in my mind. Minute after minute passed by as I lay there and envisioned the plays that would ensue the following day. I wondered if it would hurt getting tackled, and I imagined it. I wondered if I would make a big play, and I imagined that too. I imagined making all kinds of big plays.

Long runs for touchdowns, spectacular catches, big hits, and juking everyone out of their shoes with the ball in my hands. What would it be like? Would I be good? I really thought I'd be good. I had this feeling inside. The feeling that you get when you know that something big is about to happen. Eventually, despite the thoughts dancing around my head, I fell back asleep. The only thing between me and the first day I would play football was a few hours of sleep.

Mom forced me to eat breakfast, which was something I would have voluntarily skipped due to the excitement. Since Mike and I shared a room, Mom had stored my new gear in her bedroom until morning. I went about my usual routine after breakfast, which made it extremely hard to keep my secret. I went out and played with the guys for a few hours. I mainly just tried to stay focused on the game at hand to allow time to roll by so that I wouldn't ruin my big surprise.

Around eleven, I went in for lunch, and by that, I mean I ate two bites of a banana and snuck off into my parents' room while avoiding Mike. He thought we were getting ready to go to the barber, so he went to our room and got himself into his football gear and headed out about ten minutes ahead of me.

I had watched Mike put on his stuff a few times, which allowed me the inside scoop on the order in which you put everything on. I stripped down to my underwear, socks, and T-shirt. My football attire was canvas white with red numerals. As I reached toward the bed and grabbed the pants, a wave of overwhelming excitement hit me. The smile on my face was unshakable. I pulled the pants on. Next, I grabbed my all-black cleats, which were basically high-top black Converse with lumps of rubber on the bottom. I laced them up nice and tight. Next, I threw on my shoulder pads. The excitement grew inside me. I felt six feet tall and two hundred pounds. Finally, I pulled my jersey over the shoulder pads and grabbed my helmet. I tugged the helmet onto my head, not knowing to push it apart at the ear holes. It rubbed uncomfortably down the side of my head and over my ears.

Barely tall enough to see over the dresser, I looked into the mirror and buttoned my chin strap. The huge grin that was still on my face. I was nervous, but I was also excited. Butterflies flew around my stomach for a moment. I raised both hands in the air and slapped the sides of my helmet, and off I went.

As I reached the edge of my yard, I could see a few of the guys still walking up to the field: our football field was the Kivetts' side yard. It was a rectangle if you had an imagination. It had roughly 25-yard end lines and 40-yard sidelines. It was bordered on the north and the east by the creek, on the south by Springdale Avenue, and on the west by the Kivetts' driveway.

Each kid came equipped in his own uniform and the same black high-top cleats. It's all they had at the time. Once out of my yard, I started walking down the street toward the Kivetts.' If it was possible, I felt my grin get bigger as everyone started pointing toward me and talking. When I was about fifteen feet from the field, I could finally make out what they were saying.

"Who is that?" asked Steve Kivett.

"It's Steve Adkins!" exclaimed his brother Sonny in excitement.

"He sure looks big," added Steve.

I loved that comment.

It was in that moment that I decided from that point forward, my pads were going to be an extension of my body as often as possible. I'd never felt bigger than when I had my pads on. Everyone but Mike ran over to me hooting and hollering. A few of them grabbed my face mask and pulled my helmet into theirs, which was complemented by an exhilarating sound as they smashed together. They knew how long I had waited for this moment, and right then, I realized that they, too, had been waiting for it just as long.

Of course they had.

These were my buds.

I think the only excitement Mike got out of it was picturing me on the other team so that he could lay me out.

Finally, he walked over to me and asked, "What are you doing here?"

I said, "Mom got me this stuff and said I could play with you guys."

He looked me dead in the eye and said, "Don't break a leg."

I looked back into his eyes and said, "Don't break an ankle."

The first thing we did was choose captains, who in turn picked teams. I was picked to play on Steve Kivett's team. On that day, I felt fortunate that Mike was as well. At least I wouldn't have to find out on my very first day if it was my leg or Mike's ankle that was going to break. The captains met at midfield to toss a penny, and we were off.

I think every kid on that field imagined he would be the next Johnny Majors and a star player at Tennessee in front of the crowd at Neyland Stadium. At first, I just tried to get the hang of things. I'd arrive at the play after it was over on defense and try to stay out of everyone's way on offense. Occasionally, I'd run into a player on the other team as hard as I could and feel like I was blocking. About twenty minutes in, I got my legs under me and became more and more involved on each play. I recalled my thoughts from the night before.

This is my time! Show them what you're made of. You got this. You got this!

Right after giving myself a mental pep talk, we punted the ball and went on defense. On third down, they handed off to Mike Childress. I ran over and tried to arm-tackle Mike, which was a lot like trying to arm-tackle a moving cannonball. My attempt failed, and Mike Childress knocked me on my back, which in turn was followed by him running over me, his cleats literally stomping me as he moved on down the field.

How perfect is that? Hurt in the line of duty.

I should have been receiving hazardous-duty pay. I guess being heroic has its price, as in black cleat marks on my right forearm. All I could think as I lay there was *That was great!*

The rest of the guys were able to gang-tackle Mike, which brought up fourth down. They punted the ball. End over end it went, and as it came down out of the air, my brother fielded it. His attempt to return it lasted about three seconds and five yards before he bit the dust.

We huddled up, and Steve Kivett said, "Okay, let's see what Steve Adkins has got. I'm going to hand it off to him, and he is going to run a sweep around right end. Break!"

Sure enough, we lined up, he handed me the ball, and around right end I went. First, Anthony Parrot dove at me and completely missed. Sonny Kivett was playing right behind Anthony, and right before he got to me, I juked left toward the middle of the field, and he ran right by me. Finally, Jimmy Loy came flying in from the other side of the field, and as he dove in to tackle me, I switched the ball to my right hand and reached my left arm out, pushing his helmet into the dirt. I was home free, and all I had to do now was sprint to the creek. During my 25-yard run, it was as if time had slowed down.

I took it all in.

The sounds of everyone faded out, and all I could hear was the wind coming through my face mask.

I could feel the smile on my face and my feet hitting the ground underneath me as I inched closer and closer to our end zone. I ran as hard as I could and was able to faintly hear my teammates behind me yelling, "Go! Go! Go!" Even Mike cheered me on.

Touchdown!

The entire objective of the game of football is to advance the ball beyond the goal line. So when somebody achieves this, the game comes to a screeching halt. In that moment, as I ran across the goal line and turned around to see my team running down toward me, the other team bent over or lying on the ground in defeat, I realized something very important: I loved when the game came to a stop because of something I did!

I loved scoring touchdowns, and it only took one to help me reach that conclusion. It was at this time I realized something that was so important to understand in life. Later in life, I found a quote that verbalized exactly what I had understood that day.

You only get one chance to make a good first impression.

That statement isn't only true of the people around you, but also for yourself. That day, I made a great first impression on both. I could have just moped around after getting knocked on my back by Mike Childress, but personally, I thought it was awesome. I sure didn't let it embarrass me. I knew I wasn't going to do everything right the first time, and boy, am I glad I understood that! I may not have been perfect the first time, but there definitely was *something* I got right on the first shot. I ended up rushing the ball five times for two touchdowns. I also ended up with one catch on two targets and a half a tackle on about ten tries.

What?

I was still just a five-year-old playing with mostly older fellas, might I remind you. We basically played until we got tired. We counted touchdowns individually because calculators hadn't been invented yet, and nobody wanted to keep count with the scores in multiples of six. Suffice it to say, our team ended up ahead, 18–17, when everyone decided to call it quits. Nobody really cared much about who won, though. We were just glad to be playing football and hanging out with each other.

Afterward, we met in the adjacent creek bed for a celebratory smoke break—in an act of good sportsmanship, of course. Although this is the first time you are hearing about me smoking, I'm sure you've picked up on the fact that I'm talking about it like it is no big deal. Unfortunately, even though I was only five, it wasn't a big deal.

When I say smoke break, I'm not talking about store-bought regulars or menthols here. That's right, we're talking about hand-rolled grapevines. I preferred mine to be straight and about eighty millimeters long. They were pretty satisfying, but man, were they harsh. Afterward, they gave you a sore throat plus you smelled like a campfire. That's all the menu consisted of in those days, though, and you weren't going to hear a complaint out of me. It was the first day I played football, but overall, it was just another day in the neighborhood. Good times, laughs, and bad ideas came by the dozens.

Admittedly, my first love was football.

I knew it right then and there, the very first time I stepped onto the football field. Camaraderie was a close second, but football was definitely my first. From then on, with me on board, all of the kids in the neighborhood could play all the sports together.

Although sometimes we still would play a crazy made-up game, we transitioned largely into full-time athletes. I liked it that way. I had showed the guys what I was made of, and they thought I was great. Football was the usual suspect when looking at a lineup of games to play.

Each time we played, I got better. It wasn't but a few days, and I was killing it on both sides of the ball. Running back and linebacker were easily my favorite positions. Usually, when the ball was in my hands, a touchdown was soon to follow. I may have been one of the younger guys, but I was light on my feet and could run like the wind. Finally, all the time Mike had spent chasing me around the house was paying off.

I had football and football had me.

It was a match made in heaven.

CHAPTER 20

The spring of 1959 was quickly evolving into summer. I was kicking around the neighborhood every chance I got. At home, I noticed that Mom's belly had started to grow again. It was rather small at the time but was definitely noticeable. Although many of my memories include Mike playing games with me throughout the neighborhood, he still preferred television and sweet tea over being outside with me and the other kids. Susan was growing up, and in her own right, getting into whatever she found interest in.

She was two and half now, mobile as can be and cute as a button.

She definitely resembled Dad's side of the family, which they ate up. Speaking of Dad, I often wondered if he just didn't like us much. I loved to be around the people I cared about, and I figured he did the same. It just became apparent to me that either home was too much for the man or he just found more enjoyment in the people he worked with. I spent more time in a week with my friends as I did with Dad in two months.

Back on the sports scene, I sought out the opportunity to discover anything I hadn't previously been allowed to partake in. There was not a single sport I didn't like to play, and I was, in my opinion, decent at all of them. We didn't play other sports with the same intensity as football, but we made a game out of them anyway.

We had the same routine with all sports. We picked captains, they chose teams, and in a matter of minutes we were playing. I remember the first sport I played after trying out football was baseball. I had tossed the ball around a few times and was excited to finally get a chance to play.

Our backyard served as our baseball field. First base was the tree with the tree house in it. When I say tree house, I mean a small tree with two two-by-sixes nailed down to two dangerously small branches. Second base was a leg of the swing set, the end with the see-saw. Third base was the clothesline pole. This, of course, was back when everybody normally had a clothesline covered with clothespins, before dryers were in vogue. Home plate was the four-by-four concrete slab at the basement door.

I started out playing first base. As I had only tossed the ball around a few times, it only took the first few innings for a few balls to find my noggin like heat-seeking missiles.

I played it off pretty well, I thought.

The first time I blamed it on having something in my eye.

The second time, on the sun.

I got the hang of it after a few unforced errors and probably a minor concussion. I swung out the first time up to bat. When the lineup came back around to me, I took my place in the middle of the slab of concrete. There was one out, and Sonny Kivett was on second base. On the second pitch, I swung as hard as I could and connected with the pitch. It made the *crunking* noise that only a broken bat would make.

I guess it is worth mentioning that we only had one bat and it was a) wooden and b) broken.

It was the one held together by sticky electrical tape and a bent nail. We didn't mind much, though. It served its purpose just as well, and it was perfect for playing in a small yard. My first hit was a screamer. It rolled past the pitcher, past the second baseman, past the center fielder, and came to rest at the fence.

I made it all the way to the clothesline pole before I was urged to stop. The third base coach was my entire team yelling as loud as they could from the sidelines. I had driven in Sonny and evened the score. It was the least I could do because our opposition's score was definitely due to my error. Two batters later, "Big" Rick Henry drove me in with a line drive that lodged itself in the swing set.

About that time, Rusty Henry came running in. He wasn't playing that day, and at the time, we were thankful. Like I previously stated, we weren't as dedicated and intense about other sports as we were about football.

He ran straight in to the middle of the field and yelled, "Hey, the milkman is over on Springdale Avenue!"

Now let's get a few things straight here. It was nearing summer and hot as can be outside. Let's also take into consideration that Mike typically consumed about 73 percent of the milk that the milkman left at my house. At this point, Susan was still a baby, and she consumed the next 22 percent, leaving me with a mere five.

Tragic.

Also, this was during the late '50s, and there were no refrigerated trucks. It was door-to-door delivery. That's where all the milkman jokes come from. He delivered the milk in his metal carrying basket. He left whatever was on your previous order form on the porch, and you prepared your order form for the next week and he took it with him. The milk was in glass quart bottles and refrigerated by snow-cone-quality ice in heaps over the bottles they were cooling.

You haven't had milk until you've had it fresh off the milkman's truck.

I myself admit that the best milk I've ever had hasn't been available since the '60s.

Also tragic.

After we abandoned our baseball playing and gave chase, we caught up to the milkman on his next-to-last stop on Springdale. We climbed up on the back bumper and helped ourselves to a quart of milk and a glob of ice. Boy, was it refreshing! The miniature milk-and-ice bandits—including me—got away clean. I sure didn't mind an extra two percent of milk for the week.

Get it?

Through the window of the house, Mom saw us commit our crime. She went out and paid the milkman. She also got us another milk apiece from what he had in his inventory. She came out back and told us all to never do that again, and as soon as we'd promised we wouldn't, she sat the milks down for us and walked back inside. It had obviously worked out way better than expected.

As for whether or not we kept our promise to Mom, I plead the Fifth.

CHAPTER 21

As soon as we got through with the milk-truck raid, we made our way back to the ball field. Well, a few of us anyway. It was Mike, Steve and Sonny Kivett, and me. Steve Kivett had dislodged the ball from the swing set and asked, "Who wants to learn how to catch?"

I thought it was a great idea to touch up my skills, but I got a little overconfident from the tag out I'd had, as the top of the third inning had ended earlier.

"I do, I do! Actually, I already know how, too. Rear back and throw it as hard as you can, and I'll catch it. Rock and fire!"

Well, as the old saying goes, talk is cheap.

I caught the ball all right.

With my right eye, before I screamed bloody murder.

As soon as I stopped crying and came to the conclusion that I wasn't going to die, we decided to call it quits for the day. I was fine with that decision. I had ended up in worse shape after the first time I played baseball than the first time I'd played football, and it wasn't even a contact sport.

Go figure.

The next sport I tried out is now considered an extreme sport and isn't a team game. My cousin Kenny had come over. We went to Dad's workbench and walked away with two two-by-sixes, two one-by-fours, a few sets of wheels off some roller skates, and some rope. Naturally, we built a cart. First was the H-frame, and then we added the wheels. Next, we hammered on the one-by-fours for brakes. Finally, we added the rope as a steering mechanism. The only thing to do at this point was try it out.

We took off down the road, and after about fifty feet or so, it became obvious that it worked pretty well. We got to an intersection and went flying across the street. It dawned on us that we would make it to Glenwood Avenue, which happened to be a busy street, so we hit the brakes.

As we hit the one-by-fours, we realized there was one part of our cart that was lacking in functionality, and that was the brakes. As we slammed down on them, they came off. We were rapidly approaching the busy road ahead. There was only one thing left to do.

Abort!

So, we sucked it up and steered straight into the ditch. The end of our ride was both rocky and abrupt. Now, this is where the extreme sport comes into play. After the crash, we had a broken cart but that didn't deter our determination to amuse ourselves. We took a single, splintered two-by-six and, using a hammer and nail, we added two separate sets of skates at each end. It was a pretty good ride except that it wanted to pull right the entire time. It was also a huge rush. We had never done or seen anything like it, and we had fun taking turns trying it out for a few hours.

In doing so, we invented the skateboard.

You can thank me later.

CHAPTER 22

A few weeks passed by, and football had become a regular occurrence in my daily life. After a week when we had played nearly every day, I woke up on Saturday morning, and Mike and I went to pay Steve and Sonny a visit. We sat around the living room, chatting for a while. I'll never forget the graphic picture of Custer's Last Stand as the centerpiece of their living-room decorations.

After a while of talking and enjoying a glass of tea, we discussed what we might do when we went outside.

"We could always play football," suggested Steve Kivett.

"We played football all week. How about we try something new?"

A new sport I hadn't had the opportunity to partake in yet: boxing.

"Why don't we break out the boxing gloves?" asked Sonny.

Subsequently, it was decided that I would fight Dennis Turner because I had never boxed before. Let me first say that unless you are a part of organized fighting such as a boxing league, or these days MMA, fighting is for losers even if you win. With that out of the way, Dennis and I were a perfect matchup. Mainly due to being about the same size and both of us being young and stupid. After we'd located Dennis and he'd agreed to the proposal, we all went back to the Kivetts' and prepared for the bout.

My corner man was Mike.

He told me to wait until Dennis swung and then duck, then stand up and let him have it.

"In this corner, standing at four feet tall and fifty-two pounds, we have Steve Adkins. In this corner, standing at four feet two and fifty-five pounds, we have Dennis Turner."

Sonny hit a pot twice.

Ding, ding!

The main event had begun, and I did precisely what Mike had told me to. Dennis swung, I ducked, and then I stood up and hit him as hard as I could. Right in the nose! In turn, his nose started bleeding.

"Oh my God! I killed Dennis!" I exclaimed.

Only one option here: drop the freakin' gloves and run like hell. They were hard to get off, those miserable boxing gloves. I felt terrible. Nevertheless, I managed to get them off and deposit them in the Kivetts' front yard.

Mike and I departed at the same time. In our zeal to get home, we ended up going in two different doors. I chose the back door at the top of the steps while Mike flew in the front. Poor Mom had two midget pugilists pounding on the doors. Not to mention the fact that her belly was growing more and more by the day and her nerves were absolutely wrecked.

Boom! Boom! Boom!

"Let me in before the police get here so I can tell you goodbye! I killed Dennis!" I announced.

Fortunately, Mom settled me down, and I didn't go to jail after all. She even skipped the events of the morning when giving Dad the progress report on his lunch break.

No belt for me.

It turned out Dennis was okay once his mom applied a cold compress and stuffed his nose with tissues. We were welcome back to the Kivetts' with the rest of the gang by midafternoon.

Close call.

I'm Fine!

May 6, 2008

Wednesday morning came quickly, and it was time to get some double vision answers. One of my golden rules in life is to get up an hour before you have to leave. That way, you get to where you are going fifteen minutes early. That morning, I was awake about two and a half hours ahead of schedule with no desire to go back to sleep. My night had been filled with interrupted sleep, and every time I woke, I felt a wave of anxiety and fear from head to toe.

The only thing between me and some potential answers was a few cups of coffee, r and the time it took me to get ready, dressed and drive to the doctor's office. I tried to keep my thoughts as positive as possible. I must admit that this hadn't been my practice for over twenty years. Having to make a conscious effort to remain optimistic was as foreign to me as the sober double vision. Concern and worry had shaken me to the core. I needed to know what I was dealing with so that I could figure out the best way to handle it.

To move past it.

Once I arrived, I waited fifteen minutes or so before I was called in. My doctor was a familiar face as his son had been a member of the first state championship team that I had coached in 1997. He had been my family's primary-care physician for years. After I had explained to him what had led me to my visit, he ran some tests. He gave me some feedback and explained to me how important it was that I come back the following Monday for an MRI.

I guess he hadn't forgotten that three years before, he had given me some unwanted results involving my cholesterol. I had dealt with it the best way I saw fit at the time.

That had involved me not stepping foot back in his office for three years.

The severity of this issue, however, was weighing on me, and I could see the seriousness in his face when he was insisting on an MRI. I went to the receptionist and scheduled it for the following Monday and headed out to the car.

I called Bella and told her that he really couldn't put his finger on anything that would cause the double vision. He had run some tests to see if I was having problems with my blood sugar or blood pressure. I told her that he seemed concerned and that he had insisted I come back for the MRI. As we got off the phone, I received a call from Danny. He wanted to check on me and see how everything had gone. Not ten minutes after I got off the phone with him, Paul called.

Everyone was concerned. It left everyone uneasy that there had not been any certain answers as to what was going on. After Paul and I talked about my health, we talked a little Tennessee football, and I told him I would see him later. I hung up the phone as I pulled into work and went in to see what was on my plate for the day. I made some calls to a few clients and tried to escape my constant ruminations about what was going on with me.

Around three that afternoon, I got a call from my best friend in the entire world, Jim Macanudo, aka Jim Mac. He wanted to confirm that everything was still a go for the weekend. He and two other lifelong friends of mine, Tom Ward and Jackie Haun, had plans to come to the house for the weekend for some much-needed catching up. I explained to him what had been going on in the mildest manor possible, as I didn't want to sound the alarms. There wasn't anything I could think that I could use more of than some time with the world's greatest company for the weekend in order to take my mind off things.

When I got home that night, I simply relished in the opportunity to spend some quality time with Bella and the boys. After dinner, the boys had plans and went about their business. Bella and I spent some time talking until eleven or so and then went to bed. Again, my mind became a waterfall of thoughts and worry as I lay there staring at the ceiling.

My senses were acute.

I could hear the ceiling fan revolving and the clock on the wall ticking. I was wide awake, even though I was exhausted. Every time I thought I had trained my mind on something a bit more peaceful that could lull me to sleep, I realized I was again wondering what was going on with me. How could I have let myself end up in this position by neglecting my responsibility as a father and husband to ensure that I was healthy? I decided that the next day I would do some research at work and see if I could come up with something.

I tossed.

I turned.

Eventually, I drifted off to sleep. Waking up every thirty minutes to an hour with the same anxiety and fear as the night before, however, was constricting and heavy.

So much so that I wished I could get out of bed and shed the burden. It was if I had lived the last five days donning medieval body armor. I felt like I couldn't breathe, and it was wearing me out.

CHAPTER 23

Life was football, football, a random game of baseball, football, a random game having nothing to do with sports, and more football.

I was getting great.

I loved playing, and Mike hated that I was great.

Even though I was one of the younger guys, I usually led my team in every facet of the game. I was picked first every time we played. I lay the wood on defense, caught everything thrown my way, and rushed the ball like there was no tomorrow. I think the difference between me and everyone else came down to two things: natural ability was one of them, and a true passion and understanding was the other. My Uncle David taught me a very important lesson when I was young:

Find something you love and be passionate about it.

Football was the first thing I treated that way. Around the beginning of July, summer had truly set in, and I had to take a week-long break from football. It was time for a family trip to the beach. I don't remember much from the trip other than my Papaw wearing long pants and a hat the whole time. I suppose he didn't care much for getting sun. He sat on the beach in his long pants all week, smoking cigars in the constant breeze. Whatever floats your boat, I guess.

When the week had drawn to a close and we were all packed in our new Chevy Bel Air headed home, going down Highway 41 I saw cornfield after cornfield and thought about being back and hanging out with the guys. I couldn't wait.

After a game of football the first day back, it was time for me to learn how to ride my bike. Everybody had a twenty-six-inch bike, and you could tell who the veterans were because they all had bubble-gum cards applied to their wheels with a clothespin that made an engine sound. Steve Kivett taught me how to ride; he would run behind my bike, holding onto the seat, and eventually let go when I had gained speed.

"Okay, Steve Adkins, you pedal and I'll push."

The first time I went by myself, I went to the end of the road and made a left. I had something working against me, though, and that came in the form of both my tires not being inflated enough to make the turn. The next thing I knew, I had crashed and burned into the alley behind the house of a man named Jimmy Tarwater. It just so happened that Mr. Tarwater was rumored to be the baddest damn whammer jammer on the face of the planet.

All I could think was *Oh, shit!*

I thought about just leaving my bike there but finally got up enough nerve to pick it up and run away. Fortunately, I got away clean. I figured I'd better find another place to practice my riding. Yet another close call.

After a week or so of practicing, I had it down like a pro. Everyone, including myself, rode single-speed bikes. Schwinn was a commonplace bicycle make among us. That many boys with bikes in one neighborhood could only result in one thing: racing.

So, of course, we made our own racetrack.

We started by flying down Gordon Street as fast as we possibly could and hitting a rise that we commonly referred to as The Jump. Everybody could catch air at The Jump, and we kept a mental record of how high we went. From The Jump, you continued roughly sixty feet to a pair of oak trees and took a ninety-degree turn to the right. After about a hundred more feet, there was a split in the path. You could either go left, which led down to the creek at Crawdaddy Point, which did you no good in a race, or you could go right, which was level and the main thoroughfare of the racetrack. You went about another seventy-five feet and hung a sharp right down a steep decline that left the woods. Finally, you were in the flat straightaway of the alley, which led you back to the start. That's where you really had to hit the gas. In reality, it was really hard to actually race because parts of it were so narrow. Mostly, we were just legends in our own minds. However, we did keep record of who jumped the highest.

Mike was the champion by a long shot.

CHAPTER 24

As time crept on into August, we started hanging out at Christenberry Junior High, across the street from the neighborhood, more than normal. It was something we'd done sporadically up until that point. But they had real ball fields, and it was only 150 feet from where we typically played. We got the idea one day to expand our horizons and give ourselves a little more space for special football and baseball games we talked up more than normal.

We still preferred our home field in the Kivetts' side yard, but as unofficial athletes about ten percent of the time we needed a more official feel. A groundskeeper approached us one day and asked if we would like to be the first kids in a youth club he was thinking about starting up. He must have been impressed by our athleticism and obviously saw that he had a very local group. We, of course, were running around playing, laughing, and having a blast as usual. We also, of course, agreed without hesitation.

"We'll call it North Knoxville Youth Club," he announced. "The tennis courts will be down by, well, the tennis courts. We'll put the basketball courts down by, well, the basketball courts."

I had seen people play basketball but was yet to have the opportunity to play, on account of none of us having a basketball.

Finally, the man said, "All we can do today is see who can throw horseshoes the farthest. That's all I have in my trunk."

It didn't bother us any. We had never thrown shoes before, and we were always down for trying something new. We started chucking them one at a time. Everything was going great, and we loved our new club. That lasted about twenty-five minutes until Rusty Henry decided to catch one with his face. It was either the blood or the sudden departure of the founder that led to the demise of the North Knoxville Youth Club.

It was fun while it lasted.

We never saw that old man again. And

I'm sure he is pleased to this day that we never even got his name.

A couple of days later, we were all at the fields and spied some guys looking for a pickup football game. They looked like they were about our age. They lived in the neighborhood on the other side of the school's fields. There were only four of us: Mike, Steve, Sonny, and me. There were five of them, but we determined we would play them anyway. It was the first time we had the chance to play against kids outside of the neighborhood. After a couple touchdowns for each team, I ran back an interception for a touchdown. The score was 6–3, and I had three of them for my team. They came back down and scored and forced us to fourth down on our next possession and got the ball back.

The game was fairly even, and at this point it was determined that I should defend their best player. He was a pesky little guy—shifty and able to catch anything he could get a finger on.

After we shoved each other around awhile, it was decided that I was most likely going to fight the kid. I relieved myself of my shoulder pads so that I would be unencumbered should I fight. Two minutes later, he took a cheap shot at me after a play ended, and I decided it was go time. I knocked him down. He merely lay on his back and tried to pummel me with his feet every time I came in for a punch. Finally, I feigned in one direction and came flying in from the other direction. I popped him a few good times, and then everyone broke us up. Not so tough after all.

They called it quits, and we walked away victorious. The final tally was 10–6. As we walked home, we decided that we preferred to play among ourselves. A minor argument might occur sometimes, but nothing like that. Plus, due to not knowing the outsiders on the other side of the fields, we deemed that they were unpredictable. Thinking back, maybe it was me who was unpredictable. Either way, I wouldn't have traded my friends for the world. At the time, it was Shamrock Avenue 1, everybody else 0.

After we got home, Mike and I had dinner, and I enjoyed a hot bath. Instead of a bath, Mike enjoyed an entire pitcher of Mom's sweet tea. It was previously decided we would meet back up with Steve and Sonny to celebrate our victory…that's right, it was time for a smoke break. And we're not talking about grapevines here. We had upgraded to real cigarettes over the summer. It was all thanks to the Mr. Chapman's unlocked storage room next to Dennis Turner's house.

He was a local cigarette salesman. He had boxes and boxes of cigarettes. So, we were down at the creek, and Mike handed me a Marlboro. Which is not to say I knew how to smoke it. My grandfather smoked until the ashes were two inches long.

How did he do that?

Anyway, I was in the creek, but the only thing that was drowning was the butt of my cigarette thanks to my saliva. I suppose it was good. Celebrating and being around the guys was all I was in it for anyway.

On the field, I was really coming in to my own. I had a newfound confidence from being competitive with the other guys in sports, especially football. I was never arrogant about it, though. That just wasn't my approach. Even as a young buck, I preferred to be modest about it. I'd be straightforward about my production, but when that was lauded or praised, I blew it off. I knew I was good, but when people gave me praise, it was somewhat of an awkward experience for me.

Perhaps it was a by-product of my home life.

I always felt best when I was giving my all but also when I was lifting up my teammates. Seeing them get excited when they made a big play was very rewarding to me. I owed these guys for introducing me to the games and showing me the ropes. If it weren't for them, I'd still be trying to figure it out. Even Mike played a big role, in his own way.

Although some of the other guys were more like brothers to me than he was, there were times when he would stop and give me a tip here and there. I suppose that was what made us more like actual brothers.

His way of helping me was knocking me down and knowing that I would have to get back up.

I sure wasn't a fan of his methods, but in the long run, they did me good. The feeling I got when a big play was made or a touchdown was scored and the team all ran up to each other to celebrate was one of the best feelings in the world to me. It was nice to relish the moment when you had caused the game to stop, but it was the embrace of your comrades that made it really worth it.

Playing all this football had me ready to learn more about the game. See who was good at the things I was good at. I couldn't wait to see the Volunteers play come September.

The roaring crowd.

The prolific players.

The flashy orange uniforms and the headlines in Dad's newspapers. It was the first time I was really pumped for a season, but it certainly wouldn't be the last.

CHAPTER 25

Throughout 1959, some big things happened in the world—some of them good and some bad. Hawaii officially became the fiftieth state of the United States of America. The first Grammy music awards was held. Buddy Holly, Ritchie Valens, and "The Big Bopper" were killed in a plane crash, and that day later became called "The Day the Music Died," and was popularized by Don McLean's song "American Pie" years down the road.

Fidel Castro became the Prime Minister of Cuba. *Ben-Hur* and *Sleeping Beauty* hit theaters nationwide.

In the sports world, leading up to the kickoff of both the NFL and college-football seasons, there was a name that often recurred on sports news. I'll always remember waiting to hear some coverage of the upcoming college-football season on TV and all they talked about was some guy named Vince Lombardi who was about to enter his first season as the head coach and general manager of the Packers. Apparently, they had been awful the year before, so I wasn't sure what the big deal was. I didn't have a clue who he was, but he sure did seem serious when he was interviewed on television.

My general focus, though, was back in Knoxville where the Vols started preseason camp in mid-August. It was Bowden Wyatt's fifth year as head coach. Starting a few weeks before camp, Uncle David would read me the headlines and articles about Tennessee out of the Knox-News Sentinel. The opinions on how the season would go were a mixed bag.

Johnny Majors had finished his playing career in 1956, and his younger brother Billy became the quarterback in 1958. There was some competition surrounding the quarterback situation in 1959 due to a 4-6 finish in 1958 that was mainly caused by a less-than-stellar offense. And by *less-than-stellar*, I mean that they didn't even average eight points a game.

By the looks of things, the Vols were going to have a stout defense, but there were definitely some holes to fill on the offensive side of the ball. None of that was much matter to me, though. I had been conditioned to love the Vols no matter what, and more than anything, I was just ready to hear the crowd roaring on the radio. I did the only thing I knew to pass the time: play more football.

Day in and day out during the few weeks left of camp, we played once and sometimes even twice a day. Some days I wished that my uniform was orange and white instead of red and white. Finally, opening day came on Saturday, September 26, against Auburn in Knoxville. Tennessee was what my uncle described as unranked, and Auburn was going into the game ranked #3. I'll admit that, at the time, I had no clue what he was even talking about.

As coverage started on the radio, I became overwhelmed with excitement. The roar of the crowd sent cold chills down my spine. I was listening to the game with Uncle David at my grandmother's house. Even though he was a much more experienced fan, I could tell he felt the same way. It was he who truly taught me to love the Volunteers. It was one of the only things in his entire life that he cared about as much as the bottle. I had never been to a game, so I asked him what it was like.

He detailed the entire atmosphere at Shields-Watkins Field (the field inside Neyland Stadium), and yet again, the hair stood up on the back of my neck. I closed my eyes and pictured being there. Finally, we were at kickoff, and you could hear the horns blaring as the Pride of the Southland Band played "Down the Field." As the game went on, it was a back-and-forth defensive battle. As expected, the Vols offense struggled mightily throughout the entire game. Fortunately, the defense was as advertised.

Tennessee wound up on top 3–0 as time expired. The Vols were 1-0 for the season, and all I wanted to do was one thing.

Play football!

The next day, all the guys in the neighborhood got together for a game of pickup after church. I played harder than I ever had before. Three plays into the game, I made a huge tackle, knocking Hank Henry out flat. The very next play, they punted and we were on offense. On the first play of our first drive, I ran a sweep to the right. After making a few guys miss, I was out in the open and all alone. I tuned everything out like usual once I was home free. In my mind, all I could hear was the roaring crowd from the game I had listened to the previous day on the radio.

It made me run harder.

It made me run faster.

And it helped me find a whole new gear.

As I stopped at the creek bed and turned around, my team was jumping with excitement. Sonny looked at me and said, "Dang, Steve Adkins, that's the fastest I've ever seen you run."

I just looked at him and humbly said, "Thanks, Sonny."

Inside, though, I knew that my game had just been elevated. I also knew that it had been within me the whole time, but the thought of rushing down the field for the Volunteers had given me the motivation to give the extra effort. It seemed like every time I touched the ball that day, something big happened. In just a matter of one game and seven touchdowns, I became that extra effort. I knew that from that day forward my ability would be measured by my production that day. I embraced it. Internally, I accepted what I was capable of, and thereafter my effort would never be less than my new version of best.

CHAPTER 26

The following week, I asked Mom if there was anything in the paper about the Vols. It looked like she once again had a pumpkin under her shirt, and she walked to the kitchen and checked out the headlines for me. She told me that Tennessee had jumped all the way up to #9 in the national rankings. I wasn't sure what that meant, so she explained it to me.

At the time, there were 112 teams in college football, and the powers that be felt that Tennessee was the ninth best out of all of them. In 1959, the rankings only went through the top-twenty teams in the country. My uncle had said the week before that we were unranked. I put two and two together and realized this was a big deal. Although, I have to admit that in my youthful heart, they were number one, so I didn't take it as well as I should have. By the next Saturday, October 3, I was back alongside Uncle David as the Vols were set to host Mississippi State.

Radio on.

Crowd roaring.

Cold chills.

It was a routine that I loved and could definitely get used to.

The offense put it together better, and the defense was on their A game once again. Tennessee actually looked like what would be described as *good* on the offensive side of the ball against the Bulldogs. A dominant performance and four quarters later, the Volunteers finished off Mississippi State by a final score of 22–6.

I was elated and ready to get back out and play a game with everyone in the neighborhood. They all had their own routines for game day. Some of them didn't catch the games or get into it as much as I did. Their relative degree of passion was reflected in the passion and determination each kid brought to our pickup games.

Throughout the next week, every time we put the pads on, I played as I'd discovered I could the week before. I led whichever team I landed on in tackles, catches, and rushing yards anytime we stepped foot on the field. Again, during the week, I asked Mom if there was any news about Tennessee in the paper. She said the Vols had moved up to #8 in the rankings, which really got me excited.

On October 10, the #8 Tennessee Volunteers were pitted against the #3 ranked Georgia Tech Yellow Jackets. It was a huge game, and both teams were 2-0. The Jackets were coming off of a 16–12 victory over the #6 Southern Methodist Mustangs. The win was big enough to move them thirteen spots in the national rankings. They had a potent offense with multiple guys who could run the ball well. The big talking point for the game was Tennessee's defense versus Georgia Tech's explosive offense. By the time the game rolled around on Saturday, Uncle David and I were all ears as the broadcast came on the radio.

Mom had made me a sandwich with chips. When the roar of the crowd came over the radio and the announcer began his coverage, I jumped in joy, spilling my chips all over the floor of the living room. The only thing that saved my sandwich was it being in hand.

The voices coming over the radio portrayed a physical game. Tennessee's defense definitely did their job slowing down Georgia Tech's offense for the most part. The only problem was that Tennessee's offense was unable to do anything with the ball in their hands.

Big surprise.

For four quarters, Tennessee struggled to find the end zone. Inevitably, it led to their demise. When the clock struck zero, the Yellow Jackets had won the game 14–7, and my beloved Volunteers had experienced their first loss of the year. Being 2-1 certainly sounded less appealing than being 3-0. The headlines in the Sunday paper made my stomach drop.

I felt angry and let down.

This Tennessee team was never going to be world-beaters, but I believed in them. Some would say that what I was experiencing was the fundamentals of being a diehard fan. Although this was the first season I had gotten into it, I was already invested as much as most. After feeling the way I did after we had won, it was miserable being on the other end of the celebration. This is where something surprising happened within me. It was in the face of defeat that I found a new form of motivation.

Revenge is, in fact, a great motivator. Ultimately, one of the purest forms of motivation.

I am still sorry for the guys opposing me later that day as we got together for a game of pickup. I was hot to trot. Every hit was harder, and every run was faster. I hated the feeling of losing, but it was that feeling that helped me harness an even greater level of production as a player. In just a matter of a few weeks, multiple experiences regarding the daydreams I had of being in the spotlight had helped me take the next step as a player. It was embracing the way I played after the loss that again helped me move my personal meter up another tick.

It became apparent to me that, henceforth, it would be more than a game for me. I didn't just want to play. I wanted to play not to lose. I wanted to play in a way that would guarantee I wouldn't lose. I understood that if I played to the best of my ability, I typically would have enough influence on the game for my team to walk away with a win. Still, the fun of playing was what led me back to the field every day, and it's not like I ran around yelling at my teammates when they messed up.

That doesn't motivate anyone, and in fact, it makes everyone play worse.

CHAPTER 27

The following week, the newspaper indicated that the Vols had dropped in the rankings down to #14. My uncle was at the house and had read me the paper. He sure didn't seem to mind much. He kept saying that the upcoming weekend was the Third Saturday in October. I obviously didn't understand the significance of that, so he sat me down and explained. Going back as far as he could remember, Tennessee's biggest rival had been the Alabama Crimson Tide.

He told me that, year in and year out, in a game coined the Third Saturday in October, the two teams met in what was considered one of the most storied rivalries in college football. Basically, if you were a Tennessee fan, you hated Alabama, and there was no exception. Copious amounts of trash talk would occur in the days leading up to the infamous matchup. The game Saturday was our first away game of the season and was slated to take place at Legion Field in Birmingham, Alabama. Both teams were mediocre going into the season, and Alabama had a game a week prior to the first Tennessee game. Uncle David explained that this gave them an extra game to make tweaks heading into Saturday, giving them somewhat of an advantage.

The biggest message he got across was that their style of play consisted of finding the biggest guys they could and putting them on the line, then snapping the ball and running it down the opponent's throat. Power running at its finest, with players so big they had been compared to elephants by an Atlanta sports journalist in a famous article, after the Alabama versus Ole Miss showdown in 1930:

"At the end of the quarter, the earth started to tremble, there was a distant rumble that continued to grow. Some excited fan in the stands bellowed, 'Hold your horses, the elephants are coming!'"

Famous in Alabama, anyway.

As the radio broadcast came alive in my living room on Saturday, I was ready for football. In fact, I was so excited for the game that I wore my helmet the entire broadcast. A slew of questions filled my mind.

Could the Vols bounce back from their loss?

Could they stop the powerful Alabama running game?

How would we look on the road?

Kickoff commenced, and I was on the edge of my seat. In fact, I hardly sat down the entire game. It's crazy to think about how intense the game was, even though you couldn't see it. Each play broken down by the announcer, and your imagination handling most of the workload. Fortunately, I had quite the imagination.

The game was slow on offense throughout. Defensive stop after stop. Punt, three downs, repeat. The game went down to the wire with both teams struggling to impose any kind of will on the other team's defense. As time expired, I looked at Uncle David and said, "What do they do now, Uncle Dave?"

"That's it, Steve."

"What do you mean? The score is 7–7."

"It's a tie."

"A what?"

Uncle David laughed at my bewilderment and said, "The game is over. The two teams both have the same score. No one wins. Guess we'll have to wait 'til next year, little guy." Just like that, I had experienced the least favorable outcome of a sporting event.

No winner.

No loser.

A tie.

The first year I had paid attention to Vols football, and I would have to wait another 365 days to figure out who the best team was in the storied rivalry. What a hoax!

Someone needs to change the rules.

Man, was I pissed. I didn't even know a tie was possible, and it sure didn't make any sense. I was confused and at a loss for words. On one hand, I was glad we didn't lose; on the other, we didn't win. This was too much. What a terrible outcome! The epitome of inconclusive.

Game-Day Preparation

May 8 – 9, 2008

Thursday, I once again realized that if I just had some form of answer, it would alleviate some of the discouragement that I felt. I turned on the radio on the way to work and sang along to some classic rock. Birds traveling overhead caught my attention. I tried to read every billboard—anything to keep myself in a better headspace. Once I got to work, I tended to the market for an hour or so, and once I was caught up, the search began. I spent the majority of my day going back and forth between handling stocks and doing online research.

The stocks went well.

The research did not.

At the end of the day, a few of my clients were extremely pleased. The market was tough in those days, but I was still producing very positive results for those who invested with me. I knew the market well. My research had turned up nothing, and I wasn't as versed as I needed to be to perform a search that would yield more scholarly results.

When I got home after work, I needed nothing other than a good workout. I spent an hour and a half in the gym. After that, I cleaned the pool house and got the house ready for company. That included making the beds, cleaning the pool table, vacuuming the pool, and running into town for a few goodies. The goodies were a few select New York strips, potatoes, and a case of beer. I knew that Jim and the guys would bring a case themselves, but I always believed it was hospitable to match the ante. The last thing left to get was to choose a few nice cigars for the weekend. CAO Blacks were the pick.

The running around had kept my mind off things. That night, falling asleep was just as exhausting as my day had been. The night passed like the recent ones. I was ready for a great weekend. Furthermore, I was in need of it.

Friday, I felt conflicted about how I wanted to approach telling Jim, Tom, and Jackie what was going on with me. These guys and I were as close as it gets. I know they say blood is thicker than water, but we had filled the bucket of our friendship with water from the Dead Sea. Besides Bella and the kids, I was closer to these guys and the rest of the crew than anyone on earth. Unable to make it for the weekend were Curt and Kerri Jackson, Ziggy and Lana Holcolm, Jackie's wife, Caroline, Frankie and Melissa Walland, and Tom's wife Joan.

Besides holiday functions with our extended family and an enjoyable setup for Bella, the boys, and me, it was having enough space for all of them to sleep comfortably that influenced how big a house we would buy and how big a pool house we would build when we moved in 2001.

We love them, and they love us.

Multiple times a year, we would find ourselves together for weekends full of laughter and memorable moments. Sometimes at our house, sometimes at their houses. Occasionally at a chalet in the Smokies. I wished they could all be here for the weekend, but Jim, Tom, and Jackie would surely do. Hell, Jackie Haun was enough to keep up with on his own.

The day went by pretty smoothly, and I headed out of the office a little early. I was already more excited to see the guys than I was worried about what had been going on all week. It was a breath of fresh air. At 5:00 p.m. on the dot, they pulled into the driveway. Jim and Jackie had ridden in together from Knoxville, and Tom had traveled in by himself from his house just outside of Huntsville. They had conveniently met at the gas station to grab a case of beer. I already had the TV tuned to satellite radio's Classic Vinyl station on surround. It was eighty degrees and not a cloud in the sky.

The smile on my face when I saw the guys was so big it was mildly painful. A wave of memories I shared with the three of them came crashing through my mind. I felt a lump in the back of my throat. The emotions boiled up inside me, and as a few tears filled my eyes, it dawned on me that Jackie Haun, Jim Mac, and Tom Ward were now at my home, and I had better make damn sure they didn't see me getting all soft.

As this thought went through my mind, the smile on my face widened even more, and a single chuckle emerged as I wiped my eyes and walked out to greet them in the driveway. Regardless of the circumstances, there were a few things men didn't do, and crying was one of them. I guess the macho man that had led to my current situation had found his way back into my thought process. Although I was sure he wouldn't be around all weekend, he was here now. That night, though, it was about laughs, good food, shooting pool, and listening to music too loud. But I knew that somehow, at some point over the weekend, I had to let the guys know what was going on.

Honestly, at this point—and although I didn't want to admit it to anyone else yet—I knew that something just wasn't right. Something was seriously wrong with me, even if the doctors and research had turned up nothing. I could feel it.

I had lived most of my life fearing nothing.

At this point, I was scared to death about what was happening to me.

A round of hugs was in order, followed by a round of beers and a cigar for each of us by the pool. We laughed, we smiled, we sang. After ten minutes, we were on to the second beer. Tom had brought a special gift that you could only get in Alabama at the time. Her name was Sweet Lucy, and she was one of the best bourbons I've ever had the privilege of drinking. One shot, two shots. At fifteen minutes after seven, I went in to get started on dinner. As a self-proclaimed *grillmeister*, I can tell you that the steaks were perfectly marinated. I must have been pretty well marinated myself, because forty-five minutes after I put the potatoes in the oven I went in to check on them, only to find that I hadn't turned the oven on.

Whoops!

I guess we're eating late.

As the cooking progressed, so did a few more beers, a couple cigarettes, and more hard laughs. At ten o'clock, we finally sat down to eat our perfectly cooked, medium-rare strips with twice-baked potatoes.

A true testament to a well-cooked meal is how much folks are talking in between bites. The better the meal, the quieter the table. In the absolute silence I had created, I thought about my week for the first time since the guys had arrived five hours earlier. As they ate, I reveled in the moment of having a few of my best friends by my side and eating a nice meal. I thought of how we'd all met and where we'd ended up. Just a couple of wild football players in our day who had all became extremely successful in adulthood.

All with beautiful families.

All blessed beyond measure.

All best friends.

It had been hard to find, but we had it, and for that I was thankful. Ten minutes later, the table was cleared, and it was on to shooting pool, a few drinks, and another late night to put down in the record books.

CHAPTER 28

It seems like the only thing we were really interested in playing during football season was football. The following week, we played so much that I felt bad that Mom had to keep up with keeping my uniform clean while her belly was growing. She literally looked like her stomach could pop. Dad even helped out around the house a little in between shifts, and usually, this happened as often as a lunar eclipse.

On Wednesday of the next week, Uncle David popped in for a quick visit. After going over the weekly headlines in the newspaper, I was a little bummed out. Tennessee had dropped out of the rankings, and the reporters were seriously questioning how the rest of our season would play out. There were still some good teams left to play, and if the Vols couldn't generate some more offense, it could make for a bad six weeks. Our defense was well respected, but our offense was a joke. My uncle could see that I was down in the dumps about it. He told me we should beat the team we played this week. It was Chattanooga, and he thought we would have a nice outing.

Then he said to me, "I have a surprise for you."

I looked up at him. "What is it, Uncle Dave?"

As he reached into his shirt pocket, he looked at me and said, "How'd you like to go to your first Tennessee game this weekend?" He brandished two tickets.

"No way!"

As I ran over and hugged Uncle David, I shouted, "Mom! Uncle David is taking me to a Tennessee game!"

He bent down and told me to be ready at ten thirty sharp on Saturday. There was plenty to do on game day besides watch the football game. After he left, I could barely contain myself as I busted out the door to go tell all the guys about the tickets. They were as excited as I was. All I could think about for the next two days was the roaring crowd. Finally, Saturday morning came, and at ten thirty on the dot, Uncle David walked in and asked if I was ready to go. We caught a bus over to campus. Little did I know that life as I knew it would change forever that day.

I have a sneaking suspicion that Uncle David knew, though.

As we arrived on campus, I was boiling over with exhilaration. I had passed by campus on a few occasions, but I had never been in the heart of the Big Orange. We got off the bus on Gay Street. We kicked around for a little bit as Uncle David showed me all sorts of things. Occasionally, he would take a sip of "water" out of his flask.

I may have been young and thirsty, but I wasn't dumb enough to ask for a drink of the kind of water he was having.

I guess he was a pro, though, because he kept up with every step I took and answered every question I asked that day—probably about twenty thousand on both fronts. We had lunch at Frank's Brass Rail before the game and then headed toward the stadium.

Along the way, he pointed out historical monuments on campus, and just before entering he came to a stop to tell me the story of the Hill. I could see the field to the right as the Hill was just outside of the west end zone. In 1959, the stadium was a horseshoe, and the Hill was just outside of the opening. I was almost too ecstatic to listen, but I pulled it together as Uncle David continued about its history.

As the story goes, there was a college in Knoxville known as East Tennessee College. It later became the University of Tennessee. In 1826, as recommended by Thomas Jefferson, the trustees of the college decided it would be best to move to the west side of the city so that the college would have more room for growth. They ended up acquiring the Hill for six hundred dollars. During the Civil War, it was fortified and became known as Fort Byington. Inevitably, it was instrumental in the Siege of Knoxville.

Fast-forward to 1959, and the Hill was the primary location for many academic buildings. Its location on the east side of campus right next to the stadium made it impossible to miss for anyone who set foot in Knoxville for a football game. It is the oldest part of the university and is one of three major landmarks on campus to this day.

After my history lesson, we proceeded into the stadium, and boy, was I ready! All the pregame festivities were great, but the Pride of the Southland Band's six minutes and forty-five seconds of greatness as they marched up and down the field was my favorite. I had only heard them on radio broadcasts of games up to this point. I had no clue they did a pregame show, and it was really a spectacle to behold. As the band exited the field, the two teams prepared to enter it.

The crowd was roaring.

I joined along for the first time and did everything I could to take it all in. Finally, the Volunteers rushed onto the field, and in that moment, my entire view on the sport was changed. The thought of being a player down there with the rowdy crowd yelling, screaming, and jumping up and down, all because of you, blew me away.

At first sight, it became obvious to me that Tennessee had larger players in more positions. Before the opening kickoff, the two teams' captains met at midfield for the coin toss. I asked Uncle David what they were doing. He got down close enough for me to hear him over the boisterous fans, and after he finished giving me the rundown, I leaned over and gave him a big hug. I thought for a brief moment that I couldn't believe it wasn't my dad who'd taken me to my first Tennessee game. Admittedly, that was quickly followed by an even greater appreciation for my uncle. He was one of my best friends, and he always watched out for me the best he could.

As the opening kickoff was about to take place, the roar of the crowd resumed. Uncle David and I joined in, and it was as if I had died and gone to heaven.

As predicted, the Vols dominated the game. Chattanooga stood no chance against Tennessee's dominant defense. As their defense got tired from constantly being on the field, Tennessee's offense capitalized. At one point in the game, our running back broke out for a big run.

Right then and there, I came to a conclusion. I'm not sure if it was watching him blaze down the field in orange and white, both teams lost somewhere behind him, or if it was the response from the crowd that led to my determination.

Either way, I knew at that very moment that I would one day play college football. And at that point, I'd have told you there was about a 100 percent chance it was going to be for the University of Tennessee Volunteers.

On the next defensive stand, a huge hit by one of our linebackers only further solidified my decision. The hype of the crowd from a huge hit was equally as electric as the big run. At halftime, Uncle David initiated my lifelong tradition when he bought a bag of peanuts from the concession stand to enjoy in the second half.

The second half was more of the same story. Total domination by the defense, and the offense put it together enough to keep increasing the lead. As time dwindled down and fizzled out, Tennessee had won 23–0, and the crowd roared as loud as thunder one last time. Fans began to exit the gates, and I wanted nothing more than to just stand there in amazement for a few more minutes. Fortunately, Uncle David's water was catching up to him, and he was just fine with taking five before beginning the hike back to Gay Street. So, we sat there and just took in the scenery, cementing every nook and cranny of the stadium into my memory bank.

CHAPTER 29

As we reached the bus, I turned around and looked back over all the places I had traveled on campus that day. A smile crept up on my face, and nothing could have taken it away. The whole way home, I replayed in my head all the big plays from the game. Uncle David and I talked, reviewing the Vols victory. Tennessee was 3-1-1 on the season and back in the winning column. I was as happy as I'd ever been, and I had only him to thank.

As the bus approached our stop, I leaned in to him for one last hug and said, "Thanks for taking me to my first game, Uncle Dave. I'm going to play in Neyland Stadium one day. I promise you that."

As he hugged me back, he laughed and affirmed my goal. "I believe you, Steve. You can do anything you set your mind to." At this point, there was only one thing in the world I wanted to do.

Play football!

While watching Tennessee play in person, it had become clear to me that not only did the game seem larger than life but it was also actually far larger than our games of pickup. The field was obviously much bigger, but watching both teams field eleven players at a time really made our games of five on five or six on six seem so...*backyard*. I wondered when I would finally have the opportunity to play organized football.

Not today, I thought as Steve Kivett hiked the ball and handed it off to me. A nice juke later, and I found the creek bed on an untouched 10-yard run. Imagining I was playing for the Vols reached an all-time high that week as I envisioned wearing an orange uniform play after play.

I was playing lights-out, and I knew that experiencing the football season like I had was the primary reason. For the first time, that week I was chosen as a team captain, and I was one of the youngest guys out there. In order to distract Susan from running rampant in the house, she and Mom even walked over to watch us play. My mother was becoming incapable of giving chase every five minutes.

The weekly paper stated that Tennessee had moved back up to #20 in the nation and detailed the matchup for the week. Tennessee would be on the road again October 31, facing the North Carolina Tar Heels at Kenan Memorial Stadium in Chapel Hill. North Carolina was coming into the game 3-3 and had good a running game, that being common in those days. On Saturday, I was back at Grandmother's, and after a few pimento-cheese sandwiches, some barbecue chips, and a 7UP, it was upstairs with Uncle David to listen to the game.

I was glad to be back with him, and I was glad it was game day.

As kickoff commenced, it was much easier to imagine the game in my head after having seen the action in person. Tennessee went off on the Tar Heels to the tune of 29–7. No one would have predicted the Vols putting up that many points. All of a sudden, we were 4-1-1, and I was certain the win would bump us back up in the national rankings.

It was during the following week that I started to notice that my efforts on the field had started to translate into everything I did. If I was doing something, I was doing it to the best of my ability. Every time I set out with even the smallest task, I made sure to do it in a way I could be proud of. I helped Mom out a lot around the house as Mike watched television, Susan played, and Dad worked. I knew she needed someone to lighten the load a little bit. Her feet were always swollen, and I hated to see her in discomfort. My appreciation for her was immense, and I tried to do the things I could help out with in the same way she would do them.

The last thing I wanted was for her to feel like she needed to follow behind me and do them all over again. In between helping, I played football. On the rare occasions, we would play a little baseball or Kick the Can.

Mainly, it was all football, though.

Uncle David stopped by during the following week. As it had become a routine, he read me the paper. The Vols had jumped back up to #13 in the nation. My mouth dropped to the table as he told me we would be back at home against the undefeated LSU Tigers, who had won the National Championship in 1958. They were #1 in the country and 7-0. They could score points and didn't give up many. If there was ever a time that Tennessee's offense needed to show up, it was now.

On Friday, I had gone by the barber for a cleanup, and all the guys in there were talking about the big game. The commentary was pretty consistent. Was it possible for the Vols to score at all, let alone pull out the win? By Saturday, there was a buzz all over Knoxville. As Uncle David and I turned on the radio, I was all butterflies.

I was genuinely nervous for the game.

So nervous that I turned down lunch.

The game couldn't have been more intense. I'm sure it comes as a big shock that Tennessee's defense is what kept them in the game. Just listening to it, you could tell the type of confidence LSU carried. The outcome seemed to always be in their hands. Luckily, the Vols had come to play, and they surely weren't just going to roll over.

In the second half, we had evened the field and, due to keeping it close, had given ourselves a chance. Deep down, I believed we could do it, but you just knew that at any moment LSU could make a big play that changed the flow of the game for good. As the fourth quarter played out, the Vols defense played the best they had all season. And you know what? I'll be damned if Tennessee didn't find themselves ahead 14–13 when the game had ended.

"Hallelujah!" I shouted as the commentator went wild over the outcome.

I sure was glad we won.

I also sure was glad it was over—I couldn't take it anymore.

We had beat the #1 team in the country and the defending national champs. In my mind, on that day, Knoxville was on top of the world. I was so elated that we had won the game. Taken it to a more talented team. Done what no one thought we could. Those are the wins that make you believe.

CHAPTER 30

It was as if the next week the #9 Tennessee Volunteers packed up shop and turned in their uniforms. In a game on November 14, at the neutral site of Crump Stadium in Memphis, Tennessee, the unranked Ole Miss Rebels destroyed the Vols 37–7.

It broke my heart into pieces.

How do you beat the best team in the country one week and then lose to a team that isn't even on the map the next? I guess it's like they say: *Anything can happen, on any given Saturday.* To make matters worse, the next week Tennessee traveled to McLean Stadium in Lexington, Kentucky, barely holding on to the #20 spot in the rankings. After getting blasted 20–0 by the Kentucky Wildcats in the Battle for the Barrel, I felt like I couldn't take it anymore.

Fortunately, the next week, my obsession with football took a mandatory break. Just before Thanksgiving on Friday, November 17, 1959, my sister Julie Ann Adkins was born. There was too much going on with my family and at home to tune in the next day as Tennessee dropped its last game of the season to Vanderbilt.

Blasphemy!

In a home game that most expected us to win, the Vols got shut out 14–0. Was I ever glad I had other things to hold my attention so I didn't have to focus on the disappointment known as the Tennessee Volunteers. After being 5-1-1 coming off the win over LSU, the Volunteers finished the season 5-4-1. They didn't even receive an invitation to a bowl game.

Regarding my distractions from it all, Julie was a bundle of joy, and we all loved her unconditionally from the moment she got home. Susan was almost three and was absolutely enthralled with the thought of having a little sister. Mike was different toward the girls than he was me, so even he expressed interest in our new addition. Dad was back at work on Monday, and it was Mom and the four of us moving forward. Mike went to school through the week but was pretty attentive to her for a few weeks when he got home in the afternoons. Within a couple of weeks, I realized once again that there wasn't much I could do to help with the baby, so I continued to help out around the house and play football.

It was winter and cold out. I always thought it was cool to see everyone's breath become visible as it emerged from their face masks. Mom didn't allow me to play as much because she couldn't afford for me to get sick from being hot and sweaty out in the cold. It was really not that big of a deal to me, though.

We were busy. As Christmas rolled around, we did our typical family routine and celebrated Susan's third birthday. I always loved the opportunity to see Uncle David and Grandmother. I loved to sit around and talk Vols football also, regardless of how the season ended. However, it was on to 1960, and I had some more growing up to do. One thing was certain at this point in time. I knew there would come a time when my thoughts of being in the spotlight eventually wouldn't be just daydreams.

Brothers

May 9-11, 2008

Although we had stayed up late, drunk too much, and listened to music too loud, we were all up by eight the next morning. Mac had actually gotten up at six to swim laps in the pool before anyone else found their way out of bed. It was a ritual of his. The day started early, and by noon, we had already spent three hours by the pool. A few years earlier, Curt Jackson, another one of the world's greatest friends, had bought me what we called *the beach* for the poolside: it was a large, industrial warehouse fan that felt like the breeze coming off the ocean as you lay out. My anxiety came and went while we relaxed in the sun listening to some tunes. I wanted so badly to tell the guys what was going on.

They always knew what to say.

How to cheer you up.

How to make you feel better.

Jackie and Tom decided to challenge Jim and me to a game of shoes. As Jim and I found our way around the corner of the pool house and were heading to the pits, Jackie was coming out of the carport with a beer for each of us and a shit-eating grin on his face—probably because he was the king of recreational games.

Anytime you were pitted against him, you knew the game would be accompanied by a bunch of smack talk and usually an ass-whipping. Not every time, but usually. Somewhere along the way, we got on to the conversation of how everybody had been doing. I reserved my contribution to the conversation until we had finished up our game and found our way back to the pool.

As we all took a dip in the water to cool off and gathered in the shallow end to lean on the side and sip our beers, I knew the time had come. Jim Mac already had a small feel for what was going on, but out of respect, he hadn't brought it up to the others yet and hadn't even asked me about it since arriving.

Finally, I told them about the previous Saturday, the doctors' visits, and the drive home on Tuesday night with one eye shut and even asked them not to share that information with Bella. I told them I had never experienced anything like it, and that I was really worried. They knew how serious it was because they had never seen me like this about anything.

They asked if there was any suggestion about what could potentially be the cause.

I told them that no diagnosis had been made but that I had an MRI on Monday and we hoped it would shed a little light on things.

They were saddened and serious.

We hugged.

We got quiet.

We stared out on the rolling hills behind the pool deck, and everyone seemed to be at a loss for words. On cue, Jackie was able to muster up a joke and relieve the atmosphere a little, but truthfully, the tone of the weekend had shifted. As I had the night before when they'd arrived and during dinner, I noticed them relishing the moment, understanding how precious time is. How you never take a minute for granted with someone you love.

Saturday night, Bella was on her A game. She kept our glasses full and the snacks coming and prepared dinner as we spent time out on the deck. She is the best wife a man could ask for, and the guys have treated her accordingly since they met her, and the respect was mutual. As the sun started to set, we all sat out in our lounge chairs reminiscing about old times. Dinner came and went. That night was as special as any night I could remember for a long time. It wasn't just another crazy one for the record books. Instead, it seemed more sentimental. We really enjoyed the opportunity to create a memory rather than a night we couldn't remember. We sipped our Sweet Lucy and smoked our cigars, but more than anything, we just hung out and talked.

As I crawled into bed that night, I thought to myself that I couldn't stand the feeling that my life had taken on in a week's time. I was going to get past this.

Everything was okay.

I know that I felt like something was really wrong but that had to be due to the fact that I was just in unfamiliar territory. I'd have the MRI on

Monday, and they would be able to get the results, tell me what was wrong, and come up with an action plan to move forward. I wrestled back and forth with the fact that I just didn't feel right versus that everything was going to be okay. At some point, I fell asleep, and after not having a good night's rest in a week, I slept like a log.

When I woke on Sunday morning, Bella was still asleep, with her head on my chest. It was nice, so I lay there for a while and just enjoyed the moment. I could hear the guys up and about, so after about thirty minutes, I shifted and she woke. We talked for a moment and then joined the company in the kitchen. Everyone was having coffee, and Bella cooked a big breakfast. They weren't leaving until the afternoon, so we all put on our trunks and hunkered back down in our lounge chairs in the sun. Shortly after we got out there, Danny and Paul came strolling up. They looked like their Saturday night had been similar to our Friday night. Because I had been there myself when I was young, I didn't ask any questions. They enjoyed the guys and vice versa. They sat around and shot the bull with us for a little while. As time made its way into the afternoon, the guys got packed up and ready to head out.

They all gave me their *Get this thing figured out* and also their *You're Steve Adkins. You'll be just fine.*

As they were about to load up, it was time for one last round of hugs. First, they all hugged Bella, thanked her, and gave her a kiss on the cheek. The boys had come down to say goodbye, and they all shook hands and said it had been good to see each other. Then they each took their turn coming up to me and giving me a big, firm bear hug.

When they got settled in their vehicles, they rolled down their windows. Tom Ward looked at me and said, "I love you, Steve Adkins."

"I love you too, Tom."

Then Jim Mac looked at me and said, "I love you, too, Steve Adkins."

"I love you too, Jim Mac."

Last but not least, Jackie Haun yelled out, "I love you, Steve Adkins! Thanks for letting me come down here and beat your ass in horseshoes!"

"I love you, too, Jack! I'll get ya next time."

I watched them drive away. I always loved to see them come up the driveway, but I hated to see them leave. I went inside and gave Bella a kiss. I thanked her for all she'd done during the weekend and asked if she wanted to go get something to eat with the boys. She agreed, and we all loaded up and went for dinner.

That night I was a bit at ease. I was really happy to have spent a couple hours with her and the boys, hanging out as a family. After spending a weekend with the sun beating down on me with a couple of crazy old guys, drinking Sweet Lucy and beer, I was ready to get into bed early.

I was whooped.

I had overthought and overtalked the recent issues I was having. I just didn't have the desire to put myself through the wringer while trying to go to sleep. I knew there was nothing I could do right then besides hope for the best and get some rest. I hadn't had double vision since Tuesday, so that was a positive, and I had found some peace while talking things through with the guys. Bella and the boys also seemed to have taken a deep breath. To see them a little less intense was important to me. I fought off a little bit of anxiety but fell asleep rather quickly. I felt every bit of fifty-four years old after the weekend I'd had.

CHAPTER 31

The first day of a decade is something most people don't slow down enough to realize they are living. It is quite the remarkable event. Times is broken up into ten-year installments. There was the roaring '20s, the turbulent '30s, the flying '40s, aka the fightin' '40s, and the fabulous '50s. It was the beginning of the '60s.

What would the '60s unveil?

What would happen in the world?

There would be new inventions, new celebrities, new music. There would be wars, tragic losses, life-changing events. There would be many major events, advances in medicine, and changes in technology. There would be new sports heroes, some who would establish themselves as legends and others move on barely remembered. In 1960, the world was full go. The average cost of a home had risen to around thirteen thousand dollars, and a gallon of gas was peaking at twenty-five cents. A Polaroid camera was quite expensive for its time and rang in around ninety-three dollars. A can of ravioli was thirty cents, and a loaf of bread was only twenty cents. In the medical world, the pacemaker was first used in humans, and birth-control pills hit the market. *The Flintstones* premiered on television. Alfred Hitchcock's *Psycho* hit theaters everywhere.

The Olympics took place in Rome beginning in August. After having won gold in the Olympics, Cassius Clay, who later became known as Muhammad Ali, fought in his first professional fight. The most notable and popularized conversation of 1960 surrounded politics. John F. Kennedy and Vice-President Richard Nixon were in a heated battle to become the thirty-fifth president of the United States.

We were raised as devout Catholics. My grandfather was a convert from Missouri and established a deep faith that would be passed down through Mom to us kids. We went to Holy Ghost where my parents got married. Not Dad, though. As previously stated, he was Methodist, and he normally spent Sundays at work instead of church.

We went to Mass every Sunday. Back then, Mass was in Latin.

We didn't have a clue what the priest was saying. *Confiteor Deo… mea culpa, mea culpa, mea maxima culpa…* I'm sure it was all good stuff, but I literally had no clue what he was saying. Holy Ghost was an architectural marvel, though, and that is usually what I paid most of my attention to. The roof trusses were exposed, and I thought they were absolutely incredible. It almost seemed that the interior of the church was a photo negative by design. This is all to say that with him potentially becoming the first Catholic president, naturally the members of my family were big Kennedy supporters.

Coverage of the presidential race consumed the majority of airtime on the three television channels we had. Even non-Catholic Dad supported JFK. He probably didn't care one way or the other and was only trying to appease his in-laws.

The more coverage viewed inside my home, the more time I spent playing with the guys around the neighborhood. As I was approaching the six-year mark in life, my parents would sometimes let me stay out as late as eleven. I enjoyed watching Susan and Julie grow up. Mike was still Mike, but the fact that I didn't let him bother me much sort of deterred the amount of efforts he made. Still, when any efforts were made, they were solely meant as an attempt to make my life hell. In fact, it was around this time that Susan would sometimes become my tagalong. She couldn't do much around the neighborhood, but I watched out for her, and she loved to watch us play.

After my birthday in March, I was only a summer away from another milestone in life. Mom had informed me that in the fall I would begin school. I was excited by the thought of it. I thoroughly enjoyed being around the guys in the neighborhood, but I credit the natural maturation of a child to the fact that I was ready to take the next step.

At certain points in life, you outgrow the normal activities that make up your life. Now, I'm not suggesting by any means that I had outgrown playing football as often as possible. Internally though, I had a desire to learn and grow—to do more than be at home all day, every day. I could read a bit and write a little too, but I wanted to know more about both and a multitude of other topics. I knew I'd find that through my time in school.

In the summer, it was full pads full-time. I knew that school would take away from my time in the neighborhood, and I really wanted to cherish my last few months with the friends who would be left at home during the day as well as those that were out of school now for summer break. We kicked around and did all kinds of things that summer. We went to the movies, drank an Orange Julius as often as possible, road our bikes to the 7-Eleven to grab a coke for us and cigars for Dad. Catching the creek bed on fire with bottle rockets was a personal favorite in a two-month span of wonderful highlights. I had grown to be a fun-loving, funny, charismatic, and polite little guy.

I was pretty handsome, too, if I do say so myself.

I had great athletic ability but was as modest as the day is long. I was a good son, brother, and friend. I had great relationships with those I cared most about. The extent of trouble I got in could be measured by how bad a mood Dad was in on any given day and the amount of horseplay I took part in. Fortunately, I was never caught smoking grapevines or cigarettes. Since Mike indulged with me, he couldn't rat me out. All in all, I felt I was ready to start school, and come fall that is exactly what I did.

CHAPTER 32

I got to see Dad a bit more as I started school. An extra stop on his ride-sharing route to work was how Mike and I arrived there each morning. Sometimes he would even be kind enough to tell us to have a nice day.

Due to our Catholic practice, it was decided that we would go to Holy Ghost School. A few days in, I had a major realization. My teacher was, and

I realized that Sister Mary Morley was merciless That was my take on the situation, anyway. She had as much business teaching first grade as Rasputin did teaching religion. Her career was more centered around harassing children than providing them with any form of education. She believe that she was infallible.

Many days I determined that, provided the right circumstances, I would poke her in the eye with my pencil. My personal ethics and morals ultimately got the best of me anytime I felt the time could be right.

On a daily basis, you'd find me with a kid I met the first day of school. His name was Johnny McLoughlin. To this day, he is one of the funniest people I have ever met. His humor and antics are on par with comedian Jack Black's. He was completely spontaneous and always full of energy. He was my best friend—and boy, did we share a lot of laughs and good times! Hell, without him, I'm not sure I would have made it through the year. Fortunately for me, I knew that each grade had one class made up of ten to fifteen kids. This meaning Ol' Johnny Boy would be in my class for at least the next few years, and I was completely elated by this revelation.

As the school year played out, I did find that learning was something I was fond of on the few days a week that Sister Mary Morley actually taught us the school's curriculum instead of her own. Learning makes everyday life easier. For me, that meant that I didn't have to have Uncle David read me the articles out of the paper days after they had arrived.

As I spent my first fall in school, Tennessee was also playing every weekend. That year, the Vols went 6-2-2 and at their pinnacle reached a #8 ranking. Their defense fell off a little but their offense picked it up. Most importantly, Tennessee smacked Alabama 20–7, fortunately ending my need to know who the better team was in the best way possible. My weekly routine of listening to the game only became further cemented. Uncle David took me to the Chattanooga game again as the Vols left with a 35–0 victory. The other game he took me to that year was the Kentucky game. The Vols tied the Wildcats 10–10 in the Battle for the Barrel, but the game was still a joy to experience. That was the first SEC game I had ever been to. Uncle David had found a new route for getting tickets, which consisted of not getting tickets at all. He bartered with a guy who worked a gate. So, he would trade the guy some goods to let us sneak in. It was successful every time but a tad stressful on occasion.

On November 8, 1960, the popular John F. Kennedy and new first lady Jackie made waves across the nation as he won the presidential election. The folks in my family were very pleased with the outcome. It was a breakthrough for the Catholic community, and it was neat to see how much it meant to everyone I knew. After that, it was on to Julie's first birthday and Thanksgiving. Packing into Grandmother and Papaw's for the big Thanksgiving feast had never been so cramped as we brought along our newest addition to the family for the first time. She had grown like a weed in just a year's time.

Back at school, it was more of the same. Johnny and I would pay a visit to the candy counter at Sears before going to Holy Ghost. We would buy two pounds of double-dipped chocolate peanuts. When it came time to observe Lent and subsequently do our portion of the twenty-four-hour, two-man vigil, we signed up to do it together. Eventually, during the year together, we manned the two kneelers on the south side of the main altar. First, we had to go to the cloakroom and put on cassocks and surpluses; then we headed for what we called the secret walkway, which led to the sacristy. I remember it like yesterday.

On the flip side, Sister Mary Morley was just the next character in my life who posed as a foe. She had my number, and I really never got why. One day, she decided I had misbehaved in class. So, she lined up the whole class except for me. She had me stand facing the blackboard while she marched the class out, turned off the light, and closed the door. They'd practically put her in jail for that these days.

What I learned from that lesson was absolutely nothing.

Well, except that a blackboard is still black in the dark and that Sister Mary Morley was doing the world a favor by vowing to never have children.

Christmas brought family traditions and Susan's fourth birthday. Susan always cracked me up. She never saw any upside of having your birthday and Christmas on the same day. The truth is, she got a slew of presents about two weeks before Christmas and a slew more on Christmas morning. Was I jealous! She was quite the character as a kid. I liked the way she would try to keep up with me and the rest of the guys in the neighborhood when we played games. She was tough in her own right, and I loved that about her.

In January 1961, John F. Kennedy officially began his presidency. We were given a full rundown on the magnitude of it at school. On March 1, he officially established the Peace Corps. Learning a bit about that made me want to do more for others around me. Four days later, I turned seven. Miss Callie, one of my Dad's share-riders, gave me a silver dollar as a gift on the morning of my birthday. When I arrived at school, we had our daily mission collection first thing. Our goal was thirty-one dollars, and we were at thirty. I had no other choice but to contribute my silver dollar.

I guess being a hero has its price.

It sure didn't buy me any long-term goodwill from Sister Mary Morley. In fact, she seemed perturbed that I had done something to help.

What a winner.

About a week later, she was back at me first thing in the morning. We good Catholic boys started every day at Mass and were seated by class with our teachers.

"What's in your mouth?" asked Sister Mary Morley.

"Nothing," I answered.

"No, really. What is in your mouth?" she pressed.

"Nothing."

That was my story, and I was sticking to it.

Never mind the fact that my right cheek was protruding about two inches. Besides, everyone knows there is no talking during Mass. Shame on her. In reality, it was shame on me. In my mouth was actually an orange paraffin whistle that I had left over from Halloween and had found before school that morning. I had chosen to chew on it for a bit after I had relieved it of its orange-flavored sugar water.

I gave up and told her what I had, and she was livid. I told her for one reason, and one reason only: I was quite sure that if I didn't, she was going in for it. Although she would have been in perfect range for me to poke her in the eye with my pencil, I stopped myself.

Other than Mass, the entirety of first grade occurred in the basement of Holy Ghost. It was our classroom and lunchroom. There wasn't enough space to have it any other way. The last week of first grade, we were getting our stuff for lunch, and I had a major disaster: my thermos leaked.

Milk, no less, and all over the front of my pants.

There was no place to hide. I wanted to climb into a hole. There I stood in the lunchroom. *Drip…drip…drip.* Sister Mary Morley made a huge scene and embarrassed me intentionally in front of my entire class. Boy, was I glad to be done with her for the rest of my life.

CHAPTER 33

Summer was the best.

Tons of football.

Tons of shenanigans.

I was growing older and having the time of my life. Johnny even made it over to the neighborhood a few times to play with the gang and me. Whenever we played, he told me that he thought I was great at football. And other than football, we just hung out and had a great time, as usual.

We really didn't have a care in the world. There is truly no way to describe that feeling. A bad day hinged on whether or not the milk was cold or really cold. Either way, it didn't really affect us because in reality, we just didn't have the inclination to sit around having problems or complaining. We were self-sufficient young kids with all we needed in the world right at our fingertips. Or maybe I should say in our own backyards.

Literally.

The time away from school flew by. I did all I could to make the most of every second I had with the guys around the neighborhood during those few months. Second grade started and was a much smoother road than first grade. Yet again, it was me and McLoughlin against the world. My best bud! I enjoyed my time at school. I made new friends and learned as much as I could. I did tend to goof off sometimes, but it was just part of who I was.

Now that Sister Mary Morley wasn't heading the classroom, it was usually met with a laugh and a *Get back to work, Steve*. It was a good change of pace in my opinion. Truly, besides hanging out with Johnny and trying to learn, the school week was just a bridge in between Tennessee games.

That fall, the Vols wound up 6-4 when it was all said and done. The Third Saturday in October was not so kind to us this time around as Tennessee got hammered by Alabama in front of a crowd of forty-eight thousand people in Birmingham by a score of 34-3. In November, Uncle David took me to see the Vols play #9 Georgia Tech, and we walked away with a 10-6 win. It was the first time we had beaten them in a few years, so the crowd was really rowdy. After the game, my uncle continued our tradition by taking me to Frank's Brass Rail. We went for lunch and loved it. From that point forward, we went after almost every game. Plus, all the players showed up there after the home games. It was their place. I was always in awe in their presence.

A few weeks passed, and it was Julie's birthday and Thanksgiving. She was two years old, and wild as can be and getting into everything. She favored my mom tremendously. She was and always will be gorgeous. That winter, we had a big snow, and I remember being out in the alley with Dad, Mike, and Susan playing until we were too cold to go on.

Christmas came and went, and I couldn't believe that Susan was already five. As 1962 rolled around, it became really clear to me how much I was undergoing change. I was a few months away from being eight years old.

I started to care less about childish things and took on new interests. I would draw sometimes and loved to listen to music. Music was changing and I personally thought for the better. I tried new foods that I liked and got tired of others I'd once loved. I grew a good bit and wasn't one of the smallest kids anymore. One thing that didn't change, however, was my love for sports. It grew more and more by the day, and at this time, I was the best player in Knoxville to have never set foot on a real football field.

At least in my own mind.

I had the opportunity to try out for basketball, and I was a fan of it too. It had such a high pace, and each time you made a bucket, it made you feel great. Mike and I saw eye to eye on things a bit more although he never admitted it. We were never going to be those brothers who became best friends at some point. He still gave me hell as much as he cared to and got me in trouble whenever he could, but that was seemingly a lot less frequently. He was in middle school and doing his own thing the majority of the time.

In 1962, a lot was going on in the world. The Cuban Missile Crisis was one of the big ones. I remember sitting in my living room with it being broadcast on all three channels simultaneously.

On a lighter note, Marilyn Monroe famously sang "Happy Birthday" to JFK on May 19 at his birthday celebration.

But she was found dead and had apparently overdosed on sleeping pills on August 5. James Meredith, who was a former serviceman in the US Air Force, became the first black student to enroll at the all-white University of Mississippi. His enrollment led to rioting, and he was finally able to enter the school after President Kennedy insisted he be escorted by US Marshals. For the second year in a row, the US tripled its troop levels in Vietnam as the war raged on and we found ourselves more involved. Also, the US Navy SEALS were established by JFK. The first Walmart opened. So did the first Kmart. Marvel debuted the first comic book featuring Spider-Man. Brazil won the World Cup against Czechoslovakia. *Spartacus* and *West Side Story* were the big movie hits, along with *To Kill a Mockingbird*.

Bob Dylan and Roy Orbison were big in the music world. The Beatles were actually turned down by Decca Records and then came back to release "Love Me Do" by year's end. *The Dick Van Dyke Show* and *The Beverly Hillbillies* aired on TV. Telstar relayed the first live transatlantic television signal. In 1962, this affected many more than it would have in previous years, as American households with televisions reached 90 percent.

In March, I turned eight, and school was in its last leg for the year. I was looking forward to summer. The last few months of school really could be a drag, though I was doing really well and made great grades. Usually there wasn't anything I didn't understand. If by chance I was stumped by something, I would give my all to figure it out. My classmates and I always got along and had a good time together. When we had the chance to play, it was just like it was in the neighborhood.

I mean this in the sense that we would do whatever it took to keep ourselves going at a hundred miles per hour for as long as we could.

CHAPTER 34

When school let out and summer had begun, things got back to their old ways—quickly. The other kids and I played on school nights, but during the summer, I hung out with a crew of them at all times except for eating and sleeping.

In June, I had found an old fishing pole while I was poking around Dad's tool bench area with Jimmy. Since Dad had failed to teach me anything on my one and only fishing trip as a kid, I figured I should go into the bedroom and try to get the hang of things. About the time I decided to see if I could cast the line across my bedroom, Susan walked in. She asked what I was doing, so I told her to stand behind me and watch. Sure enough, the line went back and the hook went right through her hand on my attempted twelve-foot cast.

I freaked out.

Susan freaked out.

I frantically went running through the house to find Mom with my fishing pole in tote. Susan was running behind me, trying to keep up so the hook didn't rip her hand in half. When we finally reached Mom, there was blood dripping everywhere, Julie was crying because we had scared her with our screaming, Mike was sitting on the couch laughing, and I thought for sure I was in big trouble. Fortunately, my mom got the hook out and calmed everyone down. She could see it was an accident. I officially determined that, from that moment on, my fishing career was over. Forever.

Due to a growth spurt, I dominated even more on the football field in those days. I was a regular as captain and everyone wanted to be on my team. There were a few guys I would try to pick every time. When we played together, we were all in sync. Everything just seemed to run smoother, and it was due to the way that we all operated together as one—instead of a bunch of individuals flying around doing their own thing. Playing pickup doesn't really encourage the team mentality. However, when the circumstances were right and we all ended up on the same side, we played as a team and wore the other guys out.

We didn't argue over who was going to do what or who was going to play where. We understood our roles and that the outcome would be optimal if we respected them. This in turn led me to a thought that I later found a great summation of.

A team is greater than the sum of its parts.

This was a major realization for me due to the fact that for a lot of the time I played, I had to be a leader for my team. Each player really plays a significant role, and a team is only as good as its worst player. If you can get everyone to play in harmony, it really maximizes each player's personal capability. Naturally, this was due to their not having to focus on anything beyond his own task at hand. I always gave my best and played to the level I was capable of. It just so happened that my potential was greater when I played with the guys as a team instead of having an ego contest.

It was quite the revelation, and I was thankful to have had it.

The team, after all, was one of the most rewarding parts of playing, as were the feelings that were generated for everyone when a single person did something great. Narrowing in on the fact that it took everyone to make a single person do something great was important. From then on, I appreciated the others on my team whether we meshed well or not, anytime I played.

Besides, at the end of a game, it was a team that won or lost the game.

Not a single player.

CHAPTER 35

As summer came to an end, I was preparing to start third grade. I was really excited to get back to it, and on the first day of school, I was all smiles. Well, that was until I walked into my classroom. I thought I was rid of her forever, but I certainly wasn't.

Insert teacher's name here.

That's right: Sister Mary Morley. I had gotten her again for another school year. Man, was I disappointed. She sure didn't waste any time reminding me why I didn't like her. Admittedly, I found ways to stay out of her cross hairs much more than in first grade. Still, she didn't like me, and she made sure to display her feelings toward me whenever given the opportunity. I could do something as simple as drop a book by accident and she would make a big deal out of it.

One day, I spilled something on my shirt, so she made me face the blackboard in front of the class for an hour. Because that makes sense… Once again, it was my shenanigans with Johnny McLoughlin that made the days around Sister Mary Morley more bearable. When I was dealing with a tough day due to her superb treatment, he always did something crazy and put a smile back on my face.

Later, in my adult life, I ran into a girl I had gone to school with. Her name was Martha Lou McCampbell. She seemed to remember Sister Mary Morley very fondly. Maybe I could have been wrong about her, but I doubt it. I figured there was the possibility that she got along with girls better than boys. Or maybe she got along with anyone better than she did with someone named Steven Thomas Adkins. Whatever the case may be, she was a terror to me.

That fall, Tennessee didn't give me anything to look forward to on the weekends. The Vols went 4-6 and never achieved a top-twenty ranking the entire season. The guys who'd made up the devastating defense the past few years had graduated and moved on. Tennessee gave up point after point. Uncle David took me to the Chattanooga and the Tulane games that year. Tulane was actually in the SEC in those days. Fortunately, both of those games were wins, so my game-day experiences were still just as great as previous years.

It killed me every time they got demoralized by a big team. Like losing to Alabama 27–7 in Knoxville. I think my uncle and I turned the radio off in the third quarter during that one. They did, however, end the season with a 30–0 win over Vanderbilt.

It was Vanderbilt, though.

I've never seen a team find more ways to lose than the Commodores.

Everyone used to sing this little jingle about them in Knoxville that went *Little brother / you'll always be/ in my home sweet home / of Tennessee.* Throughout the holidays that year, we had our family events and birthdays for Julie and Susan. Julie was three then, and Susan six. Susan had become a pretty good Kick the Can player. In fact, she was pretty good at a lot of things she tried out. Julie just wanted to be around us whether she could take part or not. Mike would always go full speed when we played, even though they were younger and less capable. I never understood his competitive mentality when playing with a six- and three-year-old. I just loved to see them having fun. They were my sisters.

To him it was like the bottom of the ninth with the bases loaded. During that time, he'd started to become interested in other things besides sports, so maybe he just liked to show he still had it when he jumped in and played with us.

Maybe it was more about competing with me than beating them.

At the turn of 1963, the '60s were not disappointing. They were bringing all kinds of new things to the world. And t

hey were bringing all kinds of new things to Knoxville, my all-American hometown.

Times were changing, and in some ways, it was for the better. The major things that played a role in my life were on the less serious side of the coin. New music and hit movies. The prices of simple things I enjoyed went up, like candy and sodas, although only by cents, but nevertheless they went up. Sodas with pull tabs also hit the market, which were quite revolutionary.

Back at school, I did my best to fly under the radar and learn as much as I could when Sister Mary Morley wasn't riding herd on me or anyone else in the classroom. Fortunately, I made it through the entire third grade without spilling milk in my lap.

I could read, write, create a poem, do math, understand history, get interested in science, and be versed in religion. All the while, I began to understand the people around me more. I paid attention to the ways certain kids acted. The way popular kids were treated. The way bullies typically had a bad home life. Rich kids acted like rich kids. Broke kids tried their hardest to act like rich kids. Through noting it all, I determined that I would always do whatever it took to just be me, through and through.

Just Steve.

Moral Support

May 12, 2008

I woke up Monday morning in the same position and spot I had fallen asleep in. Sleep doesn't get much better than that.

There were two things in life that I wasn't a fan of: one was heights, and the other was tight spaces. What can I say? A lot of folks don't like heights, and I'm a big guy. Tight spaces and I don't get along very well. I truly am incredibly claustrophobic.

The first thing on my agenda that morning was to ask Bella to accompany me to my MRI. Like I said, tight spaces aren't my favorite.

On top of that, I was honestly scared.

It being the day I might finally receive some answers, I was anxious all over again. This time, though, I'm not sure if I was more ready to finally get some answers or scared to know what the answers would be. At the doctor's office, we were called in and took a seat in a room. The doctor came in, and I asked if it would be okay if Bella stood next to me while I was having the MRI done. The doctor said he didn't see any issues with it.

As I got on the table and was headed into the machine, I reached out and grabbed my wife's hand.

I needed it.

I was always the rock, but in this moment, I realized I was only able to be because Bella was a rock for me.

As they say, a man is only as powerful as the woman standing next to him. It is true, you know. No matter how big or bad you are, everyone needs that someone who was put on this earth for them. Bella was it for me, and in this moment, I was so thankful to have her by my side.

The table had slid me all the way into the sliver of space between the top and bottom of the machine. I wondered what the results would be. I wondered if I had been freaking out over nothing—if the double vision had been nothing more than a glitch. Insignificant. Then I thought to myself that there was no way. How I had felt lately, even when it wasn't occurring. I was too in tune with my body and mind to think that this could just be some random happening.

Again, sweat started to form on my forehead. I felt anxious. I was getting frustrated. It dawned on me that I was inside of an MRI machine, and the feeling of claustrophobia came over me at an overwhelming pace.

Bella's hand.

There was Bella's hand.

In my hand.

Her skin against mine.

Soft.

Secure.

Then a voice came over a speaker telling me it was over, and I began to slide out of the machine.

About fifteen or twenty minutes later, the doctor came into our room. He told me that the tests he had run the week before had come back and that I did not have diabetes, but that he wanted me to monitor my blood pressure moving forward and that he was going to put me on a low-level blood thinner. It wouldn't hurt anything, and in case there was something more serious going on, it could only help.

As for the results of the MRI, he said they had reviewed the images and had found nothing that could potentially be a cause for the double vision. Nothing that would indicate a more serious situation than he'd come up with at the visit last week. All I wanted was some sort of answer as to what was going on with me. Bella wanted it too. Whether I was scared to know what was going on or not, I wanted to know.

I couldn't take the anxiety of not knowing anymore.

I couldn't take the anticipation of figuring it out.

And I couldn't keep relying on my own mind to come up with the possible outcomes or issues. I kept ending up in a negative place when relying on my own opinions regarding the severity of the matter.

In the end, it didn't matter.

There was nothing more he could tell us at the time. He wanted to monitor my blood pressure and put me on a blood thinner.

"Sorry, Steve, but there isn't a clear-cut answer I can give you at this time to explain what has been going on with you."

All I could think was *Great!*

CHAPTER 36

It was 1963, my ninth birthday and Mike's twelfth came and went, and summer couldn't come fast enough. Maybe this time I would really be done with Sister Mary Morley once and for all. In spring 1963, my dad decided he was going to try to buy a house in Powell to be closer to Powell Telephone Company where he was still moonlighting. Turns out, the owner of the company lived only a few doors down from the house he had his eye on. It was decided that we would drive out there as a family and look at the house.

After being on Central Avenue for thirty minutes, I was deep in thought.

Where the heck are we going? Dad wants to live all the way out here? Are we in Montana?

After making the ride out there, I could see for myself why he didn't want to drive all that way every day. Plus his other job. He may not have been the best at doing the whole Dad thing, but he did bust his ass for our family, every day, without fail.

His hard work for the sake of our family aided me in finding an appreciation for him. He may not have been home much, but we never went a day without food or the lights on.

As we pulled into the driveway, the first thing I noticed was that it was a nice enough house. Big too. It obviously had more space than our house on Shamrock Avenue. Mom could see the saddened looks on our faces as we told her we didn't want to move away from our neighborhood friends.

She assured us that we could never get a mortgage that big because the man that was selling the house, Troy Perkins, was asking $16,500 for the three-bedroom, pink-brick ranch.

That gave me a glimpse of hope as we left that day. In all honesty though, I was torn. The house was really nice, and the thought of moving and beginning a new stage in life kind of piqued my interest too.

School came to an end, and talks of moving lingered in the air. I spent every day playing with the guys because I didn't know how much time I'd have with them if we actually got the house. The Scarbroughs told Dad that he could have free long distance if we were to move out to Powell so we wouldn't have trouble keeping in touch with our family back in the neighborhood.

See, Powell was in north Knox County, and anything over ten miles was considered long distance. Man, what we could have done with cell phones back then! Although, in some ways, life was easier without them. In July, we received word that the bank had given Dad the loan, and we were officially going to be moving to Powell.

Or as I called it growing up, *Pal.*

We would arrive there just in time for Saint Joseph Catholic Elementary School to open on Cedar Lane in North Knoxville. There were a handful of parochial schools around Knoxville at the time. The Catholic schools included Immaculate Conception downtown and Sacred Heart in West Knoxville. The new Saint Joseph was palatial in comparison, and it was something that I could get excited about. Mike and I got all of our things packed up. The only thing left to do was farm out our best excess stuff around the neighborhood.

The Blaylocks had first crack at it since they lived the farthest away. They definitely needed our old Quick Draw McGraw ball game.

The Henrys were second. Fortunately for them, we decided they needed all the old baseball caps we had andour sundry Ping-Pong paddles.

They graciously accepted.

Our little red wagon had the contents for yet another stop. It was at Greg White's house. He was in the market for a toy car with only three wheels and a yo-yo with no string. We were just the guys to hook him up.

With only about twenty-four hours left before we would say goodbye to our perfect little neighborhood on Shamrock Avenue, I was met with the opportunity to learn two very valuable lessons.

As we went to say goodbye to Steve and Sonny Kivett, it was decided we would draw up one last masterful plan. The plan was your basic bait-and-switch routine.

Someone would go find Larry Blaylock and tell him that Dennis Turner had challenged him to a fight. For whatever reason, it was determined that when he showed, he would fight me instead. I obviously went along with it. He bit, so he came hustling up to the Kivetts' front yard with his brother Tommy, smelling blood, I'm sure. We made the switch, and the fight was on.

Although the situation was somewhat serious, I smiled. This was the epitome of what I had enjoyed so much about my time living there. At any minute things could turn on a dime. The spontaneity of it all was what made it an absolute blast. Everyone was willing to do whatever, whenever for the sake of a silly thrill, a good laugh. I sure was going to miss these guys. Even Larry Blaylock, even though I was staring him in the face and he was trying to take my head off.

What Larry really had going for him was a complete lack of pain threshold. In other words, after about two minutes, somebody had to interrupt him to tell him he was bleeding profusely and that the fight was over. He stood up, and we laughed and gave each other a big hug.

The first lesson I learned there was obvious, regardless of whether I was more on the giving end.

Know your opponent.

The fight had drawn quite the crowd, and I mean every kid in the neighborhood. It was great to see everyone for the last time and give hugs all around. After we said our goodbyes and made it home, we were moving our boxes out to the driveway. Dad was finishing getting everything ready to head across town. As I was moving my stuff, I came across my favorite old toy: the telephone-company truck.

It was a miniature version of an old telephone truck that was accurate down to a T.

Dad may have been gone a lot and in a bad mood when he was around, but he was my dad, and I loved him. When I played with the telephone truck, it was sort of like being with him. So, I got it out and played with it for a minute. As I was playing, Mom called me up to the house. I left the truck and ran up to see what she wanted.

We were going to drive over to Grandmother's.

We obviously would still see them often, but it was like we were saying goodbye forever. We all hopped in the car and headed over.

After a few hours, Dad got anxious to get back to the house before sundown so that he could finish preparing everything to head out in the morning. Due to everyone saying goodbye and Mom grabbing a couple of leftovers from dinner, Dad got impatient. When Dad got impatient, he got in a bad mood. And when he got in a bad mood, he was an ass. As he pulled up to the house he spied my favorite old toy lying in the pea-gravel driveway.

I had accidentally left it out in my haste to head out earlier.

So, he decided to intentionally run over the telephone-company truck to teach me a lesson.

He taught me a lesson, all right—the second one I had learned that day.

It was a pretty simple concept if you ask me: don't leave your favorite old toy in the driveway while your Dad is in a bad mood, or this crazy lunatic in the family lemon will smash it into oblivion by running it over.

On the last night I spent on Shamrock Avenue, I lay in bed and wondered what the move would hold for me and my life.

How would the neighborhood be?

Would there be any kids? What would Saint Joseph be like?

Would I get the chance to play sports?

I wondered how Susan and Julie would take it. I even wondered what Mike thought of it all. Overall, I was pretty excited to start a new chapter, to see what was in store.

No turning back now.

We're moving to Pal!

CHAPTER 37

My first day in the new house was all about taking everything in. New sights, new smells, and most importantly, a new beginning. It wasn't that I was in need of one or had a reason to relish new beginnings. In fact, I could have really used a great game of football with the guys right about then. Nevertheless, I was going to embrace the change and see what it had in store.

It didn't take long to figure out that entertainment came at a premium. After the first twenty-four hours in the new house, taking everything in was over, and it was time to do something. I was bored as can be and needed to stretch my legs.

There was no better time to figure out what my new expanse had waiting for me.

On Shamrock Avenue, there was this whole neighborhood packed into a small space off a main road. The new area wasn't much of a neighborhood at all. We lived off Collier Road, which was also known as Route 6. In reality, it was a main road with no small neighborhoods off it, just houses that were spaced out.

Back then, it was located in an area that Mom described as The Sticks.

We didn't have a mailbox number for years after we moved there. When you turned onto Collier Road, our house was located about an eighth of mile up a hill on the right. Our house had been built in a lot across from a big, beautiful home. Our house was also located where the gentleman who lived in the big, beautiful house used to look out and see the Smoky Mountains. Criminal, if you ask me. Down the hill at the bottom of the road were the train tracks.

I loved the train tracks.

There was a house right next to them, and a gentleman who lived there would collect everyone's mail. To send it out, he would hand it up to a guy on the train as it passed by. The guy on the train would in turn toss down a bag for delivery.

We were also located two doors down from the Scarbroughs .

Across from the telephone company was a big house that had a big, bright red light. They turned it on at night. There were always women on the front porch howling at my dad when we went by.

I always thought my father was a handsome man, but perhaps by societal standards he was a heartthrob.

Either that or the women at that house just really loved middle-aged men.

As far as kids to play with, it was slim pickings. Our next-door neighbors had four daughters who were all younger than I was. Their parents were strict Southern Baptists, and after Mom put a birdbath in the front yard with Mother Mary in it the first week we lived there, they were no longer allowed to play with us. There were a few older kids who lived up and down the road from us. For the most part, it was looking like my new neighborhood gang would mainly consist of my two younger sisters.

Mike had established even more of an attitude and, if possible, an even greater hatred of me. I wasn't sure what he was going through, but man, was he a roller coaster of emotion. Mainly, it was peaks of dislike and disinterest for Susan, Julie, and me, but occasionally there was a low point that consisted of him asking me to do something with him or wanting to show me something he thought was cool.

Anyhow, it was my first day to discover the new area, and I didn't waste any time. Due to the layout, it became obvious that there would be one particular mode of transportation, and it was my bicycle. There was no traffic in Powell, so Mom gave us the green light to ride our bikes wherever we wanted to go. Mike was apparently having a good day, so he and I grabbed about a dollar in change out of our room, climbed on our bikes, and headed up the road.

We made it about five country blocks before running into J. E. Groner & Co. Grocery Store. It was your old-school type of grocery with old wooden floors. They would let you run a charge account by face. They had a meat market run by a butcher named Fred. He was a really nice guy and befriended us immediately. Talked to us like he had known us for years. In time, we learned he did the same with everyone.

He was a really nice guy, but at first sight—I'm not going to lie—approaching him was a bit of a question mark. He wore a white apron with his black-handled knives hanging from it. He cut everything to order on his well-oiled butcher's block. But I liked Fred from the moment I met him, and he was the first friend I made in Powell.

On our first trip to Groner's, Mike and I grabbed a soda and some candy. Mike's favorite candy was M&M's and mine was SweeTarts. SweeTarts cost a nickel and came in a metallic, rectangular package. My favorite has always been orange.

We sat outside and enjoyed them, and then we got back on our bikes.

Across the street, you could find Mr. Baker's Barber Shop. We didn't have anything better to do, so we decided to ride across the street for a quick cut. Upon walking in, Mr. Baker was telling a man about his son in Vietnam.

Wherever that was.

Finally, I came to understand that his son was in the war in Vietnam. I never knew his son personally, but he hadn't written in a few weeks, and Mr. Baker was visibly shaken up about it.

Back then, the barber only had one style of cut: short.

It was finished off with a straight razor.

Over my time living in Powell, I learned how to tell how long it had been since Mr. Baker's son had last written him. It was proportionate to the number of times he cut me with the razor. My first day venturing around Powell, I was cut eight times by Mr. Baker.

It truly had been a while since his son had written.

About eight weeks to be precise.

After we had been cleaned up and looked like we had been at war ourselves, Mike and I headed back out to our bikes.

The next place we came across was Weeks' Grocery Store.

In one day, we had met the establishment and the competition.

It was also official that there were twice as many grocery stores in Powell as red lights.

Weeks' Grocery was located in an old, brick building. Upon my initial entry, I found interest in the wood-burning stove that they would use to heat the place come winter. After a few weeks of living in the area, we heard rumors that the Weeks were the richest people in Powell and kept every dollar they ever made under their mattress.

I could relate to them.

As far as the standard in the early '60s, I was pretty well-off, actually.

I had a whole model-airplane box full of cash that I kept on my night side table.

Pretty foolproof plan if you ask me.

After enjoying another round of soda and candy, we headed back to the house. It was the beginning of August and unbearably hot. When the breeze hit your face while you were riding down the road on your bike, it felt like you were standing in front of a hair dryer. There was absolutely nothing enjoyable about it, and to make matters worse, it put Mike in a bad mood.

It obviously didn't take much for him to arrive there.

After dinner and some TV, I crashed out pretty early. By paying attention to all that was going on around me while I was out and about with Mike, I had effectively made a decision about what I would do the next day.

CHAPTER 38

The next morning after breakfast, I grabbed a couple of bucks and headed to the foot of the hill on Collier. I realized there wasn't that much action around the house, so if I wanted some I'd have to head downtown. After waiting patiently, I saw the bus heading up the road toward me. It was a blue and white Blue Bird bus, and it only cost thirty-five cents to get to downtown.

Once the bus made it out to Central Street, it was a straight shot until it took a right onto Broadway. We passed all sorts of stuff along the way. On my first trip, for some reason I remember passing Old Gray Cemetery, Rich's on Henley, and the First Presbyterian Church. After a fifteen-minute ride, I finally disembarked in front of the Tennessee Theatre.

I had officially arrived downtown.

My plan was pretty clear-cut. I made my way over to the Farragut Hotel. Since he was a permanent fixture behind the counter every single day, I knew my grandfather would be working. This was good ol' Burt Declue's daily routine for over fifty years. He was excited to see me and took an extended lunch. We went down to Gay Street, which had a plethora of shops. All sorts of stores, like the Kress five-and-dime and, one of my favorites, the hat shop.

My guess is that every town had a hat shop because people didn't bathe like they do today. Men took a bath every Saturday, whether they needed to or not, and nobody took showers. Some say that's where the term *hat trick* came from. No one knew how greasy your hair was with a hat on your head. Also, back in the day, they used to actually give you a hat for scoring three goals in a hockey game.

As we walked around together, he decided we would have lunch at the S&W Cafeteria. My favorite thing about the S&W Cafeteria was the floor-to-ceiling mirror. The ceiling above the tables was twenty feet high. You could see who was upstairs without actually having to go up there.

I had one of my favorites, which was roast beef, au gratin potatoes, and pinto beans. I topped it all off with a shrimp cocktail and a block of orange Jell-O, for a grand total of two dollars and twenty-five cents. I was a high roller, and I was also thoroughly enjoying the lady up front who continuously serenaded us with her organ.

Afterward, we headed back up to the hotel. As we arrived, Grandmother stopped in, and I was happy to see her. She was downtown for her weekly errands. As previously stated, they never owned a car, so she would take the bus downtown. She did all of her grocery shopping at the IGA at the Market Square mall. It was state-of-the-art at the time. The place she had previously done her shopping at, the Market House, which was built in 1854 and took up an entire city block, had burned down and the IGA basically replaced it. It was definitely considered an upgrade, although it was smaller. The last thing she always did before she finished up was grab a fountain Coke to enjoy on the bus ride home.

Once I'd said my goodbyes to my grandparents, I headed over to The Riviera for the matinee. I saw *Lord Love a Duck* with Roddy McDowall. It was hilarious, and I was recovering from a cough, so it hurt to laugh.

Once it was over, I deemed my day a success.

I walked up to the bench outside of the Athletic House and waited for my bus to arrive. I climbed aboard, deposited my thirty-five cents, and was homeward bound to Powell. The bus went straight back up Central Avenue Pike to Emory Road and then over to Collier Road where I got off.

Trip complete.

Pretty good day for a nine-year-old.

There wasn't much going on around the house, so once again, I ate dinner, spent a little time watching TV with the family, and headed to bed a little early. The next day was a bore. I went to J. E. Groner and talked to Fred while downing an ice-cold Coke and a pack of SweeTarts. He told me a little bit about his butcher duties.

I didn't really keep up.

I was still five years away from grilling for the first time, so meats and I didn't have a lot in common. I figured I could keep riding around to see if I could run into anything fun to do. I knew that I wouldn't, so I headed back to the house.

After getting back home I kicked around the house trying to find things to keep me occupied. At the time,

Julie could find more entertainment in a cardboard box than I could in a warehouse full of fireworks. I was so jealous of her fulfillment through the simplest of things. She was always exploring and discovering. Unless it was time for her nap, she never stopped. Susan sort of found herself in the same situation I was in, but you could tell she didn't mind as much. I was so used to having the guys around the neighborhood to cure my need for boredom.

Hell, it had been almost a week since I had played football. I think I was having withdrawal. At the time, though, I'd take a game of Kick the Can. Anything would suffice. Mike was still completely content the majority of the time drinking his ice tea and hogging the TV. I watched whatever he was watching because trying to get him to watch something else was a battle I wasn't willing to put any effort into.

It never worked out in my favor anyway.

I decided to walk over to the Scarbroughs' house and see if anything was going on. After all, it was worth getting to know the people who were the primary reason for my living in the middle of nowhere. After talking with Mr. Scarbrough for a while, I guess he understood the struggle I was having. Due to his own son's extensive amount of boredom at one point, he had put up telephone poles with lights in their backyard, making it good for nightly football games.

His son Kenny went to school during the school year and typically worked days during the summer, so most games were held after dinner. Knowing that some of the guys who lived near me would be coming over to play that evening, he extended an invitation to me and told me to bring Mike if he wanted to come.

I was excited and nervous all at the same time.

I definitely heard his warning loud and clear that all the guys who would be playing were mostly in high school.

Either way, I decided from the moment the invitation left his mouth that I was in. I guess it was time to test my mettle. I headed home to tell Mom and Mike. Mike decided to play, so we both watched the clock for the next few hours. I was ready to hit somebody, even if he was twice my size. Needless to say, my boredom had been replaced with anxiety as dinner rolled around.

After we ate, I was in game mode as I got ready to play. I had never played with the really big boys. I guess there is a first time for everything. They also say there is no time like the present.

I was about thirty minutes from kickoff.

CHAPTER 39

A half hour later, we walked to the field. From a distance, I could already tell it was an impressive lineup. All things considered, it was destined to be. Due to the fact that these guys were older and more physically capable than me, even if they were just a bunch of slouches for their own age, they would still be great. From left to right, Mike and I met the guys who came out to play.

There was Stump, who was about five feet tall. We later found out that he sat on top of two Knoxville phone books just to drive a car. Compliments of knowing the Scarbroughs, of course.

Next you had Chick Jennings. He was a pretty big guy, and I thought he had a cool name. After him were J. C. Neeley and Steve France. In time, I found out that Steve France was primarily a baseball player, and I ended up learning a ton from him while living there. The football gods would have really been smiling had he ever decided to focus on the pigskin. He was so fast, and boy, did he have the moves. I'm pretty sure one of my jockstraps is still lying in the Scarbroughs' backyard somewhere.

Next was Kenny Scarbrough. We had seen Kenny before but had never really met him. I thought he was a nice guy from the moment I met him. Last, but certainly not least, was Jim Courtney, aka Mr. All-South Quarterback from nearby Powell High School. I recognized him because his picture had been in the paper that I checked out for Tennessee information each week.

Color me impressed!

We picked teams of four and then it was time for kickoff. Except there was no kickoff at the Scarbroughs'. All kicks were punts, and it made things exciting. The other difference was that these guys actually played first downs. Every time you got the ball to start a drive or after you picked up a first down, both teams looked over and found a marker that symbolized the marker for the next first down.

As far as playing goes, the first thing that was really apparent was the speed of everything. Even short and thick Stump, who fully embodied his nickname, was pretty fast, in my opinion due to the age difference. I mainly just tried to get a feel for things at first, and it seemed like the older guys were fine with that. After a few series, I hadn't really had a say in things yet due to the natural flow of a game. It seemed like the plays went away from me on defense, and my team was willingly underutilizing me on the offensive side of the ball.

After we scored to finally go up 1–0, we had punted to kickoff. They fielded it for a couple of yards and on the next play, and I decided it was time to wake everyone up. I was lined up against Chick Jennings and noticed everyone looking his way as both teams walked to the line. I figured it was time for them to pick on the little guy to get the game back to even.

I figured right.

As the play developed, he ran a 5-yard-out route, and as he was coming toward me I gave him a bit of a cushion and ponied up! As soon as the ball came out of the quarterback's hand, I took off the eight yards I had in front of me, and as the ball hit his fingertips, I lit into him with everything I had. The pass was incomplete, and we both were on the ground.

Who cares if he outweighed me by 150 pounds?

Well, that's what I thought until he came collapsing down on top of me.

Somehow, he ended up landing right on top of my stomach, and it knocked the air out of me. I didn't want everyone to think I was a sissy, so

I just lay there for a minute trying to collect myself as Chick slowly got up and trotted toward his team. Next thing I knew, all the guys on my team were around me hooting and hollering. They grabbed me by the hands and yanked me up. I smiled from ear to ear as I found my bearings.

As we walked back to the middle of the field to get ready for the next play, I even heard Mike say, "I told you guys not to underestimate him." It was a huge deal, and I really gained the respect of all the older guys.

The game was back and forth for a while. Finally, we were up 13–12, they were kicking off to us, and it was getting late. Kenny returned the kick fifteen yards. The first play of the drive was a pass out to J. C. that Jim threw perfectly. It went for a 10-yard gain and a first down. The next play was another pass to J. C. for five yards. We went back into the huddle, and Jim called a sweep to the left for Kenny. I did my best to block but was lined up against Chick again, and he got around me to stop Kenny for a short gain. It was 3rd and 4 on the 50.

Jim Courtney came into the huddle and said, "All right, guys, I have an idea. Steve Adkins hasn't gotten a touch once on this side of the ball all night. Let's line him up at wide receiver and run him on an end around to the right. They won't ever see it coming. Ready! Break!"

I trotted out to the left side of the field. I was a little nervous, I must admit. I thought to myself, *You got this, Steve. No time like the present.*

All sound started to fade out as Jim shouted, "Hut one! Hut two! Hike!"

It was like I was shot out of a cannon. As Jim handed the ball off to me, I only took two steps, and Mike was diving at my legs. I jumped as he dove for me and pushed his head down into the ground, hurdling over him. It was Chick Jennings and me in a game of chicken, and I moved first *and* second. I juked outside to the right, and as his momentum went in that direction, I shifted my shoulder and blew right by him to the center of the field.

I looked left, and Stump was coming in hard and fast from the other side of the field. As he approached I stopped, jumped back half a step, and he went right on by.

I was home free, and I turned on the afterburners.

As usual, it was slow motion and complete silence.

Everything disappeared as I ran farther away from the lights and into the night. All I could see was the reflection of the lights shining off the sides of my shoes as one after the other they propelled me down the field. As I reached the end zone, I turned around, and the guys were running down the field in celebration. Had it been one of them, it wouldn't have been that big a deal, but seeing the little guy do it really seemed to inspire them. Their response definitely inspired me. I loved it when they all lifted me up.

We were up 14–12, and everyone called it quits. I had scored the touchdown to put the game out of reach.

Jim ran over to me after the game was over and said, "Man, I wish I had skills like you when I was your age. You were great out there. See ya soon, Steve Adkins. Great job tonight!"

After the game, I was grinning from ear to ear, and if I wasn't dreaming, Jim Courtney had just complimented me.

Jim Courtney had complimented me!

Yeah, I was probably dreaming all right.

I hadn't done a ton out there, but I had made a big play on both sides of the ball. Hitting the bigger guys was definitely different from the gang on Shamrock. I was sweaty, tired, and in need of a bath, pronto. As I got cleaned up, the soreness was already setting in. Fortunately, I had the world's best mom. She treated me to some milk and cookies as she listened to me tell her about my incredible outing.

The big hit was exciting, but I just could not believe I had made that run for a touchdown. As I was thinking that, though, everything clicked.

That's what you are capable of. Embrace it.

Mom was all smiles and proud of me for being tough and getting out there with the older kids. Only a few days in my new neighborhood, and I already had a good story to tell. What would happen in the next few weeks before school started? There surely wasn't much around Powell, but I thought I could make due.

CHAPTER 40

The next day I woke up, and just like that, I was bored again. Sure, it would have been nice to be a full-time football player. I'd never even played in a real game before.

Eleven on eleven was a pipe dream from my front porch.

I wondered when I would have the chance to play organized ball, if ever. There really was no use in wondering about that, though. It was time to really find something that would take up some of my time until I started school. I was really excited about going to my new school, and the three weeks I had left to wait seemed like they might take an eternity.

I had plenty of ideas. Unfortunately (or fortunately, however you look at it), when I was really bored and by myself, the majority of my ideas ended in a bang—a scenario that I could definitely see myself getting in trouble for, like thoughts of getting into my flare inventory that I still had stowed away from that day years ago cleaning at my aunt's. I relented in the end and walked out to my dad's shed to see if I could figure out something to do.

As I looked around, it came to me.

I was a sucker for making some money, after all.

You never knew when you would need a couple of bucks, and although my dad worked a ton, he certainly wasn't walking around handing out singles to us kids. And there in the corner of our shed sat his push mower. Since he was at work and not at home handing out dollars, I figured I could make a few on my own: by making good use of the mower.

It was your classic push mower consisting of a metal deck and handle accompanied by a trusty old Briggs & Stratton engine. Our new neck of the woods was a haven of two-dollar stops. I felt sure I could talk a few folks into letting me mow their yard for a couple of bucks. Given that there were no jobless kids without jobs in our neighborhood besides the girls next door and us, the people around us didn't have kids to be giving dollars out to, either.

I headed out with my lawn mower in tow. The first yard I got was Mr. Peterson's on Collier, and was he ever a skinflint, making me feel fortunate that he even agreed to let me mow his lawn. Every time I dealt with him, I came out on the short end of the stick. He had what seemed like three hundred pine trees all planted in rows of fifteen. I know this because I push-mowed around every single one of them.

My routine at Mr. Peterson's was around all the pine trees and then street to street. It yielded the big bucks, which made it worth it. My take home was five and a half dollars for the two hours of mowing. I left sweaty, tired, and happy. I had to suck it up, though: I had more business to get.

My next customer was Mrs. Moon. She lived in a big, brick house on a huge hill. I started around back and, as I pushed the mower, I would whistle aloud; I am a firm believer in whistling while you work.

The first part of her yard was fairly easy. It included mowing around the submerged garage and the sleeping porch. The second part was mowing the rest of the backyard. It was pretty straightforward, except for all the apple trees. Every time I worked there, all I could think about was eating applesauce. The smell was sweet, but the lawn mower took some serious damage back there. Sometimes the clanging as I ran over roots and apples was so loud I was amazed the machine even made it out alive. After the orchard, it was on to the side yard next to the house, which I could knock out pretty quick. Then the front yard, which was the fun part.

The front yard was huge and on the hill of the property. I divided it up into three sections.

Each part was a sure test for my Converse.

The last part was easily the worst as it was on the steepest part of the terrain. This was definitely not a yard for the morning time when the dew was still on the ground. Had I made that mistake even once, my mower would have doubled as a meat grinder. (Gruesome, I know.)

Once I'd finally finished, it was time to collect.

"How much do I owe you, honey?" Mrs. Moon would ask.

"I think we settled on three fifty, Mrs. Moon."

This conversation literally occurred every time. The yard was truthfully worth more, but it only took my first outing to find out I was a bad business manager when it came to asking sweet old ladies for money.

She would then say, "C'mon in; make yourself at home, and have something to drink while I grab my purse."

I only made the mistake of having something to drink the first time I worked for her. She poured me a glass of what I thought was lemonade, but to this day, I still have no clue what it was.

It tasted like something that should have a sign on it that read *NOT FOR HUMAN CONSUMPTION!*

Of course, before I got there she was alone and I was bored, so a bad drink was worth passing the time. After enduring the beverage in fear of hurting her feelings, I collected my three and a half dollars and headed down the road. Mrs. Moon was a mainstay on my lawn-mowing schedule.

With that kind of pay, why wouldn't she be?

I ended up with three more yards that day. When I got home, Mike was seemingly in a good mood as he approached me.

"I heard about this place called the Cider Barn. You want to ride down there with me?"

It didn't take much convincing for me to reply, "Sure!"

Collier Road was off Emory Road. Emory Road took you to Clinton Highway. If you went to Clinton Highway, you eventually ended up going straight on a gravel road. Once you traveled down that for a minute, you arrived at the Cider Barn. The Cider Barn looked like today's Cracker Barrel and was similar in what it offered. The main difference was that there were a lot fewer customers on the ten-acre forest the restaurant sat on. On a good day, they probably did about twenty dollars' worth of gross sales.

They were known for their apple cider served in a frosted mug for a whopping fifteen cents. That was nothing for my full pockets. Even if I'd only had fifteen cents, that cider would have been worth it. I can't begin to convey how refreshing it was after a day out mowing. It was refreshing anytime, for that matter.

CHAPTER 41

Over the next week, I added a few more yards to my schedule. I didn't have much going on otherwise, and I enjoyed that my model-airplane-box bank account was growing daily. About a week and a half before school was due to start back, Mike and I were given a little tip. The tip was that anybody who was anybody would find themselves at the Lakeside Pool on a hot summer day.

We, obviously being somebodies, decided we better get in on it before we ran out of time.

We grabbed our handy bikes and headed out with towels over shoulders. The pool was up the hill from the Twin Aire Drive-In on Clinton Highway. It was in the biggest curve off Clinton Highway, in fact. If you missed the turnoff, you could turn around at the Airplane Package Store.

As we walked in, I found an immediate interest in the concession stand. The menu for the day consisted of Tom's Peanut Planks and Nehi Grape soda, so naturally, that is what I ordered. Upon taking my spot on the ersatz beach, I noticed that the lifeguard was none other than Powell High's Coach Hume. He lived just a few roads over from us, and I had already had the opportunity to meet him. It was an old-school, spring-fed pool with a diving board made out of wood planks that were painted white.

After taking the opportunity to work on my suntan over an impatiently passed fifteen minutes, it was time to wade in.

The heat was unbearable, and I was a kid.

And what do you really do at the pool besides swim?

Living on Shamrock Avenue, I had had swimming lessons, but it had been a while since I had been in the water. I was no professional to begin with. What happened next was completely unpredictable. As I waded into the water, everything seemed fairly copacetic. That was until— even though it was a concrete-bottom pool—I stepped in a hole.

Perhaps it was due to the fact that I hadn't waited thirty minutes after eating my snack and drinking my soda to get in the water. Regardless, I panicked, started thrashing around like a madman, and was completely sure I was going to drown. In my peripheral vision, I could see the side of the pool on one side and Coach Hume coming to save the day on the other. I made it to the side of the pool just as he made it to me, and he pushed me up out of the water. Once I was out, I located my spot and stayed out permanently.

If I was a somebody for being there, it only took me about twenty minutes to embarrass the heck out of myself, almost die, and become a nobody.

Perfect… About an hour later, another common attraction caught my eye, so I thought I would seek out a little redemption and head over to the dancing pavilion.

Sam the Sham and the Pharaohs were rocking "Wooly Bully" over the PA system overhead.

The girls were dancing up a storm with each other to the latest and greatest music. WKGN 1430 AM was there giving away 45 RPM records. Keep in mind that 45s were about eight inches in diameter and had a hole in the middle. They were state-of-the-art at the time, and everybody wanted to get their hands on one. WKGN made that somewhat easy because, instead of handing them out, they decided they would throw them Frisbee-style.

I determined that I was going to try to catch one in an attempt to get back into the winners' circle. Of course, that only lasted until somebody else actually tried to catch one. The sacrifice was probably worth it. The young man who caught it suffered major abrasions and contusions. He is legitimately lucky it didn't cut his whole damn thumb off. I, on the other hand, was lucky I had the opportunity to learn from someone else before making the mistake myself.

I would have been 0-2 that day.

After the record catastrophe, I determined that I would live to see another day and headed for my bike. I'd be back, but not until I invested in a nice float.

When I got home, Mom told me there was something waiting for me on my bed. I went back to check it out and came away extremely excited. Word on the street was that Papaw had dropped by after going to a children's charity function at nearby Fulton High School. Everybody got a door prize, and he picked a basketball to give to us.

Basketball was one game I tried out for, but had never had the chance to play, but I did know all about it. I was completely aware of the Harlem Globetrotters and what they were all about. Along with their football field, the Scarbroughs also had one and a half other attractions.

They were the first folks around to break into the tennis business. They had telephone poles once again for lights and used chicken wire for backstops. The other attraction was split between them and the Gills: a basketball goal.

The basketball goal technically belonged to the Scarbroughs, but it was on the Gills' property. They were next-door neighbors, and Mr. Gill and his brother Linus owned the water company. Little did they know that in one fell swoop they had inherited the Harlem Globetrotters and me.

Pretty impressive pickup.

It only took me about forty-five seconds to get out to the basketball goal. About fifteen seconds after that, I was in an intense battle with my imaginary foe.

It turns out that I always won on a last-second shot.

Over the next couple days, I played a lot of basketball in my abundance of spare time. If I wasn't mowing, I was playing. Given that I had about twenty hours of practice in three days, I actually picked it up pretty quickly. Not only was I somewhat of a natural, but I enjoyed being out there playing. Getting out and doing was no issue to me.

If a nine-year-old today were to be playing organized sports, they would practice for one hour a week and play for one hour a week. In three days, I had played enough to equal a ten-week season.

As I was out there, I would play, watch people drive by, come and go, and primarily try to enjoy my last week or so of summer. Sure, I was ready to go back to school, but I knew that would wear off in a month. Anyhow, I guess that while I was playing, there were folks watching me as well. That week, while inside taking a break and grabbing some ice-cold sweet tea, I heard a knock on the front door.

Mom walked out from the kitchen and answered it.

All I heard was, "Can Steve come out and play?"

I recognized the voice of as none other than Jim Courtney.

I heard her ask his name, then she turned to me and said, "A young man named Jim Courtney is outside, and he is asking for you."

I chugged the rest of my tea as fast as possible and headed out the front door. I guess I had really been in the zone while playing the last few days, because Jim dated Mr. Gill's daughter Laura and had seen me out playing every day for the almost a week.

I was completely unaware he had been there.

Laura was the homecoming queen and Jim was the captain of the football team. He was #7, and his specialty was the jump pass. She was drop-dead gorgeous with a really bubbly personality, as you might imagine. I had a lot to learn from him and, little did I know, on that day, I would start a relationship with him.

THE WINNING MOMENT · PART 1

We walked over to the improvised basketball court, and he asked if I wanted to play a game he knew. I said sure and asked him what it was. He told me the name of it and explained how it was played.

Hmm, Horse. *That will be easy to remember,* I thought to myself.

Jim ended up beating me two games out of three, which became the norm over time, but I kept it close, which was great for a ten-year-old. It helped me build confidence, and I was certain that if I ever had the chance to play on a real team, I could drain a shot from almost anywhere.

On that day, though, we had more on the itinerary. Next up was badminton, and once we got the net up, I had to show Jim what it was all about. I was really good at badminton, and my returns were like bullets. I actually beat him 21–19, and we were tied at one game to one. The rubber match was horseshoes, which I have never been good at. That day was no exception, and Jim beat me handily.

Just like that, he carried the day.

I enjoyed hanging out with him, and although I was eight years younger than he was, I could tell he'd had a good time as well. Just like that I had a friend, a mentor, and a gleaming example of what a winner was. It also meant that from that point forward, I was included in all the stuff the older guys did around the neighborhood regarding sports.

CHAPTER 42

There were only a few days left before school started. The one constant in my schedule that continued from living on Shamrock Avenue was Mass. We still went to Holy Ghost with Grandfather every Sunday. He came back to our house with us when it was over. On the Sunday before school started, we were all in for a real treat.

Mom and Grandfather had decided it was time for our first trip to Fort Loudoun, which became a once-a-year occurrence. As it turns out, Grandfather's mother was full-blooded Cherokee. It was on that day that I found this out along with the fact that he was a full-blown Indian buff. Before we left, he showed us his collection of arrowheads that he had brought along with him. He kept them in an old collar box. (Originally, collars were separate from the shirt and were kept in their respective collar box.)

Dad was working, so it was Mom, Grandfather, and us kids. In my opinion, it was an excellent adventure. We drove forever to get there, but it seemed longer. Once we arrived, we started out in the Visitors Center. That's where we had the unique opportunity to swap some of our cash for some of their Indian replications. How lucky could we be?

After the purchases were made, we headed down the footpath, past the archaeological dig, and on to the fort. I thought it was really neat inside. One thing was for sure: there was no running around that parapet. A few nails barely kept the walls held together. After we stared at their logs sticking out of the ground for a while, we took off for the back gate. At that point, we were really in for a treat, which came in the form of a giant stone with the initials TH carved in it.

In actuality, I was just a kid and enjoyed being outside, going wide open. I was always in the lead as I was going a hundred miles per hour while everyone else lagged behind at a cool thirty-mile-per-hour pace. After the giant stone, it was down to the Little Tennessee River and back to the car.

Overall, the story behind the fort was that the British occupants of the fort signed a peace treaty with the Cherokee. Afterward, they marched out of the fort and got slaughtered by the Cherokee.

History is full of tragic endings.

Currently, that was not the case.

Just when I thought the fun was over, Grandfather hit us with one last surprise.

Sequoyah, who made reading and writing possible in the Cherokee language, lived down the street from the fort in his day. There was only one reasonable thing to do, and that was head down the road and check it out. It was about a mile south and, along the way, we passed a large cornfield and stopped and helped ourselves.

Once we made it to the house, we climbed out of the Chevy Impala to explore a bit. After walking around the outside for a few minutes, we went in to check out the main attraction, which were the remnants of some hardware belonging to various torture devices.

When we returned to the car, we were met with a more pressing matter. It only took a turn of the key for us all to realize the car was dead. Although it looked to be a bad situation, it turned out to be the highlight of the day.

Mom remembered reading in *Reader's Digest* that if you could get an automatic up to thirty-five miles per hour, you could jump it off. The next trick was to push the car down the big hill that the car was conveniently parked on in front of Sequoyah's house. I was left to do the work, and as I gave her a big heave-ho, I hopped on the back bumper and enjoyed the ride.

As the car reached the advised speed, Mom shifted from neutral to drive, and sure enough, the car started right up. She stopped long enough for me to hop in the front. From there, we were Powell-bound. On the ride home, it was decided that no word of our exploits would be shared with my dad.

Over the next few days, I knocked out a couple yards on my mowing schedule and prepared myself for school. My workload around the house was going to have to be broken up to nights and weekends, so I visited my customers and agreed on new mowing times throughout the school year.

The other exciting thing that was going on was Tennessee's preparations for the upcoming season. Articles covering the predictions on the season became more abundant in the weekly paper. I hoped to meet some new Vols fans at school.

Speaking of new, let's not forget that I was about to be a student at Saint Joseph in their inaugural school year.

I wasn't going to be the only student going to a new school—every student would be going to a new school.

In those days, I loved life and was still young enough to not have a care in the world. Right on the cusp of the transition, but the grass was still greener on my side of life for now. Things with me were surely changing, though—like the fact that girls seemed to be prettier than they used to be and caught my attention a lot more often.

What was that all about?

I had heard of these things called *girlfriends* but had only recently developed any type of interest in the idea of it all. I could only hope that my new school would potentially help me gain some clarity on that situation and, of course, the opportunity to play on an actual sports team!

Rumor had it that they would have a football team.

CHAPTER 43

Be nice, be friendly, and don't get in trouble.

These are the words that were constantly flowing through my head as I headed to St. Joseph for the first day of fourth grade. I would take minor breaks to pray that I ended up with a likable teacher who didn't hate children. I was a bit nervous, but more than anything, I was looking forward to meeting my new schoolmates. With the newfound liberty I had living in Powell, I would be able to have some buddies to hang out with outside of school if I could just make a few.

If they lived within a bike ride or a bus trip, I would have some more things to do after school and on the weekends.

Everyone walking into the school that morning had a new start ahead of them, so I knew I wasn't the only one going through that rundown. As I approached the doors to the school, it dawned on me that I hadn't yet put any thought into what I would be learning.

Of course, it was probably just going to be an extension of things I had learned in years previous. Schoolwork had never caused me any fits, and I figured I would continue to do just fine whatever the content was.

Who is *she*?

My previous thoughts of what I would learn were completely interrupted by a cute blonde who was walking across the hallway as I walked through the front door and headed to my classroom. It made me feel weird inside, but I brushed it off. I knew that it wasn't the moment for feeling weird or finding out who the girl was. It would have to wait until later.

Possibly.

If I could muster up the courage to talk to her.

As I walked into my first classroom, it became clear that the school was making a big deal of its first year being open. I was a part of the very first fourth-grade class. That also meant that Mike was a part of the first eighth-grade class.

That was all important because it took all of about five minutes for the students to find out that Saint Joseph would in fact have sports teams, and everyone is aware the school year starts with none other than ... *FOOTBALL!!!*

I was so excited.

Forget school, forget girls, forget everything.

"How do we sign up?" asked another kid in my class.

First, it was worth noting that my teacher was nice, sweet, and genuinely seemed interested in her students. Second, that I had only known her for seven minutes before she shattered my heart into a million pieces.

"Sorry, but you have to be in sixth grade to participate in football. Until then, you can go to all the games and cheer on the Bulldogs!"

My day started out in wonder, changed to confusion, came to a point of elation, and then produced heartbreak all in about ten minutes.

Sounds like life if you ask me.

It was back to *Be nice, be friendly, and don't get in trouble.* Oh and, of course, wondering who the girl was that I had seen earlier.

I also wondered what in the heck bulldogs had to do with being Catholic. Surely they could have come up something more suitable. Anyhow, I knew that, at that moment, Mike was probably signing up for tryouts, and I was bummed and kind of pumped all at the same time. On one hand, I couldn't play, but on the other, I was going to have the opportunity to cheer on my new school and get a lot more in-person action when it came to watching football. I was also going to get to watch other sports being played in person, as well.

I loved sports enough to watch whatever and whenever I had the chance. Most of all, it was nice to finally have a time frame for how long it would be until I myself could play for a real team. No more wondering if it would ever happen.

It surely would.

In two years.

Don't hold your breath.

CHAPTER 44

As we began the initial routine of a school year, which included the run-down on what we would do and learn, my attention was broken by a voice coming from the door.

"It's all right, everybody. I have arrived," Johnny McLoughlin announced as he arrived late on the first day of school.

He then tried to a do a little side-shuffle slide and nearly ended up on his face. Everyone erupted in laughter as he caught himself before turning his grand performance into a major embarrassment. It was Johnny in his purest form. He was wasting no time allowing everyone to get a feel for who he was.

"You must be Johnny. So glad you could bless us with your presence," our teacher said while giving him a good stare.

Johnny McLoughlin, Class Clown.

Her face slowly turned into a little smile as she said, "I know it can be hard to navigate a new school on the first day; I will give you a pass just this once. Please find yourself a seat and try to keep the entertainment to a minimum." Sure enough, he walked over to the empty seat right next to me and plopped himself down.

"You're crazy, man," I said as he looked over at me with a huge smile on his face. I immediately followed that up with the million-dollar question, "Did you hear the big news?"

"You mean the announcement that we are going to have real sports teams?" Johnny returned.

Classic McLoughlin.

He had intentionally stalled in the hallway in a planned effort to bestow us with his grand arrival. I knew one guy who wasn't nervous about being in a classroom full of new people. In fact, he was sitting next to me and, at lunch that day, he described the moment as an *opportunity*.

The first week of school was pretty plain Jane if not downright boring. We didn't do much learning, and the school was hardly big enough to need a full week for the staff to show us around the property. They decided otherwise, so every day was like a giant show-and-tell held by the staff. I was in dire need of some excitement, so Johnny and I figured we would go to the Boys Club after school that Friday.

As we headed toward our destination, it was our typical routine that headed the venture.

I would laugh, he would laugh, I would laugh, he would laugh.

Our routine consisted in large part of moving from one episode of hilarity to the next. As we walked into the Boys Club, we approached the receptionist's desk.

"Do you boys have a membership?"

In fact, we did from our days at Holy Ghost School. My membership number was number 10, and I was granted free admission upon giving it to her. Johnny was right behind me.

First, we did arts and crafts.

Second, we went swimming. I'll never forget that everybody waited until they were comfortable and then went swimming in the nude. It was the order of the day. After all, it was the Boys Club.

After the swimming, we had kickball and then Johnny's dad scooped us up. His family had invited me to dinner and would take me home afterward. Delicious hamburgers, chips, and pickles sounded great right about now; I was starving. We kicked around a bit while the food was being made.

Johnny McLoughlin was also the first friend I had who had a swimming pool and an accompanying pool house.

Although we had just finished swimming only an hour before, I immediately wanted to hop in. In reality, I was mostly interested in Johnny's technique of attaining a higher elevation to jump into the deep end once I asked about the absence of a diving board. He had his dad promised we could jump in for a dip after dinner and before taking me home.

Good enough for me!

We grubbed out. I had two huge burgers with cheese and warm sesame-seed buns. The burgers were accompanied by an entire bag of chips that he and I split. To top it all off, we had an ice-cold Dr Pepper, which was immediately followed by another ice-cold Dr Pepper. We were growing boys and had just played for hours, and it had been seven hours since we'd had lunch at school. Those things added up to us basically turning into goats.

Honestly, I could have gone for round three, but my mind couldn't resist thinking of what was in store for me back at the pool. As we readied ourselves to swim, I noticed Johnny doing almost anything he could to explain to his parents that we were only going to hop in for a few minutes and that we would be back in shortly. It was an obvious attempt to assure we had no chaperones poolside.

The pool was a pretty decent size. After my potential drowning just a few weeks back, the three-foot shallow end was appealing at first, I must admit. Truthfully though, I was capable of swimming, and the answer to what sufficed for Johnny's diving board really intrigued me.

As I waded into the pool, he said he would be right back. After about thirty seconds, all I heard was McLoughlin yelling, "Geronimo!"

This, of course, while he was midair at the same height as the garage attached to the pool house.

"Holy shit!" I returned before covering my mouth in fear that his parents may have heard me.

After coming up from the deep end, he looked at me and said, "Your turn."

After I went on for about forty-five seconds letting Johnny know how crazy I thought he was as he laughed hysterically, I was ready to get in on the action. It became apparent to me that the roof was reached via the hurricane fence.

Confirmation came as Johnny said, "Just climb the hurricane fence, and you'll be right up there."

A minute later, my stomach was in my throat. I didn't have many fears, and I had zero that I was willing to admit to. Heights were a fear of mine, though, and that is for certain. Somewhere between climbing trees off of Shamrock Avenue and climbing onto this garage, the fear had manifested itself and was very clear to me at the time. I wasn't going to chicken out, however.

One, two, three, jump! I told myself in my head.

Next thing I knew, I was sailing high above the ground in slow motion toward the rippling blue waters of the swimming pool. I went plunging in, toes pointed, with my hands by my side.

I felt like a human torpedo.

It was maybe a second and a half before I reached the bottom of the pool from the moment I jumped, but it felt like two minutes. As I pushed off the bottom of the pool and came busting back through the top of the water, I was already prepared to go again. Each time I got nervous before I jumped, but it was hands down worth the thrill.

As I walked into my house that evening, I felt all in all it had been a pretty good first week of school. My family was just about to eat dinner, although it was almost 8:30 p.m. I passed, as the abundance of food I had put down earlier had hit me full-fledge.

A glass of milk sounds great though, I thought.

I went walking into the kitchen and saw something my eye could never miss. Mom had set aside the local headlines about the Volunteers from the Wednesday paper. She had forgotten to give them to me over the past few days, and she'd set them on the countertop so I couldn't miss them. I hadn't kept up with them much to this point, but as the season inched closer, I became more and more excited.

That night I read them and tried to get a feel for what this team was going to be like, how good they would be. Maybe to see if it'd be another rough season like last year. Sure enough, the summaries from the reporters confirmed it would be last season all over again.

CHAPTER 45

The next week, I ran into the girl who had caught my eye a few more times at school. I had found out three primary things about her without having to muster up the courage to speak to her.

First of all, her name was Cathy Koteski.

Second, she was a year older than I was.

And third, she was the daughter of the basketball coach.

Her age and father seemed a little intimidating, but her name had a nice flow to it. What did it really matter, anyway? I was confident in myself, but in an odd way, I was also a bit shy. Every time the opportunity presented itself to talk to her, I just kind of found a way out. However, I was still trying to get the feel of liking girls in general and figured I would cut myself a break. In time, the perfect moment would present itself. Maybe it would be like the law of diminishing returns. After seeing her over and over, maybe eventually I would settle down and it wouldn't seem like such a monstrous task.

Hopefully.

At school, I met a couple more guys who were a year older than I was and lived pretty close to me. One of them was Wayne Watson, and he actually just lived three doors down from me. He said he had seen me a few times during summer but only when he had been going to do things with family or getting home for the night. He was glad to run into me at school, and I was too.

The more folks in Powell to hang out with the better.

The other two were guys who Wayne introduced me to and lived just a few minutes from us: Rocky Scott and Carrie Campbell who were both supposed to be amazing backyard football players. The thing we had in common was being plagued by the sixth-grade rule regarding eligibility to play for the school.

We started borrowing the Scarbroughs' backyard whenever we could. With Mike being on the football team and me heading home midday, I rode the bus with all these guys. We played from the time we got dropped off until dinnertime or dark. The teams were typically divided up the same. Wayne and I versus Rocky and Carrie. The games were typically a defensive struggle, like 66–60. This, assuming you could keep up with the score to the sixth power. We adopted the rules I had played with on Shamrock, so there were no first downs. You had touchdowns and Failed to Score. If you failed to score, the ball changed possession.

The best part was the amount of touches you got on offense. You literally touched the ball every snap because there were only two players. That was the best part besides just having the opportunity to play football in general.

Nothing beat it.

The week that our after-school football ritual started also doubled as my personal countdown until the start of Tennessee's season.

Five…four…three…two…one!

We had driven to Grandmother's the night before the opening game. Uncle David asked me to come up to his room for a minute. When I got up there, he had something to tell me. It had come time for Uncle David to let the cat out of the bag with the only person he really wanted to know.

He sat me down. I was a little nervous, a little anxious, but I was ready for him to shoot straight. After a brief ten-minute discussion, I emerged from the upstairs with a smile on my face larger than I thought was possible.

Uncle David worked for TVA. The guy he bartered with to get us into the games was a small-business owner through the week and worked the gates on the weekends during the fall. Over the few years that they were fine-tuning the details of their arrangement, it turned out to be very satisfying on both ends of the arrangement.

What I had just been let in on was that Uncle David would swipe all the office supplies he could get his hands on that were at the expense of TVA. The agreement originally hinged on pens but had grown to include everything from paper clips to envelopes. The man was very pleased with not having overhead for such products. Uncle David would walk them down to the gentleman's business after work. Due to the growing list of supply items, the man had informed my uncle that he was far exceeding his expectations. It was well appreciated.

Therefore, from this season forward, Uncle David had basically landed "free" season tickets for two!

We would be at every home game.

Can I get an amen?!

The following day, September 21, 1963, was the first day we took advantage of our new agreement. Our first game that year was against Richmond, and boy, was it fun to be at! The Vols slammed the Southern Conference foe 34–6.

The Vols' next three games were at home, and they got beat in all three of them.

Hooray!

They then traveled to Alabama and got brutalized by the #9 Crimson Tide 35–0. The next week, we enjoyed a home game and the beatdown of Chattanooga. Two of the next four weeks were home games that were a split. A loss to Mississippi and then, of course, a win over Vandy to finish the season.

Overall, they finished 5-5 and once again never reached top-twenty ranking throughout the season. I sure did love to spend time with Uncle David, though. We had our routines and did game day our way. The food was good, the times were great, the football was spectacular, even when it was bad.

Most of all, Uncle Dave cared about me, and he cared to spend time with me.

Even if he did drink too much.

The Calm

Tuesday, May 13, 2008
Resaca, Georgia
Fifty-four Years Old
4:45 A.M.

That's what my alarm read as I woke up and peeked over at it. I had only been asleep for about an hour.

Go back to sleep, Steve.

I would have done anything for a good night's sleep.

5:14 A.M.

Round two was not much better. The thoughts of what could be wrong with me had consumed me. Even my dreams had become a search for answers. Crazy, maniacal dreams. Running through a hallway after a man who I believed could tell me what was wrong with me. It seemed to be in a hospital, but it was as if the power had gone out and the illumination was coming from those tiny blue overhead backup lights. It was eerie, but it was just a dream.

In reality, I would have taken being that close to someone with answers, but the truth was I was no closer to solving the matter than over a week earlier when I was lying on the ground of the carport. My mind began to wander, and it went back and forth between worrying and random thoughts that were useless while I should have been sleeping.

Is it an eye infection? That would cause the double vision, I suppose. The doctor said no. Maybe he was wrong. I am thirsty. My mouth is dry. God, I hope I'm okay. I wish this would just be over and life could resume as normal. I wonder if Bella is having trouble sleeping too with all of this going on? Eagles tickets. Damn, the concert is in four days!

I guess this wasn't the most helpful moment to remember that I had purchased tickets to see the Eagles, and the concert was Friday. I had completely forgotten about it in the midst of all the chaos. At least that would be another nice break from the commotion. I was in serious need of some more sleep, though. I had work in a few hours.

Go back to sleep, Steve!

I was driving myself absolutely crazy.

6:33 A.M.

"Screw it, I'm up!" I said in frustration, avoiding waking Bella before getting up and leaving the bedroom as quietly as possible.

I made my way to the kitchen and made the coffee. Bella was up five minutes later. She came in and told me I slept funny. When I asked what she meant, she explained that I snored when I was able to get some shut-eye but that I had spent a minute between snores not breathing at times throughout the night.

Splendid.

Something else to worry about.

I went about my normal morning routine. Due to my unusual sleeping patterns as of late, it goes without saying I needed the extra time I got from waking up early. After a shave, shower and dress, I walked backed

171

into the kitchen. I walked over to the fridge with my coffee cup. Three ice cubes later, I was pouring a cup of Café Bustelo.

If you haven't ever had a cup of it, just know that it could get a man straight from the grave up and going in the morning. Premium taste and as black as a 1920 Ford Model T.

I loved it.

The ice cubes allowed me to down the first cup in less than two minutes.

Next, step two of the morning coffee ritual.

When I went to Tennessee games as an adult, I would walk around after the place started to empty out and collect the plastic cups sold for about two and a half dollars apiece at the concession stand during the game. They even came with Coca-Cola inside.

(How nice of them.)

Anyway, those were my go-to travel cups. They required six cubes of ice but could hold two cups of coffee. After I filled up, I was out the door and ready to roll. It took all of fourteen and a half seconds after I got in my car to think about the mystery surrounding my health. I tried to brush off the thoughts, so I looked around the car and made sure I had everything I needed for the day. I realized I had left my wallet on my dresser.

As I reached my room, there was a small stack of Post-it notes next to it. I knew Bella was in the shower getting ready for her day. I also knew she had been worried about me lately and could use a good smile. One of her favorite things was when I left her a little note, just knowing I was still in love with her and was thinking of her. Doing something to make her feel special. So that's what I did.

Goodbye

I love you,

Steve

Simple and sweet.

Just my style and straight to the point. I knew she would appreciate it anyway, and that is what really mattered most. As I hopped back into the boat known as my Lincoln Town Car, I had a brief moment where I thought about what Bella would do if we found out that I was in serious trouble. There was still so much to do together and, by all accounts, fifty-four was young. We had places we wanted to go and things we wanted to experience. The boys were wild as bucks, and we wanted to see them through their struggles, see them grow up and get married.

We looked forward to playing with grand kids. We looked forward to giving them back to their parents after a long weekend of spoiling them. Most of all, we were ready for the house to be holding just the two of us again and spending more time together in a one-on-one atmosphere.

CHAPTER 46

Back at school, I caught some of the St. Joseph games. Mike played, and the Bulldogs were terrible with a capital T. Literally the worst team I have ever witnessed. I hoped to change that one day when I had the chance to play. It wasn't that they didn't have some good players, they were just a poor team.

Johnny and I went about investing time in our various comedy routines. It couldn't have been more fun. Back in the neighborhood, I was showing everyone near my age who the boss on the football field was. They honestly couldn't believe it at first. They were still at an age where they felt they should be better than me just due to the natural evolution of being older.

I had other plans.

After all, I had played with older kids my entire career.

Just before Halloween, the trio of Wayne, Rocky, and Carrie decided they would go trick-or-treating together.

Forgetting anybody?

They played ball with me, but it was evident that, off the football field, I was still considered one of the younger kids. Upon being shunned, I decided to piece together my own group of ghosts, ghouls, and superheroes. It would be more fun that way and less sketchy at particular houses out in Powell's country parts.

My recruiting efforts were a success. In total, there ended up being eleven in my group. That included multiple other kids who lived near me who were in my class, plus Susan, and a few kids she knew. After three or four hours of ringing doorbells and stuffing candy into our pillowcases, we decided to head back home.

We ended up with a group of young people outside of the Watsons'. I knew that Wayne was out collecting candy, and it appeared that the rest of his family was gone as well. We decided to roll their yard. As we got busy and were approaching roll number 247, the unexpected happened.

Yep, the front light came on.

Everybody besides me took off east on Collier Road. I showed them. I just hid behind the fir tree next to the front door. In a matter of seconds, the front door opened, and Mr. and Mrs. Watson came walking out.

Can you say *busted*?

After giving me a little scare, they went about surveying the damage as I walked the three doors down Collier Road to my house. The Watsons probably had bigger fish to fry like the toilet paper in all of their trees. They never did rat me out to my parents. On multiple occasions after that, I took the opportunity to thank them for that gesture. I even mowed their yard a time or two, on the house.

That was my unforgettable and only experience rolling yards.

The next few weeks played out, and we were getting close to the next fall holiday. In general, 1963 yielded some pretty significant events.

Alcatraz penitentiary closing was on the lighter side of the significant events, and that was huge. The civil rights movement was in full swing, and James Meredith became the first African-American to graduate from the University of Mississippi. Up until then, this would have only happened in a fairy tale.

I feel it was a true sign that times were changing.

Also, I welcomed equality.

I didn't experience the strain of it much, and I was also young, but I never did understand judging someone based on the color of their skin.

To me, it seemed more like a pigment issue than a personal issue.

On August 28, 1963, on the steps of the Lincoln Memorial in Washington, DC, Martin Luther King Jr. delivered his famous "I Have a Dream" speech. The fact that it was in front of more than 250,000 civil rights supporters made it one of the more defining moments of the American civil rights movement.

It certainly had a huge impact on the world.

Years later, while in England, it was hard not to give credit to this fact. Martin Luther King Jr. was the only American I recognized in the figures above the doorways of Westminster Abbey.

He deserved it.

Then another major event happened.

Just before Thanksgiving.

Just five days after Julie's birthday.

On November 22, 1963, John Fitzgerald Kennedy was assassinated in Dallas, Texas. It was a Friday, and I was at school. I will never forget looking over and seeing Preston Walker, a classmate of mine, crying when the news broke. It happened around noon our time, and it didn't take an hour for police to have a guy in custody. His name was Lee Harvey Oswald, and he was killed a few days later.

It happened live on TV. The same day, the newly appointed President Lyndon B. Johnson, addressed the nation. At that time, I wasn't old enough to really grasp the gravity of the whole situation. I don't have anything to really add to that even now besides my opinion.

My thoughts are that Oswald was a shooter but that he didn't act alone. I always thought the guy on the grassy knoll was responsible for the head shot.

Let the conspiracies live on!

In retrospect, I think the most telling aspect of it all was that Zapruder had the only film. Today, you would have thousands of pictures and videos taken from different angles and vantage points from people's cell phones alone. In regard to the actual event, we will honestly never find out the truth.

Earlier in the year, Pope John XXIII died. That, accompanied by the Kennedy assassination, made for a rough year for us Catholics.

It yielded some rather lengthy Mass sermons as well.

CHAPTER 47

We were out of school for Christmas break. I know it will come as a big surprise, but Dad spent most of the holidays at work. This left Mom with us at the house. We went outside some, but a snowstorm was coming, so we gave up on being out in the cold and came in to watch TV. That is when *The Andy Griffith Show* entered my life. Perhaps I was a few years late, but I loved it. I had heard of it, but I guess I just never took the time to watch an episode. I joined in on the sweet-tea action with Mike and watched the sheriff and the rest of his clan get into all sorts of crazy scenarios. Living out in Powell made me sort of relate to Opie Taylor.

The Monday before Christmas, my cousin Bobby and I had the bedroom all to ourselves. His family had stopped by during the afternoon to pick up a few things from Mom to take to the family Christmas shindig a few days later.

"What do you want to do?" I asked.

"What are my choices?" Bobby Garner shot back.

After a minor debate, we decided to play with the electric train. Furthermore, we decided to play *Petticoat Junction*. There was only one good place to play without having to take the train apart.

Under my twin bed, of course. The only problem was it sure was dark under there, but what would *Petticoat Junction* be without a train?

The Cannonball Express?

After a few minutes, we decided the game was no fun without being able to see it. The logical answer was providing a light source, such as the candle on my night table, so I went and fetched it along with a match. After all, the show must go on. It didn't take long for everything to go south. Quickly.

There was tons of commotion.

Not *locomotion*.

Just *commotion*.

My brother appeared in the doorway as we had our heads under the bed twisting and shouting.

"What's burning under there?" Mike asked.

As usual, he loved to be the bearer of bad news, especially if it involved me. This time, it was understandable. Petticoat Junction was illuminated all right. At the expense of my box springs. We ended up having to take the train apart when the ash settled and the blaze was put out.

Dad found out about the incident and wore my butt out that night. The following day, I decided I should stick to what I knew best: being outside. Even if it was freezing cold with five inches of snow on the ground. I played in the snow for a little while and then headed in for lunch. Also, to thaw out my hands.

After I was back to room temperature and full, I headed back out with Mike in tow. It was time for a good ol' snowball fight. The man who lived next door walked across the yard toward us after we had been going at it for a few minutes. I had never met him, but I had seen my dad talking with him and his wife a few times. We had met his wife a couple times, and Mom loved her. Her name was Hazel, and she was sweet as pie.

"I'm your neighbor, Clyde Roberts," said the short man with a hat on. "Why don't you boys come shovel the snow off our driveway? We will pay you, make it worth your while."

So, Mike and I went in and put on most of the clothes we had in our closet. Then we went out and looked for any snow shovels we could dig up.

(No pun intended.)

Their driveway was shaped like a big fishhook. We dug and dug and dug. The longest part of the driveway was up top, connected to the road. It was about 125 feet long and, of course, covered with the five inches of snow. My Uncle David arrived at our house while we were digging and would periodically make an appearance and check on our frostbite status.

About forty-five minutes in, we got to the sidewalk that led to the front door and were really doing a great job. Now all we had to do was get down the hill, which was the hook portion. That's where things slowed to a snail's pace.

We'd literally been digging for a few hours when we decided to bear down and finish. Finally, we made it to the garage.

We had freed the Roberts car.

Now all we had to do was collect.

"Here's fifteen cents apiece. Buy yourselves a Coke," Clyde said.

Mike and I just looked at each other, then at the money in our hands, and then back at each other. We were too tired to argue, so we headed in.

After finding out how much Clyde had paid us, Uncle David offered us two dollars each to shovel all the snow back onto his driveway.

We laughed and decided to take a warm bath instead. He still gave us the two dollars he had offered. He was the best, and I certainly didn't mind seeing him a few times over the next couple of days. Christmas and Susan's seventh birthday came and went. So, did New Year's.

Finally, it was back to school.

CHAPTER 48

As school worked its way back into session, I was happy to be headed toward summer. It was 1964, but it wasn't too late for 1963 to give me one last gift. I was near the middle of the bus as everyone's attention shifted to the front. The bus driver had shifted the radio volume a few notches higher—probably in an attempt to maintain sanity and drown out the full load of crazy kids screaming and shouting.

"Oh yeah, I tell you something, I think you'll understand. When I, say that something, I wanna hold your hand ..."

The song was one I had never heard before. Neither had anyone else for that matter.

It felt different.

It *was* different.

It was clean. It was good.

It was great!

"Oh please, say to me, you'll let me be your man. And please, say to me, you'll let me hold your hand. Now let me hold your hand. I wanna hold your hand..."

The music continued and everyone was up out of their seats. It was like something out of a movie. We all rushed to the front of the bus. The bus driver stopped and started to yell at everyone in hopes we would go back to our seats. After a minute, he gave up as everyone chimed in, and sang out like a 30 member choir.

Released the twenty-sixth of December 1963, "I Want to Hold Your Hand" changed everything, in my opinion. Singing about holding hands was risqué in those days. Parents thought it was abysmal at best. I, and everyone else who was around my age, thought otherwise. In an instant, the Beatles became my favorite band.

This was a time of change in my life. I was stuck at an odd age and period.

Too old to be young, and too young to be old.

I was changing.

I had tons of friends and a few best friends. I had learned a lot about myself over the first half of the school year at St. Joseph. Most kids liked me, and if I didn't find someone's personality necessary in my life, I simply didn't engage with them. I wasn't into putting people down or making fun of folks. I was a good kid who made good grades. I stayed out of trouble, for the most part. I loved sports and exploring new things. I was mischievous, but only in the company of the people I trusted the most. They had my back, and I had theirs.

When around people I hadn't found a deeper understanding with, I was extremely strait-laced. A smile on my face, a helping hand if needed, and I followed all the rules. Of course, I learned to be like this the hard way. I had explored my options a few times and ultimately chose the path of least resistance. It made sense, and I was a common-sense kind of kid. If I had tried something out and got in trouble, I didn't do it again. It was rational, and I could fight off the temptation of doing bad things.

As the school year was winding down, I found out more and more about myself. I turned ten in March, and the personal changes hit a higher gear. Since I had moved to Powell and gained a lot of freedom, I had become pretty independent. Knoxville in its entirety was my stomping grounds. If I wanted to go somewhere, I cleared it with Mom and was on my way. I was definitely not a kid who was built to function with the help of attention.

I didn't need it.

I paid attention to the people I cared to be around. A revelatory thought at the end of the school year really emphasized my view in life, which was:

All you can do is your best. So always try to do your best, and don't be too hard on yourself or those you care about.

This was the way I felt about my friends, family, and the guys I played ball with. It always seemed to yield the best results. It was also well appreciated and extremely valuable to understand. I knew people who beat themselves up all the time, and it was weird for me to watch them operate. It was as if they were only a version of themselves. I could tell when someone was being real or not. Being fake was not my cup of tea. At the same time, I had learned firsthand the influence criticism and insults could have on you. Mike reminded me of this daily until I just quit caring what he had to say.

I also had had a go at putting other kids down when I was a young child, and it yielded undesirable results: guilt and a complete lack of accomplishment. It became apparent to me that most of those who indulged in this habit were doing it for the sake of feeling better about themselves at someone else's expense.

I had established the things I liked most in life. I loved having friends and being social. In new environments, I was always shy at first, but as I warmed up to people, I became energized through socializing. I loved being adventurous and spontaneous. I loved SweeTarts and Coca-Cola and Grandmother's pimento-cheese sandwiches.

I'd eat ten in a sitting if she made them for me.

It goes without saying that I loved to compete. I loved to win. I loved Tennessee football. I loved spending time with my Uncle David, and I loved the care of some of the elderly folks in my family.

I now loved music as well. I had discovered the artistic side of myself and thoroughly enjoyed it as well. I especially liked to draw.

I had also figured out the things I didn't like. Arrogant, disrespectful, demeaning, or belittling behavior were all things I was very unimpressed with. Whether you were family, a classmate, or part of the clergy, if you exhibited any one of these things in your daily treatment of others, I kept you at further than arm's length. It was of no use to me to really engage with someone who was willing to treat you poorly. On the chance that you lived in the same house with me and your name was Mike, I ignored you until you were willing to have a day when you treated me differently.

I didn't like Mass in Latin. It was boring, but I went anyway. I didn't like feeling nervous around girls. I didn't like the fact that my dad was always gone. I had stopped letting it impact me as much, but it still bothered me. I didn't like getting in trouble, so I avoided that whenever I could. Last but not least, I had tried licorice at school one day and thought it was awful. I surely didn't like licorice! Not to be a hypocrite and put someone down, but whoever invented that stuff had horrible taste, in my book.

Be nice, be friendly, and don't get in trouble (and don't eat licorice) was a suitable motto after all.

CHAPTER 49

More and more US military troops were dying as Congress authorized war against North Vietnam in 1964. Lyndon Johnson remained president after winning by a landslide. On the home front, killings of three civil rights workers led to the signing of the Civil Rights Act of 1964 by President Jimson. Unfortunately, this didn't stop the violent crime that was rising in many American cities.

The Beatles took the world by storm, and America was no exception.

Beatlemania was in full swing, and I was happy to be a part of it.

They made their first appearance on *The Ed Sullivan Show* and had thirteen singles on the Billboard's Hot 100 at the same time in 1964. At one point, they also held the top five positions of the Top 40 singles in America. The love for them by the younger generation was unending, and it also influenced some other bands from across the pond to give music an international shot. Namely, you had the Rolling Stones' debut album in 1964 and the rise of the Animals, who sang "House of the Rising Sun."

Charlie and the Chocolate Factory was published in 1964. Other key happenings were the first manufactured Ford Mustang, and Douglas Engelbart invented the computer mouse. Bubble wrap was also used for the first time that year, but it originally was made to be a form of textured wallpaper. After not taking off in the walls department, many companies that had purchased the material found out it was excellent for protecting products they were shipping. W e also saw the Boston Strangler, Albert DeSalvo, being captured. On the other end of the spectrum, Martin Luther King Jr. won the Nobel Peace Prize.

In regard to sports, although I never was a fan of his approach publicly, it is worth noting that Cassius Clay, aka Muhammad Ali, beat Sonny Liston to become the World Heavyweight Champion. I always agreed he was perhaps the greatest boxer to ever live, but I admittedly never understood why someone with so much talent didn't just let his boxing do the talking. I guess it was just a different approach than my own, and it garnered him even more attention than his winning did. I guess in the end all you can do is respect a talent like Muhammad Ali. He was a once-in-a-lifetime type of guy.

In Knoxville, the summer had flown by. I was in full-fledged moneymaking mode and had accrued even more yards than the year before. In fact, I had really outdone my coverage, if you get my drift, so I was working more than a ten-year-old really desired. Besides being an entrepreneur, I was getting in on any sports action I could find. I had become a regular in any local game no matter the age of those playing. I could keep up, and I was getting better all the time. All the practice and dedication would soon pay off.

Of course, other than Mom, I really had no reason to want to be home, so I took advantage of the hardship. Perhaps a lot of players I would play with, when I finally got the chance to play on real teams, would be just as good, but I certainly was going to give anyone a run for their money.

Some days, no one would be around to do anything, and I would be so bored.

"You never miss the water until the well runs dry," I remembered a man saying one time.

I severely missed my old playmates on these types of days. It was on these days that I reverted back to something I could do on my own and still find some sort of rush in. I had the world's greatest bike when I was a kid. It was a Schwinn Stingray with a banana seat and monkey bars. It also had a two-inch racing slick, a purple frame, and silver fenders.

She was beautiful, and I put some serious miles on her.

Reliability at its finest.

I had a usual route I used to ride during my alone time. It involved riding to the end of the driveway and taking a left on Collier. I'd get to Clyde and Hazel's and hang a left into their driveway. I would then make a loop around the carport and then it was down the fishhook into the bottom of the driveway near the garage. I'd make a lap around the bottom part of the driveway and come back up. When I got up to the long flat of their driveway, I got up as much speed as possible while looking both ways before bolting across the street to Mrs. May's.

Once I was at Mrs. May's, I would make a few laps around her turnaround in the center of her driveway and then head for home. The circuit ended where it began with me doing a daring slide into our carport with an electric dismount. I'd catch my footing just before running into Dad's tool shed on the other end of the carport. I figured I had done this so many times that I could do a lap around Mrs. May's turnaround with my eyes shut.

So, I gave it a go.

Would you believe that I actually made it?

The only reasonable thing to do was to go again. The second lap didn't go as well. Things were actually going pretty well at first, but that came to an abrupt end when I went crashing into Mrs. May's brick house. It hurt like you-know-what. Especially the part where I got wracked.

Getting *wracked* being a polite interpretation of ramming my testicles into the bike's bar.

Even in pain, I couldn't believe that I had even made it once.

Still feeling a bit daring and out of other activities to occupy myself with, I decided on my next act. I felt it was a good idea to lay my mother's broomstick across Mrs. May's drainage ditch and ride across it. I would start in her yard, gather a bit of speed, and ride right across.

That was the plan anyway.

The approach turned out to be spot-on. The rest, however…well, the rest didn't go as planned. Although I had hit the broomstick just right, the bike and rider combined for too much weight. I got halfway across the broomstick before I heard the snap beneath my pedals. Long story short, I did a face plant in the middle of Collier Road. As abrupt as the brick house on my blind ride I might add.

It was the quick stop that got me.

I had gone outside trying to make due with no one to play with, and not twenty minutes later, I walked back in a bloody pulp.

How fun!

For the rest of the summer I stayed a little safer during my bicycle exploits and saw myself around Knoxville when stuck with no one to hang out with. I even ventured back to Shamrock Avenue a few times to see the old clan. I was always met with a warm welcome and a good game of football.

CHAPTER 50

As school started back, it was refreshing to see all my friends again. I had also developed a new sense of comfort in making conversation. This became evident only a few days into school when Cathy Koteski dropped a book in the hallway.

The perfect moment, I thought as I bent down and picked up the book for her.

"Thanks," she said, giving me a smile.

Out of nowhere and without thinking I said, "No problem. You're Cathy, right?" She seemed a bit shocked but then replied, "Yes. You're Steve?"

So, she knew who I was, huh?

The next thing I knew, I had asked her to grab an Orange Julius with me after school and then go to the first football game of the year. A few weeks later, she was my girlfriend.

My older girlfriend, I might add.

The guys in my grade were impressed.

In reality, I was a sweet boyfriend, and Cathy was all that and a box of Cracker Jacks. Over time, we shared some fun memories for young sweethearts. She'd wear my jacket when we had recess together. I'd call her on the phone almost daily. We'd send each other postcards when we were on vacation with our families. She always thought I was a gentleman, and I tried my hardest to keep that opinion intact, even as a ten-year-old.

Once, we got in trouble because we kissed in the back seat of the bus and the person following the bus called the school and told on us. Another time, her dad caught us kissing, and I was scared to death. Fortunately, he liked me a lot, so he separated us for the time being and let me live.

At the same time I was falling in puppy love with Cathy, the Vols were gearing up for their 1964 season. Doug Dickey was about to enter his first season as head coach of the tradition-rich program. Uncle David and I were back in the saddle as three out of the first four games that year were at home. Winning the three home games and dropping the road game to #8 Auburn, the Vols were 3-1 heading into the annual showdown against Alabama that was back in Knoxville.

We were pumped when we went to the game but left deflated as the Crimson Tide defeated the Vols 19-8. The next week they tied #7 LSU 3-3, which shifted the rankings. The following week, they were home against the new #7 Georgia Tech. We reveled in the moment as they pulled off a stunning 22-14 victory. After that, it was all downhill in 1964 as Tennessee dropped their three remaining games.

Two of which I witnessed.

Thank God, the last game of the season, a 7-0 loss to Vanderbilt, had been on the road. The Vols finished the season 4-5-1. I prayed that next year would yield a more desirable result for diehards like Uncle David and me.

Meanwhile, I got invited to see Cathy's basketball game. I eventually went to almost all of her games, but this was going to be my first. The only problem was that her family was leaving in two hours, and it took me two hours to mow Mr. Peterson's yard. It was the last mow for the year, and I couldn't put it off. But the Koteskis were headed to the beautiful and oh-so-exotic downtown Sevierville.

I mean, I just had to go!

After all, Mr. Koteski was the coach, and Cathy was the star player. I didn't have time to waste, so I hustled down to Mr. Peterson's and grabbed his Toro lawn mower. This was before push mowers had an automatic shut-off. I was literally running and shoving the lawn mower. About five minutes in, I ran down a row of daffodils and decided I better regroup. Still, I finished the front and the back in record time. Now all I had left was the pine forest.

So. Many. Trees!

The first row went by in a jiffy. I was going so fast I didn't even see the hornets' nest coming. I was as shocked as they were. Primarily my shock came from the location of their nest. I had no clue those suckers lived in a hole in the ground. They stung me repeatedly before I even figured out what the hell was going on. The only thing I was really worried about was how much it was slowing me down, so I rolled the push mower over the hole in an attempt to create a sort of tornado torture device for my foe.

I had almost decided just to leave the lawn mower there before coming to my senses and realizing I had to finish what I had started. It was naturally ingrained in me. It was just the way I was and how I had determined to be. It can be summed up by a phrase that is popular, one that I have applied to life and athletics equally:

Failure is not an option.

I had to get the lawn mower. I couldn't finish mowing without the freakin' thing. I sure got it, all right. That and a handful more stings to go with it. I was still alive, though, and I was also in the home stretch. All I had to do was mow around the remaining gazillion trees.

Yippee!

Finally I finished, and according to my trusty Timex, I had fifteen minutes to spare. All I had to do was return the Toro and collect.

"How much do I owe you?" Like he didn't know.

I had only mowed his yard for two years now. I already knew where this was heading.

"I think it's five fifty, Mr. Peterson, sir."

The most predictable part of the conversation came next as he said, "Minus two dollars for the mower and gas. By the way, could you blow off the driveway for me?" he added.

"Sure thing," I said, which was followed by me mumbling under my breath how big an ass I thought he was.

After finishing up for the second time, I sprinted home. It took me about five minutes to get ready. I washed the sweat off, dragged a wet comb through my hair, slapped on some Jade East, and was ready to rock. I put my hard-earned three and a half dollars in my pocket.

I was a high roller.

No big deal.

It's a good thing I went because I was the only St. Joseph fan there. *Go, St. Joseph, go!*

Cathy was as advertised. I think she accounted for half of the team's points, and the Lady Bulldogs ran away with it in the second half. What was the final score, you ask? Oh, you know, just a heated 33–16. It was a fun day all in all, and both she and her dad appreciated my showing up to support them. He even bought me a burger after the game, and although I offered, he let me keep my three dollars and fifty cents.

Score!

When It Rains, It Pours

I woke out of a crazy dream. It was two thirty in the morning. I had dreamed about something that had been on my mind a lot over the past week but still hadn't really spoken about yet. I guess it is inevitable that you find out at some point, though, so I guess there is no better time than now to introduce you to another harsh reality that would probably plummet to a new all-time low if something were to happen to me.

It was my boys.

Danny and Paul.

They were so deeply into drugs at this time that my interactions with them were limited to going from one big lie to the next. In a way, I kind of got it. They were young, dumb, and having fun. Unfortunately, the fun they were having could have serious repercussions. The worst of which was death, and that wasn't stretching it in the slightest. I knew that it had started with a little drinking here and there when they were fifteen or sixteen. And I knew that because I was under the impression that it was better to let them drink at the house than to be out doing it and driving around. So, probably against my better judgment, I had allowed them to have a couple beers sometimes and a few friends over to the house. The drug thing didn't really enter the picture until after Danny graduated high school and found himself involved with his same old friends who had started a terrible new habit. The habit was methamphetamine, and it was devastating to see him go through.

All until…I caught him.

In my house, using meth with a complete stranger, with his little brother in the room.

Paul was only fifteen at the time.

Obviously distraught about his brother's nine-month stint of being awake twenty-three out of twenty-four hours a day and the way it affected their relationship, Paul stood there completely broken by the person Danny had become by then. I truly thought that the entire experience would push both of them in a really positive direction for good. The first year after that, things really were good. Danny was doing great in college and got involved with some great guys, and Paul and I were traveling around playing soccer all over the place, making great memories out of his last few years in high school.

And then…and then…one day, I realized.

It was the look in the eyes of my youngest son.

Paul wasn't doing so well anymore.

In fact, Paul wasn't really himself anymore.

It took a while for me to realize what exactly was going on, but that only lasted until I found some pot and a pipe hidden in the pool house. A month after that, it was a few pills in a dip can. He started smoking cigarettes and would throw the butts in the grass by the pool deck and then deny they were his. I suppose he thought I'd buy his story, but I just wasn't a big fan of the phantom cigarette-smoker theory. At some point, Paul was able to get Danny back in the fold, or Danny willingly wanted to take part. All of the positive things we were seeing from him disappeared again in rapid fashion.

Tack on the fact that Josh Bragg, who was in Paul's grade and a child I had sort of taken in, was a part of the clan. His mom was a wonderful woman who worked so hard and sometimes had trouble getting Josh to every game and practice. Bella and I had basically made him a permanent fixture at the dinner table, and everyone we knew accepted him as part of our family.

The three stooges.

Earth, wind, and fire apart.

Natural disaster when you got them together.

Paul ditched the soccer-scholarship offers out of high school in favor of joining Danny and Josh down in Kennesaw. By the end of Paul's freshman year in college, we had experienced his first overdose. We were so lucky that he was still alive and tried to get him help. When he tried out at Reinhardt College along with Josh a few months later, they both made the team, and they both seemed cleaned up. After arriving at school, it only took a few weeks for the three of them to be hanging out again daily as Kennesaw State, Danny's college, was only twenty minutes from Reinhardt. It was hard to endure, and with my own struggles in life, I knew that it wasn't going to change overnight. Paul flunked out of school halfway through his second semester in the spring of 2008.

He moved home and worked some, partied a lot, and lied every breath that he took. He ran around with guys who were going nowhere fast when he wasn't with Danny and Josh. Danny had his own set of activities, which included being a stand-up guy by day and an addict by night.

It was as if both of them wanted to be anything in the world other than themselves.

It was sad.

Worst of all, it absolutely killed Bella.

She thought about it, talked about it, and fretted over it night and day. Once Paul moved back from college, I tried to see if I could help him through it. Over the last few months, Paul and I had had some deep talks, and I really thought we were getting somewhere. I was so worried that if something happened to me, he and Danny would go off the deep end. They were so vulnerable and needed me more than ever.

Those thoughts turned to what was going on with me. It made me sick, and the anxiety of everything came rushing back in. I lay there awake, wondering what would happen to my boys. My precious sons who had done so much to make me proud over the years. Would they die out in the cold some night from drinking and driving, an overdose, or getting caught up with the wrong people? I thought that was the worst part. Knowing they were out doing dangerous things daily and not knowing if they would make it home, or back from college for a weekend visit.

The thoughts were so overwhelming that I was paralyzed by it for a few moments before I forced myself to stop thinking about it. I was exhausted and had enough to worry about to extend my attention to yet another potential tragedy.

I knew only one thing to do to keep my mind from driving me crazy.

Stop, Steve! Go back to sleep!

CHAPTER 51

Fifth grade went by in a flash. It runs so closely to when major things started happening in my life with sports, I really can't distinguish what all exactly happened in fifth grade. The holidays were upon us, and they were routine as usual. It was great watching Julie and Susan grow into beautiful little girls. They were similar in some ways and very different in others.

Susan really liked to run around with me and play in the neighborhood when she had the chance. Julie was getting older now, and she too would stomp around with us. Everyone knew they were my sisters, so they were never messed with or hurt. I suppose that was nice for them. It was also nice for the guys as well because if someone had hurt one of them, I'd have been forced to deal with it in the barbaric ways of the old days.

As always, we had one big snow that year, and it came the week between Christmas and New Year's. The snow was great, and the snowflakes were the size of quarters. David "Digga" McMillan and John Block, a few buddies of mine from school who lived relatively close, had picked a good time to spend the night. We were really cool, being in fifth grade and all.

"I heard Denise Brooks likes Joe Tom Corbell," I said.

"So, what else is new?" asked Digga.

"I also heard Johnny McLoughlin likes Martha McCampbell," I added.

"So, *what else* new?" John Block said, laughing.

"So, *else what's* new? That's rich!" I said uproariously as we were trudging through the snow.

It was still a few hours until sundown, so we had all the time we would need. We had already bundled ourselves in layers upon layers and had grabbed the sleds out from under Dad's freestanding tool shed. At this point, we were heading out to Fersner Avenue. It had the perfect hill for sledding. It was really steep, and really long. It would take us about ten minutes to get over to Fersner Avenue depending on the packability of the snow. How packable the snow was was easy to determine. If it was really good, it might take longer to get to Fersner due to us packing snowballs and throwing them back and forth at each other while we were heading over there.

When we got to Fersner Avenue, we went up to our regular starting spot. It was steep enough and easy to get to. It was at the intersection of Granville Connor Road and Fersner. You'd start there and take a 400-yard ride down to the carport in the West's family driveway. It was a blast, and we did this five or six times before deciding then was the time to broaden our horizons. Naturally, that meant going halfway up Fersner on the other side of Granville Connor.

After that, it got extremely steep getting up to the top. *Steep*, as in it probably dropped a foot in elevation every fifteen feet of road traveled. With a sled in your hand, it was almost uncomfortable to look at. Our new starting spot added a few new elements to the trip down. At least a few hundred more yards to the trip, and the little zag to the right at Granville Connor Road where the top and bottom of Fersner weren't lined up perfectly.

Still, off we went.

We were flying, and with the correct maneuvering, it was fairly easy to steer the sled eight to ten feet to the right when crossing Granville Connor. Twenty feet before the West's carport, we were already excited to climb the hill again for another run.

As is normally the case with ten-year-old boys, this just wasn't enough. The only way to beat it was simply laid out above us, so of course, we set out for the top of Fersner Avenue. It took a long while to get to the water tower, which officially marked the top.

I didn't want to overthink it, so without much hesitation after turning around and sitting on my sled, I yelled, "Here goes nothing!"

At the same time, I pushed off and was gaining speed by the inches. As anticipated, I was absolutely flying. As a matter of fact, my guess is that I was traveling somewhere around sixty-five miles per hour. This all before I had reached the zag at Granville Connor Road. As I reached the zag and tried to maneuver to the right, I became…let's say *disengaged* from the sled.

There I was, sliding on the ice and snow on my right side at sixty-five miles an hour. This is where the errant force meets the unmovable object. Hell, I was going so fast, I didn't even see the telephone guide wire. It hit me just above the knees, and at first I was certain I would need two knee surgeries. After ten minutes or so, I was fortunately able to walk it off. I immediately determined that it was time to head home. Lucky for me, I got to ride part of the way while Jim and Digga pulled me behind them. I sang "Jingle Bells" and pulled at the ropes. Even with getting hurt, it was a blast.

Well, besides almost getting killed by "dekneeification."

CHAPTER 52

A week or so later, I was back at school with a story for the ages to tell everyone around the lunch table. Cathy was extremely worried about me when she found out, but I was obviously fine.

Obviously.

I thought it was nice that she was worried about me, though. Others had stories of sledding and fun during the holidays. Only mine ended in near death. This time in my life was a blast. You had a bunch of crazy kids doing crazy-kid things all the time, and just being there or being a part of it was enough to make you love life.

I loved my friends and all the fun we had. The laughs we had, the memories we made: they were a blast, and so was growing up in the '60s.

Around mid-January of 1965, it became very evident to me that I was undergoing a change. This change was a bit different from the others I had experienced. Most other changes were more mental and behavioral. Sure, I had undergone growth spurts before, but nothing like this. In the next month, I grew two inches. By my eleventh birthday at the beginning of March, I had started to grow hair everywhere.

Everywhere!

By the time school let out for summer, I had grown another two inches, and I wasn't even done yet. Everyone noticed. I had gone from a little ol' five feet, 100 pounds to five feet four and 120 pounds in just a few months.

Along with the insane growth spurt, I had this weird thing going on with my voice. It squeaked when I talked from time to time.

It certainly proved to be embarrassing on a few occasions.

Cathy told me I was growing into quite the handsome young man as she noticed the difference in my stature. The coaches around the school took notice, as well. Just a week before school let out, the football coach walked past me in the hallway and stopped me. He asked if I had planned on playing football the following year, and after telling him that I had waited patiently for the past few years to do so, we both walked away excited. He told me he sure could use a young guy with my size on his sideline. Not to sound arrogant, but he could have used a player like me on his sideline before the changes began. Now all I needed to do was adjust to my new body, and I would be ready to rock come tryouts.

The Train Wreck

One thought about an area of my life rolled to another. All the while I was considering the effects that a serious medical issue could have on each of the three people who depended on me most.

All had poor outcomes.

For the eighteen millionth time, I thought about how badly I needed to get this figured out.

I knew it was serious.

I could feel it inside me.

I could feel it in my soul.

It was unlike anything I had ever experienced. The feeling was inescapable. Suddenly, the anxiety was grabbing hold of me again. My hands clenched the steering wheel so hard I thought about checking for permanent indentions. My teeth clenched together as well, and I could feel my jaws bulging to the point of tightness in the flesh below my ears.

Hoooooooooonk!

I swerved as fast as possible.

I narrowly avoided getting hit by a green pickup truck as I merged onto the interstate, cutting him off. I had made it eight minutes from the house and didn't remember a second of driving.

Take a deep breath, Steve. You're good. Chill the hell out, and stop thinking about this. Do something else.

Cigarette.

Radio.

Pray.

Anything!

Just stop thinking about this!

I chose the radio and a cigarette. Specifically, a mix of southern classic rock I had on a CD to go with a Winston 100. Of course, I ripped the filter off the Winston and flipped it around backward. I had always done it that way. I lit it by the torn end. Smoked the whole thing in less than three minutes.

Twenty minutes later, I pulled into my office parking lot. As I popped the door open to get out, I turned to the cup holder, picked up my cup of coffee, and finished off the last few sips of my morning fix.

As I reached the front door to my office, I couldn't remember the last time I had looked forward to a day of work to this degree. I was hoping that zoning out on the stocks and worrying about the trades I needed to orchestrate for my clients would take the place of all the bad I had been thinking about. I sat down at my computer, and that is exactly what I did. I felt a little off, but I went about business as usual.

I had become an extremely successful stockbroker. This was 2008, though. The market was as rough as concrete on a kneecap. Still, on a personal level, my success was on an upward trajectory as it had been for the past twenty years. I made less money some years than others, but that was inevitable. I had gained more and more clients each year, though. When the market was healthy, I killed it. Numbers were always one of my things. I got them, and I understood them, outside of the concept of mathematics and more like a language. Any type of calculations I needed to do for my job were just a few thoughts away from a result. I could do it in my head and quickly. It really helped with the stock market. At just the right time, I would buy or sell, and because of my ability to time it so well, I had developed an immense amount of trust from my clients.

They liked me and I liked them.

Some days I hated the job, some days I loved it.

Most days, it just was what it was: a means to an end. It kept food on the table and the lights on. Over time, it had allowed me to have a lot of food and some pretty fancy lights. I was no rich man by any stretch of the imagination, but I also wasn't struggling.

Well-off, I guess you could say.

At a few minutes after ten, my administrative assistant Renee came into my office and handed me my continuing-education test. I was required to take them every so often to keep up to speed with new things regarding the brokerage business because I ran the office. I had taken over as boss after a gentleman I worked with for eighteen years had left the previous year to move back to Louisiana where he had grown up. He was a cranky man, but he had a good heart, and I had learned a lot from him over the years. In fact, I feel blessed to have had the time with him that I did.

Renee told me she was heading out to grab lunch and that she would be back in about an hour. I set the test to the side and finished reviewing some things regarding some stocks a client was interested in. A few times, my mind wandered to my dilemma. I'd immediately try to get my thoughts to shift elsewhere. Work certainly did make that easier, after all.

By ten thirty, I was caught up with everything with the market for the moment. It was time to watch the Quotron machine. After a few minutes, I decided to use the restroom and grab a water, and five minutes later, I was back in my office. When I returned, I grabbed my test material and started to look over it. I reached over and grabbed a pen. In the top right-hand corner, I touched the tip of the pen to the paper and began to write my signature.

It was like a light switch.

I felt light.

My shirt felt like it was growing. Either that or I was shrinking inside of it. It was like everything was in slow motion. My mind felt as if it were floating, and suddenly, I felt fear seep down into the core of my chest.

I knew.

For a moment, it was almost as if I was standing above myself looking down on my body. For what seemed like two minutes, I just watched myself and tried to comprehend what I was doing and what was going on.

That was the very last time I saw who I had been for fifty-four years.

I came to and realized the pen was still on the paper and I was just scribbling. That is when I looked down and realized the first half of my signature looked the way it had for the better part of thirty years and the second half was just circles.

Loops over and over.

It all happened so fast.

Suddenly, it was as if time caught up to itself, and my senses came rushing back so fast I almost got sick. I looked from side to side. Everything was distorted, and everything I saw as my head swiveled had a trail on it that followed behind the actual object I was looking at. I thought I might panic. In fact, I thought about a lot of things.

What the hell is going on?

My body suddenly weakened. I wanted to get up and try to walk it off, but my body wasn't responding to what my mind was trying to tell it to do. I looked for the time on the computer screen, but when I looked at the screen, it felt so foreign to me. It was like I was looking at a computer for the first time in my life. I didn't know where the time or anything was.

In the amount of time it had taken me to process what I was looking at, I had forgotten that I was in search of the time. Thoughts flipped through my head in almost a painful manner.

The phone, Steve!

What phone?

Do I have a phone?

Call for help!

Who can help me?

Will anybody help me?

Please, someone help me!

I was so confused, and with each passing second, my head became heavier and heavier. It almost felt as if it were crushing my neck, and then I just gave up.

My head lolled forward, and fortunately my elbows were propped up and my palms were there to catch it. My forehead slammed into my hands. It sounded like falling boulders hitting concrete after a long fall, except it was muffled.

It echoed in my head for what seemed like forever and then…

Silence.

It was as if everything in my head just turned into empty space. It became my reality. I could hear a very faint ringing off in the distance like the ring in your ear that occurs from time to time. It felt like it was thirty or forty feet away. My thoughts became white in color with tiny blurry splotches of dark gray circles fading in and out.

Suddenly, I heard a laugh.

It was the laugh of a child.

A small child.

As the laugh faded away, I saw numbers start to trickle from top to bottom inside my head, but they disappeared as everything in my mental focus shifted over to the left side of the expanse occupying my mind. Standing there clear as day were Bella, the boys, and our two dogs. They all stood there, motionless, without saying a word. Finally, they smiled and began to wave.

Then, out of what seemed like the right side of my mind, way off in the distance, I heard a woman yell, "Steeeeeeeeeeeeeeeve!"

I came to.

"Steve," Renee yelled, "can you hear me? Look at me, Steve. Are you okay?"

As she walked over to my desk, I focused all my efforts on throwing my head back out of my palms. I managed to do so without any type of control over my movements. As my head went backward, the weight of my body followed suit and went crashing back into the pads of my office chair.

"Oh God, Steve!" Renee finally said.

I managed to look at Renee and reply, "I'm okay. Just give me a minute. I'll be fine."

CHAPTER 55

1965–1968

Knoxville, Tennessee

Life in 1965 was great for a youngster like me. For adults who worried about everything going on in the world, it was probably a lot less pleasant. Now, I am sure that they loved the $13,600 average cost of a home. It was more than it had been in the past, but it wasn't pressing by any means. Especially when you consider that the average income was $6,450 a year. Loans were shorter back then, and mortgage payments were merely crumbs compared to what they are today. I guess in some ways, it all averaged out.

A loaf of bread was twenty-one cents, and a gallon of gas was thirty-one cents. How crazy is that?

On the other hand, we had some seriously trying times. On home soil, there was a devastating natural disaster coined the Palm Sunday Tornado Outbreak. A confirmed forty-seven tornadoes hit in six midwestern states, killing about 265 people and injuring about 1,500 more. It goes without saying, though, that the majority of negativity was surrounding the Vietnam War.

It continued to get worse and worse. The United States went from having 75,000 troops to over 125,000 troops in Vietnam. In fact, the US launched Operation Rolling Thunder in 1965.

This was an air raid and the first sustained American assault on North Vietnamese territory. Really, it more or less represented a major expansion of American involvement in the war. Inversely, there were some thirty-five thousand war protesters marching on Washington, DC, in an attempt to demonstrate their complete disgust with the war.

Pressing on personal preferences at an extremely stressful time, the number-one stress reliever was finally deemed a bad guy after all. That's right, cigarette companies were mandated to put health warnings on cigarette packs, and across the pond in the United Kingdom, cigarette advertisements had been banned from television. The larger cigarette companies back in the States knew it was only a matter of time before it would happen here as well.

As far as technological advances are concerned, we can start with the small ones. The respirator was invented, and optical digital recording and playback was too. The optical disk, now known as the compact disc, or CD, was a big-deal invention by American James Russell.

On a larger scale, we had all sorts of things going on with the Space Race between the United States and the Soviet Union. The United States' Project Gemini continued its progress in testing the limits of manning an aircraft going to space. The US also had the Ranger 8 and Ranger 9 crashes in 1965.

Ranger 8 crashed into the moon after successfully photographing a possible landing site for the Apollo program. Ranger 9, which also crashed into the moon, sent back a TV broadcast of its less-than-graceful descent.

The USSR's claim to fame in 1965 was the spacewalk. A cosmonaut left his spacecraft for twelve minutes, making him the first person to walk in space.

In regard to everyday things in my life, I'd have to say the biggest news was more of a religious experience. It gained a lot of attention in the media and also at Mass. Pope Paul VI became the first pope to visit the United States, and you would have thought Jesus himself had descended from heaven. Of course, I didn't meet him, but it was a big deal in the Catholic community nonetheless.

On TV, the big deal was the debut of *Days of Our Lives*. For me, that was a big *No thanks! The Sound of Music* was a hit film in 1965, which I personally could have done without, as well.

Thankfully, the Beatles still continued to pump out great music. It was almost as if it was as natural to them as breathing. I mean, they had a song here and there that was kind of mundane, but for the most part, it was all good, all the time.

All the while, the Rolling Stones, the Animals, and the Moody Blues were picking up steam. I guess it is also worth mentioning that the Grateful Dead played their very first concert ever in San Francisco. Supposedly, Jerry Garcia killed it on the guitar.

Certainly worth mentioning is the racial tension mounting in the States. Every year in this era was a big year regarding civil rights and other things regarding the rights of African- Americans. Early in the year, Malcolm X was assassinated in New York City. Although he was a more controversial figure in regard to the rights of black people, he is still considered one of the most influential African-Americans in history. Three members of the Nation of Islam assassinated him, although the majority of his life's work was dedicated to the Nation of Islam as he traveled to various countries involving himself in works the group took part in.

After deciding that he didn't accept or desire to further be associated with the movement, he headed back to the US. Still, a wedge had been formed between him and the Nation of Islam, thus leading to his death at the age of thirty-nine.

Dr. Martin Luther King Jr. led marches from Selma to Montgomery in March. It was a peaceful demonstration that was geared toward the civil rights and voting rights of African-Americans. The demonstration was met with state troopers violently confronting them at Pettus Bridge.

After two failed attempts at crossing the bridge due to the violent troopers, the demonstration was finally backed by the US Army and National Guardsmen, and marchers were allowed to pass through.

The three thousand people who marched became another thirty-five thousand strong when they arrived in Montgomery. In August of 1965, the Voting Rights Act was signed into law, which guaranteed African-Americans the right to vote.

Also in August and just a few weeks before I started school, the Watts Riots took place in Los Angeles. The riots were the result of the arrest of a black man named Marquette Frye by a white police officer due to a failed field sobriety test on August 11. A few hundred people gathered around the scene and watched it unfold. It resulted in crowd control being brought in and the arrest of three other Frye family members.

By midnight, the riots had begun.

Although black leaders tried to restore order on the next day, the riots continued and turned into looting and arson.

On August 13, around twenty-three hundred National Guardsmen were called in. On August 14, a curfew of 8:00 p.m. was placed on the city. On the fifteenth, the riots and vandalism ended, and on the seventeenth, the curfew was lifted.

The events ended with thirty-four people dead and over a thousand people reported injured. Burning and looting damaged more than two hundred buildings and another two hundred and fifty were completely destroyed.

I lived during these events.

Whether I caught a glimpse of what was going on in passing, or I sat down and really paid attention to what was going on, they impacted society as I knew it. Change is a difficult thing for many to deal with. It is uncomfortable and breaks the status quo.

CHAPTER 56

In Powell, Tennessee, all was looking up for me, however. If there had ever been a single time in life that I was more excited, I honestly couldn't remember it. I was just a few weeks away from realizing a moment I had looked forward to for over five years. Since school had let out for summer, I had played football a minimum of four days a week, and I had become extremely coordinated at my new size for all the time put in. If I wasn't playing football, I was playing something else trying to adjust.

Not only had I grown two more inches since May, but I had also put on another fifteen pounds. Pushing five feet six and 135 pounds, I was a nice size for a soon-to-be sixth grader. There were still a few tasks left to take care of before the end of summer. First on the list, I needed a fresh pair of cleats.

Because I tried to play sports as much as possible, I didn't add any new yards to mow in the summer of 1965. I did, however, continue doing my best job mowing the yards I had. I had perfected them all and had set record times on each of them in the previous few months. Mr. Peterson occasionally ripped me off. My neighbor Clyde always ripped me off if he sought out my services. Regardless, by the end of summer, I had a brand-new pair of Spot-Bilt football cleats to break in. They cost a grand total of twelve dollars, and they were worth every penny. There was only one task left before my football career could begin: ask Dad for permission to play.

Every decision had to be run by the one person who spent hardly any time around us at all. Still, I respected the hierarchy. I couldn't ask him in person because he was working. Of course he was working. I remember calling him and being nervous for some odd reason.

"Do you think I could play football? I am old enough now."

"I suppose," he said before letting me know, "but I need to get back to work, so I have to go."

With everything on my to-do list marked off, it was just a few days' wait until preseason officially began. I had played pickup games in my new cleats every day for about a week and a half. I hadn't gotten blisters from them after about the fourth day, and my feet were all healed up by the first day of preseason.

I was ready to rock.

The time had come.

I was padded up, and my cleats were laced. I slid my helmet on and headed onto the field. The first order of the day was our first team meeting. Our coach, Denny Ledford, gave us the full rundown on the state of the program. This basically meant that he let us in on how the team had faired in the past few seasons. Mainly, this was geared to any guys who had previously gone to other schools. I knew firsthand how the team had done.

Due to Mike playing and me going to the games as often as possible, I knew how the team had done to this point. I remember going to the very first St. Joseph game against Carter. St. Joseph had won. Joe Conner coached them at that time. Their best player was Denny O'Brien. My hero!

They ran O'Brien right, then O'Brien left.

Then alternate.

Ball control was the key. No mistakes allowed. Three yards and a cloud of dust. Whatever works, I guess. They went 3-2 that year on the strength of Denny O'Brien's running. A record that would be tops for years. The following year they did a little worse, and in year three, it was a wait-and-see approach as my time to play had come.

After the memo on the program, Coach Ledford let us in on his expectations of us as players and the way things would be moving forward. The bottom line was that he wanted us to give our all, limit mistakes, and play as a team. This all made perfect sense to me as I had learned this in my pickup games.

Next, we did our first warm-up of the season, which I had never done before. Running a bit. Stretching a bit. Finally, it was time to break up into smaller groups and see what everyone had to offer. Most of the guys who had played the year before expected to gain a spot on the team again. This put the pressure on us younger guys.

It was up to us to dethrone them.

For me, that meant a challenge—and a challenge I was completely ready to face.

CHAPTER 57

Everything we did, I gave it hell. I picked the fastest guy I could find and tried to run faster. Tried to hit harder, catch better, juke better. In every drill that I was part of, I did everything I could not only to make the team but also make sure I would at least see the field at some point.

This caught the eye of the coaches, and they were singing my praises from the end of our first week of practice moving forward. On one hand, I was happy about it, but on the other, one thing had become abundantly clear to me: once again, St. Joseph would have some good players, but otherwise, we were severely lacking in talent. Just when I zoned out thinking of how much I hated to lose, I reeled myself back in and decided I'd just be grateful that I was finally able to take part.

Almost every time we did anything, it was one other guy and I who led the entire pack. His name was Jimbo Miller, and in every way, shape, and form, I wanted to be just like him.

But better.

Jimbo was a big ol' boy but also had this uncanny speed. He had started as linebacker and fullback the previous year, and he was at no risk of losing either spot. I decided I'd like to play linebacker too, and I didn't need to beat him out for that to become possible. I could just earn one of the other two spots, and in reality, from a team perspective, we had our best chance to play well when he was on the field. But I also had my sights set on tailback.

Every chance I had, I did everything I could to prove that I was worthy of the position.

At the conclusion of preseason, it was determined that I would start on offense, defense, and special teams. I was thrilled, to say the least. At the time, I felt like it was probably owed to an overall lack of team talent more than a vote of confidence for me. As in, I was warm and had a pulse. There wasn't a play I wouldn't be in on and that was A-OK in my book. As the season amped up and was underway, I had a realization of sorts after about three games.

I was a good player.

I played a big role in a lot of our big plays and led the team in scoring, although Jimbo Miller was the real star. But as a team, we were only good at one thing: losing.

Naturally, in the public eye, it didn't matter how much good I did because I was part of a losing effort. Most of the guys didn't mind much, but it ate away at me. Losing is something you shouldn't take lightly. In my opinion, frustration from losing is an obvious component that goes along greatly with the psyche that it takes to be a winner. As Vince Lombardi said best:

Show me a good loser and I'll show you a loser.

It was glorious putting on the pads, anyhow. It was more about playing and having fun than it was about winning and losing. Heck, I was so caught up in playing that I rarely noticed when Cathy would stop by and watch my games. She thought I was great, and I appreciated her thinking so. The other guys who had girlfriends would always do all sorts of crazy stuff on the field when their companions stopped by for a watch.

Mainly, those crazy things consisted of overrunning a play, trying to make a spectacular play that ended in them getting demolished, and occasionally getting hurt. If they had tried to play with that same tenacity all the time, they might have been better and, therefore, could have really impressed somebody. As it stood, they just looked like insane kids in helmets running around the gridiron.

It didn't do much good.

It did provide some good laughs, though.

We won just one game the entire season. It was an away game against Karns. Afterward, we didn't know how to act. Seriously, it almost became awkward. It is worth noting that Coach Ledford never once gave up on us, and he poured as much passion into our team when we were 1–4 as he did before the season began with a clean slate.

One day, in the middle of the week following our fifth game, I missed practice because Mom had obligations and she was the only one able to pick me up from school before practice started. It's not like I could drive, and it was sort of important to make it home to go to bed at night. As a reward, I got to run the gauntlet. This consisted of running through the entire team broken into two halves facing each other about three feet apart. Everyone would hit you relentlessly as you made your way through. At the end of the gauntlet, I looked down to discover that I had a new joint in the middle of my forearm.

My arm was severely broken.

I freaked out.

This was just one of the many injuries that football would end up affording me. It was obviously enough to end my season with only a few games left.

CHAPTER 58

For the rest of the season, I gave my all, cheering for my comrades from the sideline. It was an odd experience for me. I was confident in my talents, but I didn't like to talk about it much. I was an extremely modest player and almost became uncomfortable when I was complimented. It became apparent to me what I meant to the team. We went from bad to worse when I wasn't out there.

It was undeniable.

Internally, it made me kick my future commitment into overdrive. I knew I was a skilled asset, and although I didn't flaunt it like others did, I understood what I meant to my teammates and the team, even if we did lose. I wasn't going to play everyone's position and belittle the others around me by doing so. I would, however, do everything I possibly could in my positions to ensure I was setting a good example and contributing to the team playing as well as possible.

Outside of my own football endeavors, I only had spare time on the weekends. I would wake up early and mow my yards until that season was over. After mowing on Saturdays was done, it was my favorite time of year.

Football time in Tennessee!

Uncle David and I were living the high life down in Knoxville with our bus rides, good meals, peanuts to crack, Cokes to drink and, of course, our beloved Tennessee Volunteers.

In Doug Dickey's second year at the helm, the Vols entered the season unranked. Still, there was a lot of buzz in the air about the team. Times had been tough in Knoxville regarding the success of the Tennessee program, and everyone was ready for the ship to turn around. On September 18, 1965, they opened the season with a 21–0 win over Army at home. The next week we witnessed as the Vols tied Auburn 13–13. After a bye week, we were back in Neyland Stadium as Tennessee trounced South Carolina 24–3.

Heading into the Alabama game on October 16, 1965, we were 2-0-1. Alabama had entered the season #5 in the country, but after a shocking 18–17 loss to Georgia in week one, they had fallen completely out of the ranks. They bounced back and had reeled off three straight wins. Therefore, they entered our annual meeting 3-1.

Who's ready for the Third Saturday in October?

Although we were bummed the game was at Legion Field, we listened with anticipation as the broadcast came over the radio. With 65,680 folks in attendance, the game was a back-and-forth defensive struggle. Once again, a Tennessee versus Alabama matchup ended in my least favorite way.

A tie.

Sure enough, 7–7 was all she wrote.

Back in Knoxville the following week, the Vols beat the Houston Cougars 17–8 and were still unbeaten rolling into the November 6 clash with Georgia Tech. The crowd was rowdy and relentless as the Vols handled the #7 Yellow Jackets en route to a 21–7 victory. The players were pumped at Frank's Brass Rail after the game. So were all the fans that turned out to congratulate the team on a job well done.

Next up, Tennessee traveled to Memphis Memorial Stadium for a neutral-site game against the unranked Ole Miss Rebels. Our boys must have gotten ahead of themselves after getting bumped all the way up to #8 in the nation, and they paid for it. A 14–13 loss brought them back down to earth. That would be the only loss of the season, though. After beating

Kentucky in Lexington, the boys in orange were back at home and back to #9 in the country.

The next week, they would be going head-to-head with the black and gold from West End. Vanderbilt gave it a go but really didn't stand a chance in the Vols' 21–3 win.

On December 4, the Volunteers were back at Memphis Memorial Stadium. This time, it was #5 UCLA that would come into the state of Tennessee to take on the #7 Volunteers. They were hoping to hand them their second loss in Memphis.

The game had really been played up in the media and newspapers. I sure did wish that this one had been in Knoxville. I was certainly thankful for the full home slate for the season, but the East Coast versus West Coast contest was full of excitement leading up to the game. It didn't disappoint, that is for sure. The edges of our seats were warm as my uncle and I listened to the game at my grandmother's.

After four quarters of highly entertaining airwaves, the Vols pulled out a 37–34 victory, sending UCLA packing. Finally, the season ended with a 27–6 win over Tulsa in the Bluebonnet Bowl. For all intents and purposes, it was deemed that the Vols were back, and that provided nothing but smiles for Uncle Dave and me.

CHAPTER 59

Other than the usual birthdays and holidays, the end of 1965 was filled with another new venture: basketball. My arm had taken about six weeks to heal, and that meant that I was cleared for action just in time to still take part on the basketball team with the help of a delayed tryout. My games of Horse with Jim Courtney really paid off.

Although Jim had moved on to Mississippi State to play college football in 1964, the time he spent with me on the court proved to be extremely valuable. I don't think Jim ever really knew just how much his time meant to me. For a short while, it had been like I finally had an older brother who was appealing to be around.

One who cared about me.

I always took his advice when he taught me the ropes. He taught me everything from how to hold the ball properly to how to release my shot using my wrist instead of shooting from the hip. In some later one-on-one scenarios, he taught me how to guard and not get called for the foul.

I was flawed just from being so young. However, I was good for my age, and I owed that to the hours he put in with me. Competition and camaraderie were like addictions for me, even at such a young age. Contributing with productivity was a standard of mine. In my first season, we did pretty well, and I received a good amount of playing time.

St. Joseph's schedule consisted of about twenty-five games a year. Due to that, I really loved basketball. My thought process was simple regarding athletics, not about actually playing them but the commitment of being on the team. To fulfill your commitment, you had to be there. Of course, we all know I loved the games, but accompanying the commitment to play on the team was one very attractive add-on.

When I was on the field or the court, I couldn't be anywhere else.

And if I couldn't be anywhere else, then that meant that I wasn't at home.

Being at home was not a very glamorous experience for me in many ways, and this became more and more cemented the older I grew. Perhaps this explains why I was so eager to be in a positive atmosphere that centered on a team, a group of people working together to reach a common goal.

Teammates.

Comrades.

Brothers.

The laughs, cheers, and celebrations.

The feeling you get when you have worked together for the length of a game regardless of the outcome. The bond you form with your teammates and coaches. It was so opposite to my home life. When I say that, I don't mean to take away from how good my mom was to me, but I could have been a serial bank robber at the age of eleven and she would have loved me just the same. Hell, she would have told me how good I was at it.

Like they say, *There is no love like a mother's love.* It only took a few months of playing football and beginning basketball season for me to realize all of this. I didn't stop there either. As the season ran from fall to spring, 1966 brought another first-time experience.

I was new to organized baseball and was on the way to Badgett Park, which had just recently been completed. This meant it was a brand-new ballpark for my very first game. It was exciting, to say the least, for a young buck like me. I don't remember all of my inaugural season, but I will never forget my first game and a few other impressionable moments.

Mom (who signed me up for all the sports), my grandfather, and I were headed down the road in our blue '59 Impala. The windows were down, and life was just right. Another sport to master was exactly the task I was up for.

My team was called the Hustlers. We were adorned in navy blue and light gray. The light gray was better known as wool. The other team, the Comets, wore green and light gray. Which was also wool. I was picking up on the trend...

I guess the parents all got the memo about cleats at Almart, which was a store that we frequented before the existence of Walmart. They had these super-cheap cleats that everyone wore. I played left field, and in the first three innings, it was a hot spot for the Comets. I would go sprinting— better yet, clomping—over to get the ball so I could throw it to the short-stop. The shoes were terrible.

By the fourth inning, all I could think when I looked at them was *All these blisters just to save a buck.*

There was more game to be played, though. A few innings later, and the hot spot had cooled off completely. Compared to the other sports I had played, I couldn't help thinking that there wasn't very much total action during my first game. That, of course, was before the big moment.

Throughout eight innings, the game was close. As a matter of fact, it was all tied up at 5–5. In the top of the ninth, we took the field on defense and forced the Comets to go three up and three down. This left the game tied, and after two batters had been called out at first, I was up to bat. With two outs and no one on base, the first pitch was a fastball, which I missed as badly as I did football season at the moment. I stepped back for a second and got dialed in. The next pitch came rocketing in, and I swung the bat at what seemed like a snail's pace by comparison. I learned a lot about base-ball in that moment. Well, batting anyway. You didn't have to swing the bat as hard as possible to hit the ball really well.

Sure enough, the bat connected as well as it could with the ball. The ball went soaring toward the outfield. Before in landed, I was halfway to first base. The Comets were still chasing it down as I ran past first, so my coach signaled for me to keep going. At that point, I lost my footing and went sprawling headfirst into the dry dirt known as the infield. I was too embarrassed to stay down there long, so I jumped to my feet and took off again. When I was rounding second my third base coach signaled for me to keep going, and I was glad to oblige. As I approached third, my coach looked to the outfield where the Comets must have really been royally screwing things up, and then he turned back to me and told me to keep going. I had home plate in my sights, so I hit the gas.

The moment was so exhilarating, and the mission was simple: beat the ball to the bag.

Bring it on!

I crossed the plate with about three seconds to spare. It was officially my first home run, and we won the game 6–5 to everyone's delight. With my first game out of the way, I tried really hard to be one of the guys. My goal in life was to be one of the guys—the talented, the ones you could rely on, the assets.

A guy who all my teammates were glad to be playing with.

This, of course, was all coupled with a never-ending objective to downplay my own talents for the sake of not coming across as one of *those* guys.

I'll tell you one thing: my goal of being one of the guys was no small task on this team because of the plethora of talent we had.

CHAPTER 60

A few weeks and about four games later, we were set to play. Upon arriving, I laid my eyes on something I had seen recently.

"Where is your uniform?" I asked Freddy Russell, who arrived to play in his cutoffs and a T-shirt.

"It's in the washing machine," offered Freddy.

"Wasn't it in the washing machine the last time we played and it was ninety-five degrees out? Couldn't have anything to do with the fact that it's made out of wool, could it?"

I got no reply.

"Who's pitching today?" asked Freddy.

"Tommy Beaver," I replied.

Tommy Beaver was a great pitcher. Honestly, though, his real claims to fame were 1) he was a southpaw and 2) he used to smoke cigarettes on the mound. He would lay them on the mound in between pitches.

At the age of eleven.

Well, he's a badass, I thought the first time I saw him do it. That thought was immediately followed by another thought. *Where the hell are his parents?*

Either they never showed for a game or just didn't care that he smoked. No matter what the case was, Tommy Beavers went through some Marlboros during our season. They certainly never hindered his performance. When he started as pitcher, we knew we were in good hands. When we were in a pinch and he came in, we knew we were in good hands.

Tommy was the product of another era and time in my life. If a player in modern-day Little League baseball was seen taking a smoke on the mound, the entire league would probably fold. For that, my memories of him are symbolic in many ways as to what life was like back in the day.

Our sixth game went just like the rest of them. We finished the season undefeated, which in turn was the most lasting memory from my first season playing baseball. Going undefeated is something that most people never get to experience during their entire lives, and I was blessed with the experience in just my first year of organized sports. Being undefeated was something I really wished I would have the chance to get used to, but I knew that wasn't likely.

I'd have loved to never lose a game in any sport for the rest of my life as a player.

Going undefeated left no room for doubt.

It left no room for someone to say that you weren't the best. And

I liked being the best.

So, naturally, I loved being undefeated.

Again, it wasn't the in-your-face *I'm the best and you suck* kind of mentality. It was really just a standard I had developed through realizing things could click at a higher level than most people knew. Why not be the best if you can put in the work and become capable of it?

It was almost as if moving forward in life from the moment our last game ended, I was seeking the answer to what it took to be undefeated.

To win.

To be a winner.

Not just in sports, but in life.

I never got the guys who didn't care about winning or coming out on top—middle-of-the- pack kind of guys. They were better than they knew or gave themselves credit for. They didn't believe in what they could achieve. They lacked the commitment it took to find out how great they truly were.

I mean, I get it. It's all about having fun. Really, though, there is an important note to make about all of that. You can have fun and still keep your eye on the prize. Later in life, I summed it up in a simple suggestion:

The reward for discipline is success.

For me it was simple. I loved winning. Now, I loved the camaraderie and the bond I formed with players and coaches no matter the result, and I loved the competition. Furthermore, I didn't even view losing as a failure. It is just that winning had so much more of a rewarding feeling when it was all said and done. It gave the bond you had formed with your team-mates and coaches a more lasting meaning. This is due to the fact that you achieved the common goal that you all set out with in the beginning. You know, *Veni, vidi, vici*:

I came, I saw, I conquered.

And you had each other to celebrate with after the whole thing was over.

CHAPTER 61

As summer drew near and sixth grade ended, I had no clue that I was in for more growth as a person. Although I did continue to grow physically at a steady rate, I started to grow mentally too. Realizations came in abundance, and it was enlightening.

I started to understand myself, other people, and life in general a lot more clearly than I had before. It was as if a switch had been flipped. I was turning from a boy into a young man. Only, it was accelerated by the life I lived. My commitment to being the man of the house, per se, when Dad wasn't around, made me realize from an early age the responsibilities that accompanied growing older.

I had my sights focused on playing athletics as long as possible. After a lot of thought I began to realize the responsibilities it would take to be the kind of player I wanted to be. I never forgot my promise to Uncle Dave about playing football at Tennessee, either. I remained focused on it every day.

Speaking of my uncle, we continued to get closer. I knew that his drinking was getting worse and worse, but at my age, it never affected me personally, and I loved the relationship we had. He was genuinely interested in my life and well-being. He was interested in the boy I had been and the young man I would become. In some ways, I could also tell he was interested in my not making the same poor decisions he had in life.

Around me, he was great. The all-American uncle who was more like a dad than anything I had experienced otherwise. In his personal life, though, when I wasn't around, he got drunk and made terrible decisions.

He hurt those close to him during moments he would regret when he sobered up.

He was hurting and angry inside.

Around me, that side of him never came to light at this point. When he was with me, it was as if he was doing the one thing he felt would make up for the other bad things he did. I certainly thought he was doing a damn good job at it too.

I tried to get better every single day in all things I did. With football, in particular, I really homed in on getting better all the time.

By the summer before seventh grade, it already seemed as if I was frantically fighting against time to accomplish goals that I had made for myself. Goals that wouldn't come to fruition for five or six more years.

Ecclesiastes simply lays out what any good and motivated person should remember in athletics or in life when trying to reach a goal or win a contest.

The race is not to the swift, nor the battle to the strong, neither yet bread to the wise, nor yet riches to men of understanding, nor yet favour to men of skill; but time and chance happeneth to them all. (9:11) I can relate this in life to folks who procrastinate as opposed to those who are proactive. It is never too early to start working toward an accomplishment once it is made a goal. Sure, it can be nice to take a deep breath and relax, but I would rather get to where I want to be, achieve what I am trying to achieve, and then relax with a sense of accomplishment. Athletically, you can bet that every second you waste sitting on your ass, there is someone out there who is working their ass off. Be dedicated to yourself and to your craft. In fact, later in life Julie had a son named Spencer, and one time he shared a quote with me that he saw on the wall of a Jimmy John's, of all places. The quote is the epitome of what I'm talking about, and it goes as follows:

Do what you have to do when you have to do it, so that one day, you can do what you want to do when you want to do it.

Overall, my enjoyment of the things I had to do to reach the level of play I wanted to reach aided me in not wasting any time. The fact that it catered to other parts of my being made it easier as well.

The other sports I played were a blast, but they all took a back seat to my true athletic love. There was something about football that spoke to my soul in so many ways. The team aspect of football brought about a lot of connection with folks that I didn't experience in a lot of areas of life. It also provided me a viable outlet for other things. I took my frustrations from life out on the field. For every person who I cared about who never told me how proud of me they were, I had a coach who did. For every time I had been put down or discouraged, I made sure to do my best on the field so I would know deep down that I was worth more than those people would ever know.

I became sure of myself instead of relying on the opinions of others, and I learned to recognize my true value.

Most of this was geared toward my relationship with my Dad, but I don't think I realized that wholeheartedly at the time.

In many ways, he was such an admirable man, but it was like he drew a blank when it came to having kids. He hadn't showed up to a single athletic event of mine in an entire year of playing sports almost every day. In fact, it would be a long time before he showed up to a contest of mine.

I guess I became okay with it over time.

I accepted it, and I knew that there was nothing I could do to change it. Because of that, I stopped being concerned with it. I just did my thing and let the pieces fall into place around me. And, if I'm being honest, my approach paid off significantly in the long run.

It did, at times, come with the price of not being intricately involved with my sisters' lives, or Mike's for that matter. Not that Mike wanted anything to do with me more than the rare occasion, and my sisters were understanding of my commitment to sports. My mother, with my grandparents at her side, Uncle David, and a few friends were close to my heart, though, and they were always there when it counted.

The Storm

Tuesday, May 13, 2008

Dalton, Georgia

Fifty-four Years Old

When I told Renee that I would be fine, I think I was really just trying to convince myself. She called my bluff and called 9-1-1 before going to get a more immediate form of help. A doctor from the office park we worked in came over to the office and stayed with me until the ambulance arrived. Somewhere in the midst of drifting off into dreamland and doing my best to respond to the questions the doctor was asking me, off in the distance, I heard Renee on the phone frantically explaining what was going on.

My brain wasn't working right, but I managed to come up with the probable candidate for who would be on the receiving end of that phone call: Bella.

In that moment, my heart sank. I knew that something was terribly wrong. It was a devastating realization but inevitable nonetheless. The thought of Bella hearing the news saddened me deeply. These thoughts turned to a dream of sorts. I no longer heard the doctor or Renee. Somewhere else in my mind, I looked straight out over a field of green grass with weak sunrays lighting her image through dark and daunting clouds. All I could really focus on was Bella, crying, broken down on her knees. I tried to yell out to her, but she couldn't hear me. I tried to run to her so that I could comfort her, except I couldn't move.

I was stuck.

I was voiceless.

And then everything went completely black.

Pitch black.

And then it was as if I'd gone blind. For what seemed like only a moment, I fumbled around feeling my legs and chest to see if I was still there. And then I wasn't. Then my thoughts and my ability to make memories faded away.

Like the prettiest of sunsets turning to night, everything that I had ever been just faded away.

As Danny later explained to me, the ending of my memory was the start of a storm that was completely unexpected. For him, it was met by a phone call.

"Hello?"

It was just after eleven as he remembers it. It was a Tuesday. Any normal Tuesday as far as he was concerned. He was attending Kennesaw State University and was living just off campus. He and Lindsay, now his wife, had just started dating a week prior. She was on a study-abroad trip in Belize at the time. He had the girl of his dreams, finals had just ended, and he was out of school for the summer.

Life was good.

Then he went on to vividly portray how the words he heard next would spark a change, a monumental shift, in his life, our family's life, and for all who knew us. In fact, his exact words were pretty telling. He said that it was *like taking a dramatic right turn while cruising down the road at a nice and comfortable seventy miles per hour.*

None of us ever saw it coming.

"Well, Danny," Paul said as he paused for a moment, which he often did when discussing something serious, "Dad is in the hospital. And, umm, it's not good, man. They say Dad had a stroke. I don't know what you are doing, but you need to get here as fast as you can."

He went on to tell me that he really only had one response to what had been laid out in front of him.

He told me that at first all he could do was think *What?! Dad had a stroke? Steve Adkins had a stroke? This can't be real. He is invincible.*

He was speechless. He told me that he honestly wasn't sad, mad, scared, or any other kind of emotion. He was just shocked. He didn't know what to be. Furthermore, he didn't know what a *stroke* was, due to lack of personal experience.

"Where are you?" Danny asked.

"I just got to the hospital."

"What hospital is he at?"

"He's at Hamilton Medical Center in Dalton."

"I'm on my way," Danny responded. Then he asked, "What even happened?"

"Mom got a call from Renee. She said everything was fine before she stepped out for lunch. When she got back she came into his office, and he was slumped over his desk. She told Mom he wasn't responding clearly and knew she needed to call 9-1-1. Just come up!" Paul said with urgency.

"I'm coming. I'll call you when I'm pulling into the hospital," Danny said before hanging up.

Once he arrived, he called Paul, who talked him through finding them in the hospital. After meeting up with the others, they told him that I had been there for about forty-five minutes already.

He must have flown up to Dalton because the hospital was sixty miles from Kennesaw State.

They also told him that, upon my arrival, the hospital staff did a brain scan. After receiving the results, they had consulted with a stroke specialist at Erlanger Medical Center in Chattanooga, Tennessee. The specialist saw signs of stroke but wasn't positive that was the whole problem. Erlanger had the staff at Hamilton Medical put me on a life flight to Chattanooga pronto. Danny said he felt fortunate that he had made it before I was in flight.

When he was finally able to see me, I looked at him and asked, "What are you doing here?"

When revisiting that day, he told me that moment broke his heart and still does to this day. He said that it wasn't as if I didn't want him there. Rather, it was evident I just didn't want him to see me that way. I didn't want him to see me broken, no longer in control, afraid, and hurt.

He replied, "You're my dad. Why wouldn't I be here?"

Then he told me I looked at him and in a muffled voice said, "Everything is going to be okay. It's going to be okay. I'm fine. I'm going to be okay. I'm sorry this is happening. I'm so, so sorry."

From his recollection, I went on to say those words a hundred times that day. For Bella, Paul, and him, it was so sad. He said it was like Superman had encountered his kryptonite. He went on to tell me that it was because I had always been there for them. I had always provided everything they needed. I was their strength. In his opinion, I was for countless others, as well.

In my darkest moment, I was still trying to comfort them.

I was still trying to protect them.

Though, in my words and in my face, he could see how terrified I was of my current situation. Why? Well, I didn't really know if I was going to be fine.

I didn't know if I was going to be okay.

CHAPTER 62

Through the beginning of summer, it was evident that I wasn't the only one undergoing changes. Mike played football at Powell, but he had become quite the outdoorsman. Right after he turned fifteen, he got a job at J. E. Groner's where he made sixty-five cents an hour and worked his days away as a bag boy. It was crazy when I thought about it: I had to be making more mowing yards than he was working a real job.

Thank God for entrepreneurship.

To me, his changes became abundantly clear in early summer on a Sunday after Mass when my grandfather came to the house. As a ritual on most Sundays after lunch when he came, we made our way down to the arrowhead spot on the other side of the train tracks. It was my experience that arrowheads were readily found in small ponds and puddles that formed on rainy days. It hadn't rained in weeks, so I was hoping another form of entertainment would present itself because I knew the arrowhead-finding probably wouldn't yield a great result.

This is where Mike really didn't disappoint.

He was donned in his full-woodsman getup and sporting his new Ithaca 20-gauge shotgun that he had saved up for by working at Groner's. He'd spent every last penny he had on it.

Usually I didn't find my amusement in Mike, but this day was completely the opposite. As we strolled past the tracks, we came up to the creek on the other side. Beaver Creek, that is. As usual, my grandfather was saying that his theory was that this area was an ancient Indigenous hunting camp. Meanwhile, Mike really got entertaining. He started shooting his gun and never stopped.

He shot everything.

Everything!

If it was living, he was killing it. He held no prejudice. Turtles, birds, squirrels, rabbits, and so on. It was a full-blown rampage, and we were only fifteen minutes in. Finally, my grandfather told him to get a grip.

The shooting halted for a bit. I was disappointed, I must admit. In reality, I was as impressed with his shooting as much as I was amused by it. The fact that he was just walking through a field only about four hundred yards from people's homes blowing the ass off of every animal that he came across was funny (not that I'm an advocate of killing animals unless you are going to eat them). The fact that he killed everything he shot at on the first shot was undeniable talent. Of course, it was a shotgun, but still.

As it turned out, it was a pretty good day to be an arrowhead hunter after all. In just the matter of a half hour, we found seven as we were walking. Finally, we reached the end of the field, and to the east, as always, there was a large shed with a plane inside. The only difference this time was that there was a shotgun in our possession.

Once my grandfather realized there was no talking Mike out of the idea, we all took turns shooting the plane repeatedly. After all of the ammo was spent, we headed back to the house just in time for my grandmother's hot Mexican corn bread to be brought out of the oven.

I could chalk this day and experience up to a good one with family. I welcomed them whenever they came. I especially loved the ones that involved Mike and I getting along, even if we did typically avoid each other. All in all, it was certain from this point forward that Mike had found new interests for himself.

He was typically at work, out fishing or killing whatever he could lay eyes on. He had found a true passion and stopped at nothing to pursue it.

Well, he had two new passions, actually. He had also gotten into cars. If you didn't know where he was, you could find him in the woods or at the drag strip. It was kind of odd to see him love something like he did hunting and cars. I thought he loved football but just wasn't dedicated to it. It immediately went onto the back burner once he found his new hobbies.

As time went on that summer, I found pickup games or initiated them as often as possible. Preferably football, but I was down with any sport. I even kept up my weekly regimen of beating the Harlem Globetrotters at the buzzer.

Some things are too good to pass up.

In times of boredom, I got extremely desperate but equally creative. More than anything, I found some good fun to have with my youngest sister Julie. I would pay her twenty-five cents to play football with me. The catch was that I had to play on my knees while she tried to play full steam ahead on her feet. It didn't really make me a better player in the grand scheme of things, but I did relish the time I spent with her. Just watching her give her best effort was worth a thousand smiles.

CHAPTER 63

Around the beginning of May, I had the opportunity to hang out with Mike again. I had asked if he wanted to put down the sweet tea and shotgun long enough to toss the football around. He obliged, and immediately after we had stepped foot in Mrs. May's side yard, he found a way to turn it into a competition.

He decided we should play setback, which is where you spread out about thirty-five to forty yards apart. The basics are that you are both punters, and you punt away while the other guy tries to catch the ball and punt it back. You win by getting the ball and punting it back so that it goes over your adversary's head in an uncatchable manner. Mike and I were versed in playing this with each other, and the few times a month when we got out in the yard together, it was one of our favorite games if no one else was around to play with.

Playing this game with Mike led me to a realization that was later summed up pretty well like this:

You are really only as good as the people you practice against.

Regarding athletics, I always found this to be true. Good opponents bring out the best in you if you are up for the competition. In this case, I had my work cut out for me. Over the first twelve years of my life, on about three or four separate occasions when Dad was feeling like a spirited father, he got out and punted the ball to us. In his heyday, he was a highly touted punter at Knoxville High School.

Although there was strain on our relationship with him, Mike and I tried to be like Dad whenever there was something positive to emulate. With punting, we both hoped to be just like him.

Mike was currently the punter for Powell High School, and boy, he must have really taken notes when Dad came to play.

He could boom it!

Every punt was a spiral that averaged close to fifty yards.

That kept me fetching the punts and racking up the losses. I tried to keep up and wasn't too shabby myself. But I was no match for Mike. He knew as much, which is why he always wanted to play setback. If there was one thing he couldn't stand, it was losing to me. About the time I lost for the twelfth consecutive game, we heard a car flying down the road.

Beep beep!

"Who is that?" I asked

"Johnny Mixon," Mike replied with a laugh.

Johnny Mixon was about six feet tall and weighed around 120 pounds. He would have needed to be about six feet five and weigh about 210 to match the way he thought of himself. He parked his '59 white Comet with a T-shifter at our place. He and Gene Hammer hopped out and made their way across the road to Mrs. May's. Johnny was a regular acquaintance of my brother's and one of the Powell local yokels. Johnny would take Mike to the drag strip on Friday nights.

Gene's claim to fame was that he introduced us to Buddy Holly's music about a decade after he became popular.

We decided to play a game of two-on-two, and because Johnny was in his good clothes, he took it upon himself to deem the game two-hand touch. Due to Gene's talent as a football player, it was more like two-on-one. They exploited his weaknesses every time they had the ball, so I just did whatever I could to score when we were on offense and try to keep up. After a half hour, they were beating us by about five scores.

At one point, we had the ball. When it was snapped, Johnny came at me as fast as he could, and in turn, I juked him nearly clean out of his shoes. Mike followed behind and tagged me down after a good 10-yard gain. On the next play, I was trying to get around Mike on the edge, when Johnny ran up from behind and knocked me clean off my feet and straight into the peonies that marked out of bounds.

I was pissed.

Johnny was always a bully, and I couldn't help but think this was a bit over the top for two-hand touch. He was admonished by my brother, although that didn't make me feel any better. So, on the next snap, I got the ball, and Johnny was running right toward me.

Instead of trying to go around him, I had other ideas.

I picked up as much speed as possible as he closed in, and right before he got to me, I lowered my shoulders and knocked him flat on his back. He hopped up ready to throw blows, and even though I was four years younger, I wasn't backing down. Our faces were inches apart, and we were yelling who-knows-what at one another.

Finally, Mike came over laughing, looked Johnny in the face, and told him not to bite off more than he could chew. I wasn't as tall as he was, but I definitely outweighed him. My brother's advice to him made me feel taller. Truly, I felt vindicated, and even more so when Johnny took Mike's advice. The fiasco ended the game, though, and we lost.

Booooo!

CHAPTER 64

In the coming weeks, I thought of that moment a handful of times. I thought about how not too long ago, given the same situation, I would have potentially become a bit timid with someone who was older than I was. My reaction to Johnny was almost instinctual. I realized that this too was due to the mental change I was undergoing. It was as if I felt more of a man, even though I wasn't even a teenager yet.

It further helped me realize what I was made of and what I was becoming. I wasn't backing down from Johnny, and I wasn't backing down from anyone else for that matter. I wasn't a hothead by any means, but I wasn't going to be pushed around. I also wasn't backing down from a challenge or task.

Now, if you'd told me to jump off a bridge or steal a car, I would have backed down. Really, both of those things are idiotic and not doing them isn't what I consider backing down. It was just accepting the challenge of making a good decision for the benefit of my life and, when applicable, the others around me.

Most people would fold under peer pressure.

I was my own person who was capable of making my own decisions.

It also became apparent to me that I had extremely high expectations for myself and held myself to a very high standard—even higher than others had of me. This is when I realized I trusted myself with my own decision-making process.

I could take care of me.

I could take care of standing up for myself.

I could take care of my responsibilities.

I could take care of making the right decision, and I could live with the decisions I made.

For the most part, I almost always got it right. When I did make a bad decision here or there, I chalked it up to the fact that no one is perfect. That is, in fact, why they say *Live and learn.* Overall, as a family, everyone was going about life in various stages. I mean, the parents were doing parent stuff. Dad was working. Mom was raising us the best she could. We kids were spaced out just enough to be involved with completely different things.

Mike was finding his passions.

I was evolving in every way possible.

Susan was desperate to get to sixth grade so that she could play sports like her big brothers.

Julie was just a few years into school.

Susan really liked to hang out with me anytime she could. Julie would tag along too whenever possible. Understanding the struggle of being the younger sibling, I always took time out to play with them. All the old games from Shamrock Avenue. Kick the Can, Fox and Hounds, and so on. I was an athlete, and I was approaching seventh grade, but I never turned down a good ol' fashioned, crazy adventure either. These are the things that Susan and Julie liked to be in on more than anything at their age. Really, you could tell that their favorite thing was just being included.

Through August, I prepared myself for preseason practice back on the football field. As each day passed, I got more and more excited about the season. I hoped we would be better. When I say *I prepared myself,* I really mean I just did what I did all the time.

Played football as much as possible.

Played other sports when I wasn't playing football.

And stayed in shape.

By the time September rolled around, I had grown another inch and was officially ten pounds heavier. Add that to the slow growth I had made during my sixth-grade school year, and I was five feet, seven and a half inches and weighed 155 pounds. I was excited by my maturation when camp started, and I was ready to use every bit of my size to my advantage.

I had heard through the grapevine that we would have new coaches. Sure enough, we were met with a new staff upon arriving on the first day of preseason practice.

Under the tutelage of Eugene Hill and Bob Arden, we got to work. Due to always playing with different groups of guys who were various ages in my pickup games, my abilities shocked me when I got back on a level playing field with the Bulldogs.

I was faster.

I was quicker.

I could hit harder, and I could punt further (Thanks, Mike!).

The coaches took a bit more time before singing their praises, but after a week and a half of practice, they approached me and asked if I had ever played quarterback. I told them only in pickup games, and they asked if I wanted to try it out. I wanted to do anything I could to help the team win, so I went for it.

I just wanted to win.

But winning…we just didn't do. Not much, anyway. We racked up a couple, and again the coaches never wavered despite our not-so-winning ways. In fact, they managed to make things interesting in their own way. We ran (for lack of a better term) a T-formation offense. I was the primary running back and quarterback. I also got my fair share of chances to chuck the ball. Our games resulted in a similar outcome usually—the outcome where we were losing when time expired, but the way they decided to do things made for some pretty fun plays here and there.

I gave my best effort every game and made sure to leave it all on the field.

On the sidelines, I always tried to keep my teammates in high spirits, even if I knew that we were going to lose. I always attempted to exemplify a high work ethic in practice. We just lacked talent in too many areas. It wasn't as if I viewed losing as a total failure.

I was still progressing weekly as a player. As an adult, I was asked a question that brought back a multitude of memories. Some of those memories were times at St. Joseph. I think it is an important lesson for any highly competitive athlete to learn.

The question was: "Steve, how do you deal with the failure of losing?"

My answer was simple.

I never saw losing as a failure. As a matter of fact, some of my best efforts were in losses.

In any given league, there can only be one champion each season. And even a champion loses at some point during the season. In most cases, only the champion has the opportunity to go undefeated. One exception would be if you played under the BCS rules from 1998 to 2013 in college football.

Sorry, Boise State.

Sorry, TCU.

For the most part, though, this is usually the case. Losing sucks, but for most teams, it happens.

That's why winning streaks are such a big deal.

They are rare and special.

At St. Joseph, I wanted to do everything I could with a team-first mentality, but on a personal level, I wanted to continue preparing myself for the next level. No matter the outcome of our games, I could do that. I was only a few years from high-school ball, and all my efforts were geared toward my dream of playing at Tennessee one day.

The '66 season was upon us. With everything I had going on, it was nice to have time with Uncle David on the weekends at Neyland Stadium or at Grandmother's listening to the games. The season zipped by. I attributed it to my full schedule outside of Saturday afternoons.

The Vols started out 2-0 before losing to Georgia Tech and Alabama in consecutive games. The Alabama game ended with a score of 11–10, and that one hurt! We were there, and I was deflated after the game.

After the Third Saturday in October, the Vols reeled off three straight wins and were sitting at 5-2 before losing to Ole Miss for the second straight year.

This time it was in Knoxville.

This time I was there.

I was deflated after it, as well.

The Vols won their last two regular-season games over Kentucky and Vandy. After going 7-3 in the regular season, they earned themselves a trip to the Gator Bowl. Although they had some games on TV dating back to the LSU game in 1963, this was the first time I caught the Big Orange on the tube. The family huddled around the TV as Tennessee beat Syracuse in the nationally televised event on ABC. The Volunteers ended up with an 8-3 record and in the middle of the pack in the SEC.

CHAPTER 65

In the classroom, I was having some more realizations. I had yet to struggle with any material I covered. It was actually quite the opposite. I made good grades and most everything came very easily to me. Math was one of my strong suits, and there wasn't a subject I didn't like. I did all my work. I never forgot about an assignment or turned in my homework late. I was good at test-taking. All this made things much easier for me to just focus on athletics. I was happy to be blessed with intellectual abilities that allowed my time in school to go this way, and I never took it for granted. Doing all that I was required to do was my way of saying thanks to God for affording me the ability to get by without issue.

As football season ended, I phased into basketball, and then it was Christmas break. Looking back on things, 1966 had proved to be yet another busy year around the world. The Space Race continued and was talked about all the time. Vietnam protests really picked up steam. They were met by hardly an ounce of consideration by the United States government, though. By the end of 1966, we had 500,000 troops in Vietnam.

Miranda rights came into existence that year, and the US Department of Transportation was created. Although hope springs eternal, my relationship with Cathy Koteski didn't last. That was followed by the fact that miniskirts came into fashion in '66, however, which did wonders for my curious mind and eyes.

The *Batman* and *Star Trek* series debuted on television. The country's population exceeded 195 million people, and some citizens of that population formed the Black Panthers. Black Power became a big deal, and there were race riots in Atlanta.

Charles Whitman, an ex-Marine, killed fourteen people and injured another thirty-one on a killing spree at the University of Texas.

The Beatles were still the biggest thing on the music trail. Also in music was the introduction of Simon and Garfunkel along with the Beach Boys. Kevlar was invented by Stephanie Kwolek.

Fiber optics were also invented.

Last but not least, one of the most-purchased items of any generation was created. I know you are probably thinking something really fancy or crazy. Nope. Pampers created the first disposable diaper. Pretty big deal if you ask me.

No one could imagine what 1967 had in store. I mean, some really big deals on multiple fronts. Of course, Vietnam raged on as did the protests.

Muhammad Ali was actually stripped of his heavyweight title and charged and found guilty of draft evasion. He was adamantly against the war and stood up to The Man and openly refused to be drafted.

It was an important year for many reasons that affected my generation and me. First of all, the Beatles released the album *Sgt. Pepper's Lonely Hearts Club Band*, which has become one of rock's most acclaimed albums in history. In large part, this was due to a high level of creativity and experimentation that went into the sounds and lyrics.

It was revolutionary. Music completely revolved around the Beatles.

Also happening around the same time was the release of the first issue of *Rolling Stone* magazine. John Lennon was on the first cover, and it sought to reflect a youthful perspective on issues ranging from music to politics.

It became popular from its first issue and even today hasn't lost a bit of luster. Otherwise in the music industry, stars were bursting at the seams.

I mean just read this rundown of groups and artists that broke onto the scene or continued to be popular throughout '67.

Ready for this?

The Beatles, the Rolling Stones, the Doors, the Monkees, Bob Dylan, Aretha Franklin, the Grateful Dead, Elvis Presley, the Beach Boys, the Bee Gees, Jimi Hendrix, Pink Floyd, and David Bowie.

That isn't even all of them.

I lived that.

It was an incredible time for a kid my age. And although not providing the same type of lasting effect, television was evolving as well. *The Beverly Hillbillies, Jeopardy, Bewitched, General Hospital, Doctor Who, I Dream of Jeannie,* and *Tom and Jerry* gained popularity throughout the year. Between the music and television, you really had a turn from the old ways of the world to influences of modern-day society being born.

CHAPTER 66

Back on the court after Christmas break, we were playing in the Clinton Invitational Basketball Tournament.

"What time are the finals?" I asked.

"Seven o'clock," answered Jerry Washburn.

So, that afternoon, we had a few hours to kill in beautiful downtown Clinton. It was the dead of winter, and it was snowing. Everybody was going to the local soda shop, so I figured I'd tag along. The only problem was that my street clothes were in Coach Jimmy Mabry's car, which was where we changed clothes between our first and second game.

Maybe chalk this decision in the mistake column. I went in my basketball togs—short shorts and a sleeveless jersey. I was freezing after about twenty feet, not to mention that I was wet from sweating in the game we had just finished. Once we arrived, we all grabbed ice-cold Cokes and slurped them down. After we finished up our sodas and chatted for a bit, we ran back in the snow, arriving in time for the big game.

Tweeeeeet went the referee's whistle in the second half.

"Foul on the defense. Shooting two," said the referee.

"I didn't even touch him," I pleaded with Coach Mabry.

The other team's forward had my number. He would go up for a shot and slap himself on the wrist. The referee in turn would call a foul on me. With five minutes left in the game, I fouled out.

Boo hoo!

On top of that, we lost the game. Regardless of what I have said in the past about losing, I hated to lose. It had become personal. Fortunately, I kept myself in check after the game and made it back home around nine that Saturday night. A couple days later, the unthinkable happened.

Illness struck me on Tuesday, and on Friday, I felt so bad that I didn't even get off of the school bus when we got to St. Joseph in the morning. I had a fever and was congested, so I just stayed on the bus and went back home. The bus driver was glad to take me back to the warm confines of 7714 Collier Road, which had been recently, and finally, given a mailbox number. What do you do on a Friday when you are home alone and sick as a dog at the age of twelve?

Try one of your dad's Camel non-filters.

Duh.

Dad smoked three packs a day, so he bought them by the carton. A carton of ten packs cost roughly ten dollars. Not bad. I didn't know how he did it, though. After a few drags, I thought I was going to puke. I didn't even know how to inhale, but I had to lie on the couch and hold on for dear life for a solid ten minutes. The entire room was spinning.

After I recovered from my therapeutic smoke break, it was time to check out Dad's *Playboy*s. He kept them in two big stacks under his bed. The mags were compliments of my Papaw and Firehouse #7. Nakedness was different back then. Nudie magazines were mainly all about breasts. They rarely showed hair that accompanied the lower half of a woman's body, and it would have been completely unacceptable to show what the hair was hiding.

My fascination with the magazines lasted all of about three minutes, so I put them back where I got them. About ten minutes after my smoke, I suddenly felt much worse, and it wasn't nausea. I did the only thing I could possibly think of, which was crawl back in bed and need my mom. She nursed me through the weekend as I got a little worse, and on Monday, she got me in to see Dr. Lawson. He was the only doctor in Powell at the time. After a chest X-ray, his diagnosis was simple.

"Steve has pneumonia, Ann. I'm going to have him admitted to St. Mary's Hospital."

So, straight to St. Mary's we went. It really wasn't all bad. My grandmother stayed with me all week. I also sort of enjoyed the extra attention, if I'm being honest. Uncle Dave brought me a pizza from the Brass Rail one day, and on Friday, a package was dropped off that contained letters from everyone in the seventh grade in an attempt to cheer me up and help pass the time.

I guess it paid off to *be nice, be friendly, and not get in trouble.*

My friends and teachers were concerned about me, and that was much appreciated. About halfway through the stack, I got to a letter from Johnny McLoughlin. He detailed how he had brought a Frisbee to school for the first time. When pressed by Larry Blaylock as to what it was called, he told him it was a *sizzletanger*. He then laughed at Larry as he told everyone to check out McLoughlin's *sizzletanger*. I could see the whole thing in my head and cracked up for a good five minutes picturing the event unfolding.

That Sunday morning, I got a clean bill of health. I knew that my updated status had come just in time for the finals of the Parochial School Basketball Tournament. It was being held at Knoxville Catholic High School.

The finals included St. Joseph versus Immaculate Conception.

Although I had just spent a day shy of a week in the hospital with pneumonia and completely against the doctor's orders, I pleaded until I was taken to the game. Mom told me that I could try to play but not to take it too far.

Try?

Yeah, right.

I know that this is a pretty silly source of a highly important thought pertaining to sports, or anything else for that matter, but it is very applicable, in my opinion. The quote is from Yoda in *Star Wars*, which came out years down the road, but it is identical to what I was thinking at the time. He said:

Do it. Or do not it. Just trying is not an option.

It rings true, though, if you are a dedicated teammate. Now, I know that medical clearance is taken much more seriously nowadays than it was in the '60s, but if you are given the green light, you should be out there. Why would you want to miss a game anyway? You only get so many a season. So, if you guessed that I played every minute of the game, you guessed right.

It was a really high-scoring affair. We were leading 12–10 at halftime, and I had six of our twelve points.

Damn the pleurisy!

Full speed ahead.

On the strength of layups, we blew them out in the second half. Killed them, really. The final score was 24–18. I ended up scoring fourteen of our twenty-four points. I owed my teammates for the letters they had sent me, and I had been ready to rock after my hospital stay had kept me out of the first few games of the tournament.

We were the champions!

Just another one under Coach Mabry's watch. We didn't go undefeated, but we sure weren't strangers to winning games and tournaments. He was a great coach, and he sure knew his basketball.

CHAPTER 67

After basketball ended, there was baseball. It was also on to my teenage years as I turned thirteen in March. My baseball team was good again this year, but we didn't match the outcome of the Hustlers. I was still glad to be participating in something through the spring, however. I wasn't in love with baseball, but I surely don't know what I would have done without it. It ended at the beginning of summer: time for mowing and finding ways to kill time.

Typically, it was just more of the same stuff. I'd travel to the other side of town to play in a good pickup game. There was nowhere I wasn't willing to go to get in on some action. We would play basketball at parks, schools, and anyplace else we could.

After the season was over, a group of us would still plan to meet up and play baseball throughout summer. Each week, we would set the game time for the following week. When it came to football, it really just came down to a few of us to play. If we had a large enough piece of grass to play on, we were down to play. Hell, sometimes we would even play two-hand touch on a black top. I guess all we really needed was a football, and we *always* had a football.

Otherwise, I did the normal stuff anybody my age did. I guess these things haven't been highlighted as much, but they were always a big part of my life. When I wasn't playing ball, I was typically at some sort of family function or passing time the best way I saw fit.

With McLoughlin.

Going to movies, stomping around with friends, grabbing some good grub at a diner, and hanging out with girls. Kids our age were much freer back in those times. The anxiety-driven need to be able to reach anybody, anywhere, at any given time hadn't become a thing yet. Sure, parents worried, but as a whole the world was much more trusting and trustworthy.

Maybe ignorance is bliss, but there wasn't tragedy spilling out of multiple news outlets all day every day, and the world acted accordingly. It was more peaceful that way too, in my opinion.

More carefree.

More natural.

Technology is great, but we are human. The advances we have made are incredible, but some of them can actually limit our experience as a person as much as they make other experiences more limitless. The world being at our fingertips is amazing, but it has come at the expense of face-to-face social interaction.

My generation thrived on social interaction. We would take the bus into downtown early in the day with no real plans. Before we got home at night, we would have made the best of our time and done all sorts of things.

It was cool back then. Because no one had cell phones, there was no way of telling who would be somewhere you went unless you'd made prior plans—which we hardly ever did.

With that said, most kids my age hung out at the same places all the time. There were hot spots all over town, and we would just go to them. It was cool to show up and run into whoever was there at the time. They would be surprised to see you. There were times when whoever you came with would go do something with the people you ran into. I was all for the way things were, and I certainly had my fair share of friends. I liked everybody, and everybody liked me. I wasn't judgmental or superficial. I didn't care where you grew up or what house you lived in.

If you were a good person and fun to be around, I would hang out with you.

It was my experience that most people were cool to be around. In fact, I later developed what I called the *3% Solution*. Once again, it pertains to my experience on the field and in life. It simply states:

3% of people are buttholes 97% of the time, while 97% of people are buttholes 3% of the time.

It holds true for my life, anyway, and I've been around a while now. As a thirteen-year-old, I was around kids all the time. Sure, kids could be mean, but really the rule held true. You would have a bully or two in every grade, and everybody else just wanted to avoid them and get along.

As summer dwindled down, I really got to thinking about the fact that I was only one more school year from being in high school. That really got me pumped up. I didn't know where I would go to high school or what it would be like. All I knew was that I had been preparing to play high-school athletics for a few years now, and I was inching closer by the day. Ultimately, I just hoped I would go to a school where I could play football and win some games!

Was that too much to ask?

CHAPTER 68

I really had no way of anticipating the way my life would change once school started. While sitting around wondering where I would end up going to high school, it didn't really dawn on me that the high-school coaches were wondering the same thing. Before we made it to our first game in eighth grade, it was impossible to miss. Coach Hill had brought it to my attention that high-school coaches had been in touch and that each time I stepped on the field, there was a set of eyes on me somewhere.

It was official.

I was a prospect.

A high-school football prospect.

My hard work and game-time performances had paid off.

I really tried to do all I could to downplay the whole matter. I just wanted to play my game. I knew if I did so, I would catch the eyes of the powers that be. Inevitably, just a few weeks later, it paid off, and I began receiving invitations to take a look at the high schools in the area. Multiple coaches from the district urged me to attend the preseason jamboree. I thought this would be a good way to get a feel for multiple programs at the same time. I probably would have gone either way, if I'm being honest. Mike was playing for Powell, and they were on the slate of teams to show off their talents for the year. Regardless, I went.

Mom dropped Johnny McLoughlin and me off at Evans-Collins Field where the jamboree was set to take place. Evans-Collins Field was home to two local high-school teams, one junior-high team, and the local semi-pro team named the Knoxville Bears. It was the Friday night before Labor Day, and folks from all over town had gathered for the event. Every team played a quarter against a team they didn't normally play during the season. Mike and the Powell Panthers were set to take on the South High Rockets in the first game.

Powell was wearing black and white while the Rockets wore all white with fancy red numerals. It was great to see all the teams just sitting there in their uniforms waiting for their fifteen minutes of fame. My imagination ran wild as I pictured myself in each getup.

Powell ended up winning 7–0. After their game, we watched as a few more games were played. About halfway through the night, the jamboree held a punt, pass, and kick contest. With Mike being the punter at Powell, he participated. He fared well on the punt portion but lost by a long shot after the other two events. The next two teams up to play warmed up at the north end of the stadium.

I had an interest in the next two teams. It was time for the Knoxville Catholic High Fighting Irish to play the Young High Yellow Jackets. Mom was an alumna of Knoxville Catholic, and their head coach was one of those who had urged Coach Hill to point me toward the jamboree. Before they took to the field, Johnny and I made our way down to the closest point we could near the sideline. From there, we watched the end of the Fighting Irish warm-up. I thought the jumping jacks they did were pretty cool as I was trying to be as objective as possible while scoping them out.

Coach Hill told me beforehand that if I made it to the jamboree, Knoxville Catholic's coach, Donnie West, would find me on the sideline before they played. Sure enough, he walked up to me like he had known me his entire life. It was almost surreal for these coaches to think so highly of my playing ability that they knew exactly who I was. Coach West was full go in his best flat-top persona.

"So, how do you think you'll do?" I asked.

"The best thing that could happen would be for us to lose. We played Central High in a scrimmage and accidentally ended up winning," he responded.

Wait a second. What? I thought to myself. *The best thing that could happen would be to lose?*

I thought you always played to win!

Down the road, I was let in on a certain verbiage that really summed up how I thought about this encounter. It is a really important point to be made regarding the mental aspect of being a winner. That guy Vince Lombardi, who took over as the Packers head coach when I was five, must have really done things right. Not only did he become the epitome of winning ways, but people also repeated his mantras everywhere you turned in the sports world. He said it best when he pointed out:

Winning is a habit. Unfortunately, so is losing.

I was seeking the opportunity to win football games not lose them. I had already experienced playing with a team that did plenty of that. For this reason, I had some serious questions regarding Coach West.

Realistically, what the hell was he talking about? I think he was trying to downplay his team to the scouts for his regular-season foes. If they lost in the jamboree, the scouts would report that Knoxville Catholic was having a down year when they got back to their respective social circles.

I thought he should do the exact opposite. If you could win by five touchdowns in fifteen minutes, then do it. Then the scouts would go back and tell everyone, "You don't want to play those Catholic boys this year! They are a tough bunch."

It was my thinking that you should always try to win. Losing would happen at some point for most teams, but trying as hard as you could to not endure that outcome was a substantial part of winning. Giving your best effort to come out on top. In fact, Vince Lombardi also made a great point about this as well. He said:

Winning isn't everything, but wanting to win is.

As far as I am concerned and the longer I live, I believe an unwritten rule of sorts. It was the player's job to give it their best effort at all times, and it was the coach's job to put his team in the best position to win.

Anybody can lose.

It doesn't take any talent to lose.

But always remember:

The only thing there is to learn from losing is what you need to do to get back to winning.

Even at thirteen years old, I realized that winning was an art. Poetry in motion that flowed together seamlessly. It was the product of each and every player knowing their role and doing it to the best of their ability. Which brings me to my next point, which is simply:

An all-star team will always beat a team of all-stars.

You can have the most talented players in a league all in the same uniform on game day, but if they can't come together as a unit, they won't reach their potential. This will almost always prove to be true, so you should give yourself the best chance by building chemistry with your teammates and buying into the system. It will pay off with hardware on the playing field and other desirable luxuries in a later life. All of these concepts can be applied to a life perspective if you allow them to be.

As far as Coach West was concerned, he got his wish. Knoxville Catholic lost 13-0 in just one quarter. Color me unimpressed. Looking back on it, I could go on and on about what I thought of this outcome. A great friend of mine named Frankie Walland once said:

You only shoot as high as you aim.

All of these sayings were applicable to the Fighting Irish at the jamboree. I was bummed about it too. If I had to put a number on things, Knoxville Catholic was easily one of my top three choices for high schools to attend. Now I really needed to take a deep breath, sit back, and think about everything. One of the other schools that I was looking at had won.

The Powell Panthers were close to home, and they definitely seemed to take a more serious approach to their test drive in the jamboree. The decision wouldn't have to be made for almost a year, though. At least I had time on my side.

Ouch

"Welcome to Erlanger Medical Center. How can I help you?"

"We're here for Steve Adkins. He was just airlifted in from Hamilton Medical Center. Where did they take him?" Danny asked the receptionist as Bella and Paul stood by his side.

From his point of view, they couldn't get to me quick enough. It was approximately 12:30 p.m., and they had me in an emergency cubicle. Other members of our family started rushing in from all over the map.

By early evening, I was transferred to the Intensive Care Unit, and Bella finally got to speak with the stroke specialist. He explained to her that I had suffered a brain-stem stroke. There aren't good strokes, but there are worse strokes. A brain-stem stroke is one of the worst ones you can have.

The way they explained it to Bella was that a stroke of this kind was like a hard reset on a computer. Everything your mind and body knows, and knows how to do, is reset. All that he and the rest of my family knew was that I was alive and that I would live to see another day.

Thank God!

I'm told that I was awake and responsive to an extent that day. I had undergone various tests. Some were small like raising both of my arms as high as I could. Some were more intensive like the brain scan. My most noticeable ailment was the drooping right half of my face.

This was told to me by multiple people who showed up to be by my side that day.

In all, I probably saw over a hundred faces.

Nurses, doctors, and techs. My wife. My boys. My other children, Staci and William. My sisters and my mother. Family on Bella's side. I spent very little time alone, and I'm sure I liked it that way.

In time, I have heard many accounts of what I underwent that day. All of them ended in the same way.

I had fear in my heart.

I was scared.

I was sad.

In the twenty years previous to that day, I can remember crying twice. On that day, I'm told I cried more than two dozen times. I'm sure I was heartbroken at the thought of what type of impact it made on those who meant the most to me.

I was heartbroken at the thought of what it meant for me.

I still am. I have tried to conjure up some type of recollection of the events that unfolded on that horrific day, to no avail. Honestly, I don't remember a single second of it. Nothing past lying on the floor of my office that morning talking to the doctor before everything faded away.

Like a leaf blowing in the wind, I was just along for the ride.

CHAPTER 69

A few weeks later, the Volunteers opened their season out in Los Angeles. They entered the season #9 in the country, and they were set to play #8 UCLA. As I was growing older and getting closer to playing in high school, I knew that college was only five years away. Thinking about it all and playing had me really ready for the season to ramp up. Unfortunately, Uncle Dave and I sat in disappointment at Grandmother's house on September 16, after Tennessee's opening 20–16 loss.

The next week though, we were fired up again to watch Tennessee take on Auburn at Neyland. Auburn was a great team during my childhood. They slumped a little throughout the 1960s, and I was always glad when the Volunteers capitalized on it. In 1967, the Volunteers capitalized on a down Tiger team to the tune of 27–13. The next week, we got to see them knock off Georgia Tech 24–13. This bumped the Vols back up to #7 in the country heading into the Alabama game.

The game was at Legion Field in Birmingham, so we sat at Grandmother's and tuned in to the radio broadcast. During the game, I noticed that my uncle was really putting back the whiskey. Before the game had ended, it was undeniable that he was completely trashed. Instead of celebrating with me after the Vols 24–13 win, he stumbled to his room and passed out.

I hated to see him that way, but I shook it off. The next week, Tennessee climbed to #4 in the ranks before taking on LSU back in Knoxville. Uncle Dave still had his flask in hand at the game but was back to his more normal ways as we contributed to the electric atmosphere inside Neyland

Stadium. The game was close, and when time expired, we had edged the Tigers 17–14.

While watching the game, I was really drawn into thoughts of playing for the Vols one day. I always thought about what it would be like to play for them, but this was more like the thoughts I had when I was a child.

Making the big play.

The crowd roaring because of something I had done on the field.

Celebrating with my fellow teammates at the end of a game inside Neyland Stadium.

I wanted it so badly I could taste it.

Most importantly, I knew that in time I could achieve it.

The following week's paper confirmed that the Vols had climbed another spot in the rankings to #3. After destroying Tampa 38–0, they climbed another spot to #2 before beating down Tulsa 35–14 to which Uncle David and I bore witness. The next week we avenged our previous two losses to Ole Miss in a 20–7 win. Finally, we ended the season with a 17–7 win over Kentucky before handing Vanderbilt a 41–14 shellacking.

This put us at 8-1 for the season and undefeated at 6–0 in the SEC. The Crimson Tide finished just behind us at 5-1 in the SEC, thanks to us. This, of course, meant we were SEC Champs. Our #2 Volunteers were invited to play the #3 Oklahoma Sooners in the Orange Bowl down in Miami. They were also 8-1 with their only loss coming to their rival, the Texas Longhorns. As ecstatic as you could imagine, we tuned in to NBC to watch the big game.

The game was a huge deal, and there were over seventy-seven thousand people in the stands. The game certainly didn't disappoint, but Vols fans ended up disappointed, nonetheless. We lost the game 26–24 to end the season at 9-2.

CHAPTER 70

About halfway through our season back at St. Joseph, I was finally approached by a familiar face. Across town at Sacred Heart, my good friend Bill Murray was also a prospect. Bill and I both were given an opportunity or invitation, so to speak.

You remember Bill, right?

He was the one who hit the car with a rock in our younger years.

Good ol' Bill.

We would see each other from time to time. Fortunately, upon my first invitation to attend a specific high-school game, Bill was also invited.

We traveled together to see West High School play Knoxville Catholic at West. That is, Knoxville Catholic High School, aka Knox Catholic, aka KCHS, aka Catholic.

Just *Catholic.*

It was *the* Catholic high school in the area and needed no other accompanying moniker on the local scene. We had both been invited during in-person visits from Coach West. I was still interested in Catholic, although I questioned the losing-jamboree effort. I owed it to myself to give them a second chance to impress me. Bill and I traveled shared a seat on the back of the team bus.

Off we go!

"How's your team doing?" I asked Bill.

"Pretty good. We're sitting at 6-2. How about you guys?"

"We're 2-3, and for St. Joseph, that's pretty good," I answered. "How did you and Kay Moorman do in the big eighth-grade waltz?"

"We came in third. How did you and Suzanne Shrader finish?"

"We won," I said before our conversation moved on to the task at hand.

Bill and I both thought Catholic was pretty appealing. They had lots of good athletes. My personal favorites were their backs: Joe Proctor at scatback, and my hero Denny O'Brien at fullback. We arrived at West High and took our spots at the end of the bench.

"I know you like Knox Catholic, but where do you think you'll end up playing high-school ball?" I asked Bill.

"Pretty dead set on Catholic. How about you?"

"I'm really undecided right now," I told him.

Our attention then turned to the captains heading out for the coin toss. I was taking the whole thing in. I even stopped panning the scene to admire how impressive Denny O'Brien's girlfriend was. Her name was Kathy Rogers, and she was easily the best-looking girl on Catholic's cheer squad.

To say it was a track meet would be an understatement. Catholic scored first on a 43-yard run by Joe Proctor. That was followed by West scoring, then Catholic, then West, and so on.

Denny O'Brien got hurt and had to go to the locker room with Dr. Reed, and this was all before halftime. The suspense was killing me as West was winning 21–20 going into the half due to a missed Catholic extra point. I knew they still had Proctor, but what was Catholic going to do without O'Brien out there making plays?

Just before the second half started, it began to rain—it came down in buckets, and all of the dust turned to mud. I remember early in the second half, Coach West got pissed and threw a helmet through a blackboard.

Another distinct memory, halfway through the third quarter when they needed him most, Denny O'Brien trotted back out onto the field, and the Catholic crowd went wild. It was the spark they needed to get their heads back into the game.

There was a lot going on, and I was soaking it up like a sponge. The whole atmosphere. The way they played. The most impressive thing was everyone's speed. I was also particularly impressed with a guy named Nick Pappas. He was Catholic's center and middle linebacker. He played every snap with perfect technique and posture. To me, he was the perfect Catholic soldier on that night.

Catholic was fired up when Denny O'Brien returned to the game. Unfortunately, so was West.

Challenge accepted.

The lead changed repeatedly. Again, Catholic would score, and then West, and then Catholic. Proctor and O'Brien went for over two hundred yards on the ground, an offensive player's dream. Catholic ended up with the ball 4th and goal at the 2-yard line, with ten seconds left on the clock. Coach West apparently had no faith in the kicker after the missed extra point in the first half. Subsequently, they went for it. They handed the ball off to O'Brien for an off tackle for the win. Just when it looked like he was going in for the score, a player from West came flying in and knocked him out of bounds at the half-yard line. In doing so, they won the game 41–40.

Are you kidding me?

All of that for a freakin' loss?

It was exhausting just to watch.

West picked one hell of a time to make a defensive stand.

How do you score forty points and lose in a high-school game?

Can you spell *defense*?

Although the outcome was undesirable sitting on the Catholic side-line, it was still a heck of a game. Bill and I had a blast. Watching the game really got me looking forward to being on a high-school gridiron more than ever. I also must admit that Coach West's passion and coaching presence left me with a completely different opinion of him than our previous encounter had. I really needed to get down to the nitty-gritty in regard to making a decision about where I would go. It wasn't easy for me, though.

Catholic had certainly helped their cause on this night. Still, I knew everything would point in the right direction, so I decided to be patient and trust the process.

CHAPTER 71

Toward the end of the season, I visited other schools for games. Each one had a unique set of qualities. Some good and some bad. There were really small schools and really big schools. There were annual powerhouses. Schools that were known for being a team you scheduled for homecoming. Some that were affiliated with religions, and some that were public. There were all sorts of different options to weigh.

But every school had one common trait.

It was something that you didn't experience on a typical day at mighty St. Joseph. I guess this was because when we played, we were all really just focusing on trying to get better and get through the games. The common trait with high schools, though, was probably the one thing you had to understand to be able to make it as a ball player back in those days. It was summed up fairly easily.

Rough and tough!

It was fast, physical, and brute.

Around anyone other than my mom and perhaps my grandparents, I was already accustomed to being a certain way. If you were a boy, there were rules to life. You didn't cry. You didn't tattle. You didn't go to the doctor unless it was life-threatening or due to a broken bone that needed a cast. If you did have to go to the doctor, you followed that up by doing stuff like playing sports in said cast or with pleurisy despite getting out of the hospital after a week with pneumonia.

Parallel to all of this was another way of being in my day. If you had a problem that couldn't be talked out, you took things *outside*. In the case that you were already outside, you just stopped what you were doing and duked it out on the spot.

My youthful confrontations with the likes of Dennis Turner and the kid from the neighborhood on the other side of Christenberry Elementary would eventually prove to be useful. Of course, they were also accompanied by probably a handful of other fistfights I had in my life. None of which I am proud of.

In fact, back in sixth grade, I even got whooped by an eighth grader over a misunderstanding. I also still had my daily dose of Mike to deal with. All of this is important because it went a long way for me. We all grew up like this, though. To varying degrees, we all had a similar experience by the time we were this age. It was accepted, and everyone from poor folks to the privileged rich respected the ways you handled yourself and particular situations.

Of course, some kids had it worse than others. By *worse* I just mean that they were forced into tough situations more often or grew up in tough environments period. We all remember the stories of Dad's daily behavioral check-in. It would turn out to be quite painful anytime he didn't approve of our actions. For other kids, however, it was much worse at home. Some kids would get the hell beat out of them by their fathers. Truth is, it was more accepted than it should have been, and people were rarely charged with child abuse. So, we all learned to suck it up, toughen up, shut up, and move on.

I never thought it would ever amount to much, but once I'd seen some high-school games and practices, I knew that the mentality of growing up that way was what you really gained. Hitting hard, playing physical, and being bullish were all ingrained in me instead of being something I had to talk myself up in order to do.

When I visited high schools or was around teams, it became very clear to me that football carried this to another level of life. A lot of coaches acted more like dictators. They were in-your-face, rough, and insulting. For the most part, it was geared toward motivation, but you'd better have some mettle if you wanted to play high-school football in those times. This was incredibly true when it came to injuries. A concussion meant that you were going to be back in the game within a few plays if you weren't unconscious or throwing up.

Actually, you may have been back in depending on the way the game was going even if you were throwing up. If you broke a bone, it better be protruding from your skin if you thought you were coming out of the game. Most guys didn't want to come out when they were hurt, anyway. It was just the way we had been taught. The way you had instinctively learned to think.

Honestly, I loved it!

Call me crazy, but I thought it was exactly how it should be. It eliminated a lot of the less talented players from playing. It just wasn't worth the abuse to be a bad player. For those that stuck around, it could get pretty ugly. Therefore, what you had left was a bunch of high-school football teams that were made up of players who were game. They were ready to play whenever, wherever, and there was no backing down.

Perfect if you ask me.

CHAPTER 72

When our football season finished at St. Joseph, I played basketball again. When the holidays rolled around, we did our usual routines, and it was over to 1968. I was interested in playing as many sports in high school as possible, so I continued to venture out to visit schools to see how their other athletic teams fared.

My decision was coming down to just two schools. Knoxville Catholic had begun to really impress me. But Powell was close to the house, and they were equally as impressive. They both had good athletic programs, and they both would have some of my current classmates attending them.

Although we hardly got along, I knew if I went to Powell I would get to play football with Mike for a year. It would be pretty cool, and as it stood, he was actually gaining some attention due to his size and athleticism. He even had a few college coaches talk to him, which I was extremely impressed with. Mike was a big ol' boy. I'm talking over two hundred pounds and about six and a half feet tall as a junior. As a bonus, he was the fastest guy I knew. In fact, even as athletic as I was and with the size difference, I never beat Mike in a foot race. The colleges that were talking to him weren't scrubs, either. Florida State was the only one he paid much attention to.

On the other hand, Knoxville Catholic had definitely done more than anyone else in trying to get me to come there. It was certainly a tough decision, and time was now running out with only a few months before I was expected to begin summer workouts with one the two football teams.

Another thing that was consistent in my life during the winter months was Uncle David. He was always ready and willing to spend time with his favorite nephew.

As each year passed, I continued to view him as the main father figure in my life.

In turn, he viewed me as the son he never had.

We were a good team.

We went to all the Knoxville Knights hockey games that we could make our way to. If the game dates fell when our schedules were open, we were there. Sometimes we would go together, and sometimes we would plan to meet there. Typically, it was the former and we would meet at Grandmother's house. We were huge fans to say the least, and every game was a blast.

The games were held during the week at the Civic Auditorium, and we always sat in the same seats next to an elderly black gentleman and his grandson. The seats were general admission and cost a buck.

Literally one dollar.

The four us were always the only ones in section AA, which was just south of the buttered-popcorn machine on the southeast balcony. I know all of this because I spent a lot of time scoping out the specifics while I mustered up the courage to ask for thirty-five cents to buy some popcorn and another fifteen cents for a Coke at every game we attended. Even though my uncle had a drinking habit to pay for, he was always happy to spare me the two quarters.

For the majority of my tenure as a fan, the Knights had two star players. Their names were Don Label and Gil Champlain. Those two guys were great and never failed to entertain. Of course, the Knoxville Knights games were always entertaining. They were even more entertaining on certain occasions. Those occasions were when their nemeses, the Nashville Dixie Flyers, were in town.

There were always fights when they were in town. One time they blew the whistle to start the game, and every player on the ice dropped their gloves and started brawling. It was more like we had gone to a fight and a hockey game broke out.

I remember one time I had to go to the restroom very badly, but the game was really close. At an opportune time, I took off. I went blowing into the first available spot, which happened to be a stall. I finished up and went to wash my hands and dry them off. As I looked at the other spectators coming in and out, I stood there wondering why all these women were in the men's restroom.

Fortunately, my embarrassment didn't last long because just as I got back to my seat, I snagged a puck that was shot over the glass, and I was overwhelmed with excitement.

Lucky me!

After the games, we crossed the viaduct to Frank's Brass Rail. Gus Constantine knew us well from all of the Volunteer and Knights games. He didn't even ask what we wanted before dropping off a cheese pizza and ginger ale. It was the greatest time, and I grew to love Gus. He was like family, and he always treated us extra special. When we finally made it back to my grandmother's, it was usually late, so Uncle Dave would let me crash with him. I'd make my way to school from there the following day.

Back at the schoolyard, it was turning from winter to spring. I turned fourteen and hit another growth spurt. By the time May rolled around, I was five feet ten and weighed in at 170 pounds. I was ready for what the future held for me. I weighed the pros and cons for Powell and Catholic daily. It was really tough to determine which one was the better option for me.

That gleaming moment that made one of the two the undoubtedly right choice still hadn't come.

Outside of school, I hung out with all my friends as often as possible. Anything we could do together, we did. I knew some of them would go to other high schools, so I wouldn't get to see them as often, moving forward. Mainly, I spent a lot of time with Johnny.

Funnier than ever, he made my time spent with him time well spent.

He was always dropping one-liners on girls and goofing off. His hilarity never ran out. We were like the perfect one-two punch when we were around each other. He was the outlandish comedian, and I was the more reserved, nice guy. Both charming in our own ways.

Handsome too!

I had my fair share of cracks as well, but I definitely didn't measure up to Johnny. He too had undergone a lot of change in the last few years, but growing older never changed his magnetic sense of humor.

Finally, school came to an end and decision time had come calling. Only a few months now, and I would be either a Powell Panther or a member of the Knoxville Catholic High School Fighting Irish.

I talked it over with those close to me.

I got my parents' thoughts. I got my grandparents'.

Uncle Dave's.

I ran it by some of my friends and took inventory of where those I was closest to had decided to spend their high-school years. They all gave me some good feedback, but in the end, they all said the same thing.

"It is your decision to live with, Steve. We understand you have put a lot of thought into this. Ultimately, it is all up to you."

I trusted my decision-making.

I knew I would make the right decision.

CHAPTER 75

1968–1970

Knoxville, Tennessee

High School

At the time, I hadn't realized the magnitude of the monumental decision that was looming. My world had me sitting at a crossroads, and I knew that it would be a big deal. I thought about playing time and girlfriends. I thought about winning games and school dances. I thought about what the teachers would be like and how much fun I'd have at school. The decision between Catholic and Powell was a big deal in the eyes of the young teen that I was.

Not a single fiber of my being could have possibly realized the tectonic role this decision would play in my life.

The people I would encounter due to it.

The ways I would grow and mature.

The relationships I would be blessed to build—and avoid. I had, however, recently spent some time thinking about just how big one moment could be in a person's life, and because of that, I wanted to do everything I must to get it right.

The thought of what a single moment could mean to a person's life stemmed from two rounds of tragedy that struck the world in 1968. Now, there were tons of tragedy going on in '68, but to me, there were a few that really brought things home on a personal level. Yes, Vietnam continued to rage on. Yes, the Space Race continued to accelerate. These events however, had a much smaller bearing on my personal thoughts than the assassination of two American men.

Martin Luther King Jr. was assassinated on April 4, in Memphis, Tennessee—my home state—by a man named James Earl Ray. Now, at this time in my life, I still didn't realize the true heroics of King's efforts. I did know that a man who stood for something good, and something I agreed with, was killed because of his influence, not only on the United States but also on the world. He believed in something.

He had a passion for something and ended up making the ultimate sacrifice in the name of it.

Civil rights.

The equality of all men.

The announcement of his death made me realize just how fragile life really is. How, no matter what you have or haven't done, accomplished or failed, triumphed over or succumbed to, it could all be taken away in a moment. This further pushed my thoughts toward how important each and every moment is. How important each decision you make is.

There are no guarantees in this world, and it is easier to go through the effort of getting things right on the first go around. Even if at first you waste efforts in the wrong decision, it is never too late to make the right decision.

Martin Luther King Jr. had got things right and had gone about things the right way.

The honest way.

That was admirable in and of itself, but what he stood for was, in my opinion, something worth standing for. Why divide the human race for the sake of singling out a particular skin tone? Why take rights away from a man due to the pigment of his skin? Think of the minds wasted that could have helped so many fields. Think about the ideas that never came to fruition because of the color of the face that was in front of a brilliant mind. It is criminal.

It is unreasonable and irrational.

Martin Luther King Jr. is one who I think everyone wishes they could have back. James Earl Ray spent the rest of his life in prison. In my opinion, you could have a hundred James Earl Rays waste away in prison, and it still wouldn't do justice for the life he took. The life of a world changer.

The life of a highly influential man.

The life of a true hero.

The life of a believer.

The life of a man who was taken away in one terrible, sad, and tragic moment.

On June 5th, just two months and a day after King was killed, another tragedy occurred. The assassination of Robert F. Kennedy, JFK's brother. Just short of five years apart, they had both been shot dead. He was better known as Bobby Kennedy, and he was quite the politician himself.

Posthumously, Sirhan Sirhan took the fall. The Palestinian/Jordanian immigrant shot Bobby in the head and back in the kitchen corridor of the Ambassador Hotel, where Kennedy had just given a speech. After being rushed to the hospital and undergoing brain surgery, Robert Kennedy was pronounced dead twenty-six hours after the attack. He was only forty-two years old.

This, once again, got me thinking about how pivotal a moment can be. Of course, the decision that was in front of me wasn't life-threatening, but it is in these big life decisions that the future is paved. I aspired to play football at Tennessee one day, and this decision would place trust in one of the two schools to get me there. At the very least support my ambitions along the way and help develop me into the caliber of player I would need to be.

Not just physically, but mentally.

Other major things happening in the world at the time included the airbag being invented and the beginning of the emergency 9-1-1 telephone service. Later in the year, Apollo 8 became the first manned spacecraft to orbit the moon. Otherwise you had some great things happening for a person of my age: once again, the Beatles and the Rolling Stones blew up the music scene. Fleetwood Mac, Marvin Gaye, the Doors, and multiple other big names hit home through the beloved radio waves.

Planet of the Apes hit theaters in 1968. In more pressing matters as far as I was concerned, you had the fashion world flirting with see-through blouses to accompany miniskirts.

From where I was sitting with Uncle Dave in McDonald's, you also had another great first, the Big Mac. At a grand total of forty-nine cents, it was exactly what I was ready to try out as my decision was only getting closer. As we enjoyed our burgers, I once again went over the pros and cons with my trusty uncle.

Again, he just told me that the decision was really up to me and that his only advice was to go where my heart took me.

CHAPTER 76

Through that summer, I kept up my mowing gig. I had become obsessed with making the right decision, and it was through earning my weekly income that I found even more time to ponder everything.

I visualized myself in the uniforms.

I visualized making big plays and the crowds going wild.

I thought of the friends I would have at each school. I thought of the friends I would lose by going to a different school. I imagined the new friends I would make, and I imagined interactions with the coaches. I also kept up my conditioning by, once again, finding any and every athletic activity in the area and taking part in it—mainly football.

As I lived in Powell, I even played pickup with some guys who I would be playing with at Powell High if I went there.

They told me more about the school and the other players. They told me about girls and what it was like to be a Panther on Friday nights under the lights. How the whole town would shut down and come watch them play.

I have to admit, it all seemed intriguing, and their sincere love for their alma mater helped me see that there would be good times to be had at the school less than a mile from my home. The fact that it was so close didn't hurt either.

Maybe my family would come watch me play. I was determined to be a star player, and if I succeeded at doing so, it would make me the new Jim Courtney. And again, Mike played for them, and even though he and I didn't get along much, I thought it would be a valuable experience. It could do us some good getting to play together for a year.

As the days went by, I found out that some of my friends had made a decision about what school they would go to. Johnny McLoughlin going to Catholic was a big one for me. I had also received news that Bill Murray would, in fact, be going to Catholic also. I had always hoped there would come a day we got to play ball together. Catholic was Mom's alma mater, and I had been raised in the Catholic school system throughout the years. Coach West had also really impressed me with the passion he displayed during my trip to see them play, as well as other times later in the year when I watched.

He was intense.

He also thought very highly of me and expressed his opinions willingly.

Coach Henley at Powell was a little more reserved in that sense. That wasn't a problem for me, but it was nice to have someone so pleased with your skills, so willing to tell you all the ways you were great. The other thing that Catholic had going for them, as silly as it may seem, was the fact that they were called the Fighting Irish.

I loved it.

I thought it was cool.

As summer drew to a close and I was ready for the big decision to be behind me, I came to my conclusion. I did the only thing that would free me from the constant obsession over where to go, the only thing that would relieve me of weighing the pros and cons, the one and only thing left to do.

I made a decision.

Or so I thought.

CHAPTER 77

Upon walking up to Powell's practice field for the first time, I felt ready to make the big leap to high school. With school starting in just a few weeks, it was time for preseason football practice. Coach Henley had made it clear to me that I was one of the top five prospects they had. After being there for only a few minutes, it was evident that they had ended up with four of the top targets they were aiming for: Mike McConkey, Ronnie Franklin, Bubba Woody, and I all stood there with chatter all around and eyes giving us a gaze. Of course, we were in the middle of a pack of other soon-to-be freshmen, but we stood together. There was a buzz surrounding us with the older guys who really seemed to be glad we were there.

I guess we were some great prospective additions to the team heading into the season, and it was understood that we could, in some way, help their chances of winning a bunch of games.

The four of us highly touted guys knew each other from word of mouth or meeting one another during our time checking out schools as prospects. In the event that there was any question, it was also easy to know who was who because everyone knew where the others had played ball in grade school. Only having our grade-school garb to practice in, it only took seconds to figure out who was who. We didn't have much time to get acquainted, though. After a brief speech by Coach Henley, it was time for some highly anticipated high-school conditioning. With the depiction I had played out in my mind over the summer, I figured it would be unbelievable.

Impossible!

Take us to the brink of death before slowly reeling us back in.

After twenty minutes of it, I couldn't help thinking that I was right to a degree. It was unbelievable. I couldn't help thinking how unbelievably nonchalant the whole thing was. I certainly wasn't dying, and if the team came with me on my daily routine during summer, they would probably consider it intensive by comparison. I was extremely unimpressed, and I wanted things to get better in a hurry. I had put so much time into my decision to be at Powell. I couldn't imagine it going the wrong way.

I wanted to be pushed.

I wanted to be spent.

I wanted to hurt.

I wanted to be sore.

All of this for the sake of wanting to be better.

I was in the middle of practice on the last day of our opening week. Every practice to this point had had the same level of intensity, and I was ready to pick it up. After Coach Henley came over and said that he needed a couple guys to play full-speed defense in a scrimmage, I felt my eyes widen and a smile sneak onto my face. I was still a bit reserved with it being a new environment and all, but at the urging of my brother and a couple of his buddies, I raised my hand. To my dismay, Coach Henley wouldn't have anything to do with a freshman getting the first reps of the year at full speed.

In fact, it was almost as if he was insulted that I would think he would consider giving me a shot. He looked at me and half laughed before telling me to put my hand down and calling out a junior who was standing behind me.

The next week didn't get any better. When I left practice on the second Friday I had spent practicing with Powell, I was exasperated.

To be forward, I thought it was bullshit.

I wasn't being pushed to get better, nor was I being given the chance to show that I was good.

I could only wonder why you would waste so much effort trying to get a kid to come play for you only to belittle him and make him feel like he was no big deal. For Coach Henley, that spelled trouble. Trouble in a few forms as a matter of fact. First of all, I knew what I was capable of, and I knew the kind of skill set I had. I had played ball with some of the best Powell had to offer in pickup games and had done more than hold my own.

The second problem he had pulled into my driveway as I got to my front door after returning home from practice. It wasn't the car itself that was the issue to Coach Henley. Instead, it was the man exiting the car.

This brings me to a very important point. It is one of the biggest things you need to understand about coming out on top in life and on the athletic field. It is the one thing that you cannot control by preparing, playing hard, or carrying yourself in a winning way. It is simple, has a few different ways of being viewed, and it goes as follows:

The Lord works in mysterious ways.

—and—

Sometimes God has different plans for us than we have for ourselves.

I knew the man as Jim Hannifan. Jim had watched Powell's practice but only for the sake of seeing how everything was going with me and one other incoming freshman. Jim's allegiance was to Knoxville Catholic High School, and he knew my parents. He knew that my dad worked tirelessly, that we were barely a lower-middle-class family, and that Mom had gone to KCHS.

The cost to enroll at Catholic was five hundred dollars.

In those days, that was a lot.

Hell, I still consider that to be a lot.

Even with my parents raising me in Catholic schools, continued education at Knoxville Catholic was always going to be a strain on them. I guess you could describe that as a variable leading up to my decision about where to go to high school.

From both athletic and academic standpoints.

It was like the outlier that withdrew Catholic from the running, even though I had spent so much time considering them anyway. I decided on Powell for other reasons, but I always knew that I would have to cross the price-of-tuition bridge with Dad had I decided on the Fighting Irish. Even then, I could have been forced to go to Powell, due to the price of tuition alone. I didn't like asking my dad for things nor the way I felt when I had to. All of which made my decision of going to Powell seem much more comfortable.

Regarding that topic, it was my stance that Dad worked all the time, and I didn't want to be the reason for him working even more. A few days prior, I had discussed my current discouragement with Powell and how things were going for me on the practice field. Dad didn't pay me much attention, but I could tell that Mom wanted more for me. She also had always enjoyed the thought of me going to Catholic like she had. When it came down to it, my Dad's only issue with Catholic would have been the money.

I could hear the whole conversation between Jim and my parents playing out on the front porch. Catholic still wanted me, and it definitely wasn't too late. When the topic of money came up and the fact that I was already spending time with the kids at Powell, Jim knew exactly what to say.

"If he goes to Catholic, you won't have to pay a thing. Plus, there are kids enrolling at Catholic High from St. Joseph every day. He will know a lot of the kids in the incoming class. Think about it. We would love to see him out there."

I smiled as he backed out of the driveway and my parents came in. They sat me down to talk. My mom told me about the conversation I had just overheard, and I tried to act like I was hearing it for the first time. Dad finally looked at me and said that Catholic was offering me a scholarship.

After that came out of his mouth, I drifted off into thoughts as they continued talking. I heard them but couldn't tell you a single word that was coming out of their mouths. At some point Dad stood up, went to get ready, and headed off to work. Mom disappeared into the kitchen a little while later.

The whole time, all I could think about was one thing.

It is never too late to make the right decision.

The Observation

Wednesday, May 14, 2008

Chattanooga, Tennessee

Fifty-four Years Old

As I lay there in the hospital bed, I was both aware and unaware of the sheet pulled up to my chest, the monitors hooked up to me, the curtains pulled to, and the nurses coming in and out to make sure I was okay and chart my status. The thought of having been lucid and conscious without the ability to recall anything happening is a bit eerie. I truly can't speak for myself regarding how I felt about what was going on. I will say that my family has told me that I was in shambles. For the first time in my life, I appeared broken and afraid. It is an odd thought of sorts.

The people who viewed me as the foundation of our family were facing the fears that dwelled within me. Medicated, emotional, completely out of control, begging for mercy, and most of all, sorry.

All things that were completely foreign to those I cared about the most due to living the life of a man's man.

I wonder if it were truly ever worth it—to try and be a conqueror of all things I experienced my whole life, to always seem level and centered in the midst of chaos. The true problem was that it was indeed not always the reality. Still, I didn't want to come off any other way. I am sure that in the strength I conducted myself with over the years, my family gained a false sense that I was bulletproof.

To let yourself prevail over the worst of situations, to overcome hardships and shortcomings: in a way, I truly had done those things. But i

n the end, it was foolish to think that I could overcome everything that life had in store for me at the exact moment it happened. Sure, you can overcome things in time, but you have to work at it, if you are even given the opportunity. The opportunity is not guaranteed, and we never really know when we will take our last breath. I certainly learned that lesson as I lay in my current state wondering if I would live.

The demeanor and ideology that I had lived with for so long was taken away in mere seconds. This, of course, allowed a more important lesson to be learned than the one I'd taught for so long. That was that no one man is bigger than life, and in my experience, I would go even farther by saying that God is the ultimate director of our tomorrows.

No matter what we try to create as our self-image, we are truly, deep down, only what he created us to be. All of that is in accordance with what he has in store for us to do in life. Free will allows us to deny our true purpose or seek it with haste. Either way, in an instant, God can restore order to our path if he chooses to do so.

If we are honest with ourselves, we will see the magnetic force that we experience on a daily basis to create our own version of ourselves and take pride in it. Pride should really only be taken in what God has chosen for us, and all of the glory should go to him for what he has let us accomplish.

Through the experiences of my life, I would now say that resistance will only lead to our personal demise.

The ultimate demise would be living an entire lifetime and never even realizing why you were sent here.

I had prayed for a long time to have the ability to slow down and stop bad habits. Admittedly, those prayers were sent to a God that I wasn't sure of. I wasn't sure of what I believed in and spent a lot of time learning about all sorts of belief systems and religions. In time, I was given the answers to my prayers by the one and only God. Although, it was in the form of something that I would have never planned myself—my stroke.

Nevertheless, my prayers were answered, and that, of course, showed the true power God possesses.

Dr. Thomas Devlin made the decision for me to be airlifted to Erlanger Hospital so that he could treat me himself. He told my wife that he did so because of some odd effects caused by my stroke. He was a highly regarded and incredible doctor in the field of neurological pathology, so she trusted him completely. His forward and brutally honest approach only furthered her ability to believe what he told her. She has told me that he certainly knew that I had a brain-stem stroke. He also told her that some of the characteristics of the stroke were indicative of something more than just a brain-stem stroke.

The day after my stroke, things actually appeared to be looking up, I've been told. The doctor told Bella that I could potentially be out of the hospital in a few days if all stayed the course. She was told that I would need some care regarding getting back to normal, but that I would probably be able to fully recover.

The optimism was useful at that time, for her and the rest of the family. What everyone truly wished to come out of the trial that had been put in front of us was for me to get back to the way I had always been.

They say change occurs when you take a single step outside your comfort zone. In this particular matter, a change wasn't desired, and Bella was hoping that stepping outside the comfort zone would be something that wasn't necessary.

In regard to her personal state, she also went on to tell me that she did all that she could to remain strong while around those who needed her strength. That too was something that she was feigning rather than experiencing in reality. In her few moments of isolation—alone, and with her own thoughts—she cried. She hurt, deeply. She was in fear of what would happen to the man she loved so dearly. At the time of the stroke, we were just a month away from our twenty-fourth anniversary. Our lives were completely dependent on one another, and we loved each other in a way that is truly indescribable. To even see me the way I appeared in that hospital bed completely broke her heart.

It ravaged her soul.